NATIONS OF THE MODERN WORLD

CEYLON

S. A. Pakeman
*Formerly Professor of Modern History, Ceylon
University College. Appointed Member, House of
Representatives, Ceylon, 1947–1952*

ENGLAND

John Bowle
*Professor of Political Theory
Collège d'Europe, Bruges*

MODERN IRAN

Peter Avery
*Lecturer in Persian and Fellow of King's College,
Cambridge*

IRAQ

Brig. S. Y. Longrigg
*Formerly of the Government of Iraq and the Iraq
Petroleum Company and one time Political
Officer, Iraq*
and
Frank Stoakes
*Formerly of the Iraq Petroleum Company,
Lecturer in Government, Manchester University*

JAPAN

Sir Esler Dening
H.M. Ambassador to Japan, 1952–1957

MALAYA

J. M. Gullick
Formerly of the Malayan Civil Service

MOROCCO

Mark I. Cohen and
Lorna Hahn

PAKISTAN

Ian Stephens
*Formerly Editor of The Statesman
Calcutta and Delhi, 1942–1951
Fellow King's College, Cambridge, 1952–1958*

SOUTH AFRICA	John Cope *Formerly editor-in-chief of* The Forum *and South African correspondent of* The Guardian
SUDAN REPUBLIC	K. D. D. Henderson *Formerly of the Sudan Political Service and Governor of Darfur Province 1949–1953*
TURKEY	Geoffrey Lewis *Senior lecturer in Islamic Studies, Oxford*
THE UNITED STATES OF AMERICA	H. C. Allen *Commonwealth Fund Professor of American History, University College, London*
YUGOSLAVIA	Muriel Heppel and F. B. Singleton

SUDAN REPUBLIC

SUDAN REPUBLIC

By

K. D. D. HENDERSON

FREDERICK A. PRAEGER, *Publishers*
NEW YORK · WASHINGTON

BOOKS THAT MATTER

Published in the United States of America 1965
by Frederick A. Praeger, Inc., Publishers
111 Fourth Avenue, New York, N.Y. 10003

© K. D. D. Henderson 1965

Library of Congress Catalog Card Number: 65-27084

Printed in Great Britain

Preface

THIS IS a personal, but not, I hope, a subjective account. The introductory chapters try to avoid lingering on ground already mapped by more expert cartographers, while filling in a few additional details. The middle section is mainly eye-witness reporting, with the inevitable defects of such as well as the advantages. Where bias exists an attempt has been made to identify it and allow for it.

It is intended primarily for the English reader, but in the hope that it will also be read by Sudanese, some of whom contributed the information and comment which shaped and filled the closing chapters. It does not directly answer some of their questions, but may help them to find an answer to most of them. Why was General Abboud invited to Britain in May 1964? Because the British preferred a friendly autocracy to a critical democracy? Because they wanted to secure transit facilities to Aden? Because they wanted to sell their goods? Or because they felt that his new Central Council was a genuine step towards the reintroduction of representative institutions in a country tied to Britain by the tenuous threads of many personal friendships? Why did the British stay on in the Sudan unless it paid them to do so? Had the Gezira Scheme a less selfish motive than the supply of cotton for Lancashire or spite against Egypt? Could the interests of the Condominium Government conflict with, or prevail against the interests of the United Kingdom? Does the British Government, or anybody in Britain, care today what happens to the Sudan, provided it still provides an export market for British goods? All these questions have been raised at one time or another.

The spelling of Arabic names made familiar by fifty years of use has been retained in the text, and elucidated where necessary in the Index. The vowel sound 'e' in Edward may be absent from classical Arabic but it is common in Sudanese and has been transliterated accordingly. To call the Beni Bedr 'Banu Badr' is surely no more necessary in a book of this kind than to write Daibhidh Macantoisich for David Macintosh.

Events have decreed that the story should leave the new Republic poised on the springboard, ready to plunge into a new adventure.

9

It is not so much a biography of the new Sudan as an account of its training period and its preliminary trials. It is dedicated to the memory of three men, Gamil el Imam, Yusef Saad, and Ali Abu Sin, with whom the narrator once walked and talked 'in black Rioupéroux'.

Contents

Maps

Chapter 1

The Country and Its People

T HE SUDAN REPUBLIC is more of a geographical unit than most
of the new African states, being roughly co-terminous with
the Nile basin below the Ethiopian escarpment between
latitude 4° and latitude 20° North. It is the largest state in Africa,
though the cession of the Sarra Triangle to Italian Libya in 1935
deprived it of the distinction of covering a million square miles.

In the west the frontier runs along the far side of the watershed.
In the east it follows the Abyssinian foothills north to Tokar, at the
mouth of the Baraka river, and then along the Red Sea coast for
four hundred miles to Halaib.

The northern frontier runs straight across the desert, crossing the
Nile just where it enters the long defile between the second and first
cataracts, the country of Lower Nubia, destined after five thousand
years of history to disappear under the waters of a succession of dams.

The southern boundary is mainly the result of adjustments made
when the Lado Enclave reverted from Belgian leasehold in 1910
after the death of King Leopold. It includes a good natural barrier
in the Imatong Mountains, crosses the Nile at Nimule, the first
river port above the Fola rapids, and follows the watershed westwards.

Geographically speaking the only real anomalies are provided by
the inclusion in Ethiopia of the swamps of the Baro Salient and the
Eritrean Basso Piano.

Ethnically the boundaries are less satisfactory. The Eritrean
frontier divides the Beni Amer, the Baro frontier the Anuak, the
Equatorial frontier the Madi, the Kakwa and the Azande. West
from Lake Rudolph the boundary goes straight across the line of
north-south seasonal grazing previously shared by the Toposa of
the Sudan with their cousins, the Turkana of Kenya and the
Ethiopian tribe variously known as the Bume, Donyiro or Nya-
ngatom. Thus came into existence an area known to diplomats as
the Ilemi Triangle, a modest but always potentially effective irritant
to interterritorial relations ever since the various governments
concerned began to move up on to their frontiers in the nineteen-

15

twenties. The Ilemi Appendix, a finger of Sudan territory running down to Sanderson's Gulf, at the north end of Lake Rudolph, being cut off from the rest of the country by the Lotagippi Swamp, was a constant source of recrimination until the Kenya authorities agreed to police it after the reconquest of Ethiopia in 1941–2.

A similar common-sense agreement in the north extended Sudan administration beyond the political frontier to cover the Bisharin grazing area around Halaib. An attempt by the Egyptian Government to cancel this arrangement nearly caused a war in 1958.

In the far west the boundary was demarcated after the 1914–18 war along what is virtually a cease-fire line, the limit of French expansion eastwards into Darfur. This section of frontier, which bears a curious resemblance to the profile of the late Lord Oxford, left the Sultan of the Masalit and other resistance leaders safe inside the Sudan but with more than half of their hereditary domains over the border in what is now the Chad Republic.

Also over the border, on the far shore of the little lake at Umm Defog, is a plot of ground which is forever England, the grave of Colonel Pearson, Chairman of the Boundary Commission, which was permanently ceded to Britain by France. Over this six feet of English earth a small Union Jack used to fly, and English visitors were invited by the French administrator to open the gate of the *zareeba* which surrounded it and precede him on to their own soil.

From north to south the Sudan presents a cross-section of northern Africa with the Nile as a base line. The Nubian and Libyan deserts which cut off its inhabited areas from Kufra and Egypt give way slowly and reluctantly as they enter the belt of seasonal rain to scrub and bush and grassland and forest. Out of the Sahara the Tibesti-Ennedi massif thrusts a diagonal spur south-eastwards for two hundred and fifty miles into Darfur, culminating at the southern extremity of the Marra range in a ten-thousand foot extinct volcano with two lakes in the crater, one salt and one fresh. On its topmost peak is a group of pre-historic graves, locally reputed to enshrine the remains of two sons of Alexander the Great, and their dog. Thanks to them Marra is well-watered and, since the excavator's spade would destroy their blessing, no one knows whether these barrows in fact contain Greek forerunners of Ordinary Seaman Frederick Gowler, or merely some early Daju kings.

On the other side of the Nile the gaunt Red Sea hills run south out of Egypt into Eritrea, climbing steadily to join the mountains of Abyssinia. The Imatongs in the south include the Sudan's highest peak in Mt. Kinyetti (10,456 ft.). They are rich in gallery forest and their podocarpus stands were exploited during the

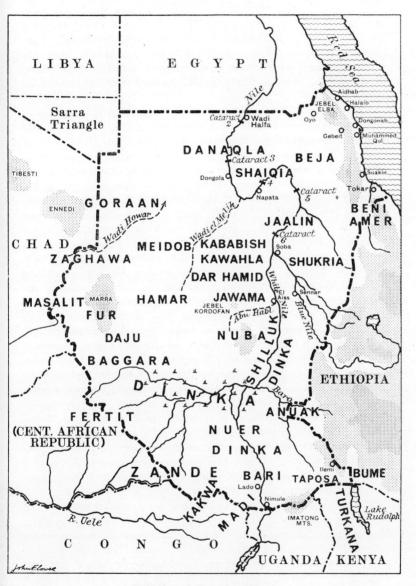

Tribal and Frontier Map.

1939–45 war when imported soft woods were no longer obtainable.

Elsewhere the country consists mainly of rolling plains and rocky outcrops beloved of coneys, rising again south-west of the swamps of the Upper Nile to the ironstone hills and mahogany forests of the Nile-Congo divide. The rainfall increases southward from the infinitesimal and occasional at Wadi Halfa to six inches at Khartum, fifteen at Wad Medani, thirty at Malakal and over forty in the far south.

The country and its people are roughly comparable with those of Mauretania in the west but the Nile has provided a basis for civilisation, and a means of communication as far upstream as the papyrus swamps. These swamps, known as the *sudd* area ('the block on the Nile'), have prevented the river from providing a route into central Africa; turning back, among others, a survey expedition sent by the Emperor Nero in the year A.D. 60. It seems to have been by way of the high ground east of the Rift Valley that prehistoric northerners found their way to south Africa. Penetration downstream never presented such a problem to the Negro and the tide of his expansion has ebbed and flowed through the Nile Valley down the millenia.

Broadly speaking, the popular conception of the Negro paddling his canoe through swamp and forest and the Touareg ranging the desert on his camel are fair criteria of judgement when it comes to conjecturing the racial affinities and way of life of lost African civilisations. Where the Negro is, there is usually decent rainfall. Where the Arab flourishes, the desert (or the sea, if he is a southern Arabian) is never far away. All across Africa these two stocks, Hamo-Semite and Negro, have confronted each other between the tenth and the twentieth parallel and their mingling has produced a chain of successive hybrid kingdoms from the Niger across to Ethiopia. The dependence of most of these states upon Negro infantry for their armies and Negro girls for their concubines has led to their portrayal by Egyptian artist and Arab historian as predominantly Negroid, though their cultures were usually of northern origin and the features of their ruling class sometimes northern too. Pigmentation seems to change more easily than physiognomy.

Most of the Negroid peoples inhabiting the Sudan today are of much the same stock as their neighbours, the Sudanic-speaking Negroes of west and central Africa, but the so-called Nilotics present a remarkable exception. Their origin is obscure. The Nuer claim to have been created in the swamps. The Shilluk, or Acholi, say that they and the Anuak came north through the *sudd* about twelve generations ago, followed after an interval by the Dinka. The Nilotes are blacker than the west African — dead black — and their skulls are narrower. They are a tall lean race with beautiful hands and chiselled faces, wanderers on savannah and swamp, worshippers of a supreme spirit, idolisers of their cattle. They have provided, with their cousins the Masai and the Watussi, a ruling aristocracy over a large section of Africa and, although their conservatism has relegated them to an inferior status in the contemporary picture one may venture to predict that their role in African history is not yet ended.

At the beginning of history, from five to ten thousand years ago, the rain-belt extended north of the junction of the Niles and the Negro hunted and fished up to the sixth cataract, and possibly beyond. Here he met a brown race of nomadic hunters whose blood was to provide the stock on which the Arab culture of the modern Sudan was grafted.

Some of their descendants still flourish between the Nile and the Red Sea, north of the Atbara river, where the stony desert washes up into the mountains and the vegetation of a bygone age lingers on in favoured valleys. These are the Beja, the ancient Blemmyes, who live today much as they have always done. Solitary in habit, warlike and predatory, shock-headed and handsome, they have sought the lonely mountain glens and turned their backs on sea and river for thousands of years. Like any other people in these latitudes they have absorbed black blood. Immigration from Arabia, and possibly Armenoid influences from Anatolia, have also played a part in their make-up. But basically they, like the pre-dynastic Egyptians whom some of them resemble, are kin to the hunters and artists who ranged the Saharan steppe before the rainclouds withdrew to north and south. The Bisharin are famous for their riding camels, the Hadendoa for their military exploits under Osman Digna in the 1880s. The Amarar are familiar to travellers as stevedores at Port Sudan. The Beni Amer recently produced a Rob Roy, Ali Mintai, who terrorised the Eritrean border in 1942–5. But only the mixed tribes of the Gwineb (the Red Sea coast), the merchant princes of Suakin, the Hadareb and the Halenga, have contributed much to the national prosperity.

From the Beja country came a large proportion of the gold in the Pharoahs' tombs and the palaces of Rome. The deserted mines are to be found scattered from Oyo to Gabeit. The last of them was worked until recently, a honeycomb of ancient galleries where thousand-year-old implements and clay lamps were trodden under foot by the twentieth-century miner. Forgotten vegetation lingers on Jebel Elba, east of Oyo on the borders of Egypt, and a few cedars survive on the high hills behind Tokar. Tokar itself is famous for cotton and dust storms, with moving dunes of silt which swallow up houses and bury the roads so deep that a traveller trying to get a sand-track under his car once uncovered the top of a telegraph pole. The Ptolemies had an elephant remount depot near Tokar. Eighty miles to the north the mediaeval Arab port of Suakin moulders picturesquely on its island, inhabited chiefly by cats. North again Port Sudan quays are the twentieth-century Sudan's front door on the world. A hundred miles farther, at Muhammad Gul, a little Turkish fort sleeps between the mountains and the sea.* North again, beyond the deserted oyster beds of Dongonab, where a houseboat from the Thames once sheltered hopeful pearlers, is Aidhab, 'Old Suakin'. Here pieces of Chinese celadon and Saracen glass still lie about amongst the charred rafters of the port destroyed by Renaud de Châtillon in A.D. 1182.

Along the coastal plain, watered by winter rains, the Beja graze their white camels, leaving the fishing to Arabs from Egypt or Arabia and the gypsum deposits to whoever chooses to exploit them.

The history of their cousins on the Nile presents a very different picture and indeed the Nubians have a fair claim to have provided the weft on which the whole history of the country has been woven. Kushites, Nubians, Danagla, Berberines — the Nile enabled them to progress in agriculture, Egypt was a perennial source of civilised contact, the Libyan tribes to the west refreshed them with frequent injections of vigorous blood, the Negroes to the south provided slaves and soldiery, and all these, plus the Beja and occasional invaders from Abyssinia, kept them on the alert and prevented them time and again from sinking into decadence.

So after centuries of subjection to the Pharoahs they were able in the eighth century B.C. to strike back and provide Egypt with its 25th Dynasty. Defeated by the Assyrians in Palestine, the Nubian armies had to evacuate Egypt, but from their capitals at Napata and Meröe they held off Persians and Ptolemies and Romans for the thousand years of the Meroitic Kingdom. It fell at last in the fourth century A.D. to the King of Axum, who found the 'black Nuba' infiltrating amongst the red; but Christian missionaries sent by the Emperor Justinian ushered in a renaissance, and new kingdoms based on Dongola and Soba (a few miles from the site of Khartum) successfully resisted the Arab invaders of Egypt from the seventh till the fourteenth century.

The influence of these successive kingdoms was remarkable. Through the Wadi Howar and the Wadi el Melik, ancient tributaries of the Nile flowing east and north out of Darfur and Kordofan,

* Birthplace, on 26 October 1900, of the future President, Ibrahim Abboud.

it spread westward and southward into the heart of Africa. In modern times there are Jellaba colonies west to Chad and south to the Bahr el Ghazal and Uganda (where the name 'Nubi' is still applied to them). '*Jellabi*' means a man in a shirt, as opposed to the nomad Arab in his '*tob*' or toga. In the days of the slave trade they were the '*Bahhara*', the sailors, and their skill in navigating the Nile has carried them in modern times via the forecastles of merchant ships into most of the world's ports.

Shortage of land at home has also forced them to add yet another skill to market-gardening, date and citrus growing, trade and navigation. The Berberine domestic servant is in demand everywhere in Egypt and the Levant for his honesty, intelligence and deftness. They combine the capacity for travel with a deep attachment to the land of their fathers, a narrow ribbon of palm groves hemmed in by towering orange-coloured sand dunes or rocky crags crowned with castle walls and ruined churches.

The original Nubian stock has of course been considerably diluted with Arab blood since the fall of Dongola or even earlier, though the Danagla still speak their original languages in their homes. Their conversion to Islam resulted, as it did amongst the Berbers of North Africa, in the swift emergence of men distinguished for piety and learning. Today they retain this reputation — the famous Mahdi came from Dongola — and they also provide the Republic with a large proportion of its professional and governing classes. In appearance some of them strongly resemble the figured profiles on the frescoes of dynastic Egypt.

The Arabs came into the Sudan by three routes — across the Red Sea, up the Nile, and, after a long detour, from the west. Infiltration by sea from southern Arabia has been going on for thousands of years but it is only a century since a complete tribal unit, the Rashaida, made its way across into the Beja country. There it still wanders between the Atbara river and the coast as an unappreciated guest, breeding racing camels which carry off all the prizes at local race meetings and surprising the traveller with the kerchief-and-cord headdress and the crooked scimitar of Arabia in a country of turbans or fuzzy heads and cross-hilted Crusader swords.

From the seventh century, when the Arabs occupied Egypt, until the fall of Dongola in the fourteenth, there seems to have been a steady infiltration of individuals through Nubia and up the river. Some of these were the ancestors of the Jaalin, related on the mother's side to the Danagla but claiming paternal descent from the Beni Abbas and rivalling their northern neighbours in every Jellabi activity. 'The Dongolawi' they said 'is Satan enclosed in the skin of a man,' and to this day they find it difficult to preserve amity in proximity. But the two of them, together with an intervening group, the Shaigia, of whom more anon, constitute a majority of the educated class in the contemporary Sudan.

The Jaalin settled mainly on the Nile north of Khartum, but many of them and many other Arabs penetrated farther into the domains of the Christian kings of Alwa.* The flourishing city of Arbagi in the Gezira between the Niles was founded, according to tradition, in A.D. 1485, perhaps by Hadareb merchants from the Red Sea coast.

After the capture of Dongola the Arabs broke through on both sides of the river, driving the desert-dwelling 'Nuba' south through the arid plains and scrub covered sand dunes of Kordofan into the Dilling hills, and the Negroid peoples of the Isle of Meroe, beyond the Atbara river, back to the confines of Ethiopia.

In both areas their descendants still live, making, through their export of camels on the hoof into Egypt, a much more important contribution to the balance of payments than was fully realised until recently.

They differ from their cousins across the Red Sea only in that many of them have exchanged the wiry frame of the Arabian *bedu* for a portlier and more robust appearance and a rolling, unhurried gait. Such are the Kababish and Kawahla of northern Kordofan, whose leader Ali el Tom was the *beau ideal* of a nomad shaikh under the Condominium; Dar Hamid, whose country surrounds the Danagla oasis of Bara; and the Hamar, who came in from Darfur in the eighteenth century with the Fur armies. Many of these are now sedentary, or semi-sedentary, cultivating amongst the dunes and tapping the gum trees but congregating at well centres or water-bores in the dry season. The great treeless grassy plain of the Butana, east of the Blue Nile and south of the Atbara river, has been dominated since the eighteenth century by the Shukria, led by the Abu Sin family, who by virtue of having 'town houses' at Rufaa on the Blue Nile and Gedaref ('*Suk Abu Sin*') on the Ethiopian border have played a more prominent part in history and government than any other sheikhly family since the days of the Abdullab.

The Abdullab were a branch of the Rufaa section of Juhayna, and their power dates from the obscure period of two centuries which intervened between the fall of Dongola and the conquest of the Kingdom of Alwa. They took a prominent part in this conquest, but only as allies of a new invader from the upper Blue Nile.

* Soba was its capital.

The origin of the Fung is a mystery. They were Muslims and claimed descent from the Beni Umayya, but to the Arabs they were known as the Black Sultans. Their military strength rested on their mailed cavalry. Like other black sultans farther west, they probably owed their position to Arab intermarriage into a matrilinear royal house. O. G. S. Crawford* has argued plausibly that they were dislodged from a homeland in Eritrea. They were strong enough to secure the allegiance of the Abdullab, whose '*Mankil*' governed as viceroy of the north from Gerri, on the south edge of the Jaalin country, and also of the merchants of Suakin. They appear to have had a garrison up the White Nile at Demoth, near Fashoda, and another at el Aiss, near Aba Island, to secure a bridgehead for expansion into Kordofan. Hence they pushed westwards up the Khor Abu Habl to establish client kingdoms in the northern fringes of the Nuba Mountains. The contemporary Sudan owes to this conquest the 'Kingdom' of Tegale and the establishment of the Jawama tribe between Jebel Kordofan and the river. The name *Jawama* means 'brought together' and they incorporate Jaali and other Arab stocks. Their name is familiar farther west as founders of dynasties as far away as Wadai. Their country is sandy and over-cultivated today, depressing the railway traveller with acres of sodom apples until at Rahad station, where the branch line takes off for el Obeid, his eye is refreshed by the great *haraz* trees of the west and the jagged peaks of J. Daier, northern bastion of the Nuba Mountains. The Jawama are an able and disciplined people, fond of service in the army and the police, and playing a larger part than most rural communities in the national life.

The triumph of the Fung had considerable repercussions in the Islamic world. It is alleged to have come just in time to prevent a Turkish invasion by Selim I, and it brought men of learning and piety hurrying to Sennar from Dongola and Egypt and Arabia and even, if we are to believe tradition, from as far afield as Baghdad and India. Most of these men were members of a *Sufi* brotherhood and they set the pattern of Islamic life in the Sudan. Whether or not it be true, as some modern Arab theologians assert, that the decline in Muslim power and culture was due to the fissiparous influence of the rival orders of Sufism, they have certainly exercised a divisive influence in the Sudan. The later rule of the Fung was marred by bitter rivalry between the established Qadria and the immigrant Sammania, and political progress in Condominium days was hampered by friction between the *Ansar* and the Khatmia (Mahdist and Mirghanist). These missionaries were settled by the Sultans on

* *The Fung Kingdom of Sennar*, John Bellows, 1951.

the Blue and White Niles and in the Gezira, the 'island' which lies between them. The Gezira area, still known locally by the ancient and no longer intelligible name of el Huoi,* is a great plain of heavy clay, capable, when wet, of snatching the chains off a too-adventurous car in one glutinous grab. It enjoys a fair rainfall (fifteen inches at Wad Medani) and seems to have been the granary of Soba as well as of later regimes. Presumably it was farmed under the Fung by the subject population, working occasionally in the more remote areas for themselves but more usually as slaves or serfs of the baron or abbot to whom the land was granted.

In the result the Gezira became the first and only inland area containing privately held land. When, in the twentieth century, it was desired to irrigate it, a complete survey and registration was carried out preparatory to renting the land from its owners, many of whose titles dated from the Fung. By that time they had become the most efficient growers of grain in the rain-belt, living in family groups which grew into small tribes with a strong local attachment. This again had its results when the irrigation scheme was no longer able to provide tenancies locally for an expanding population, and found the sons of tenants reluctant to move fifty or sixty miles into foreign parts.

The boundaries of the old plots were ridged to retain the rain-water, a process which made map-making easier, and wells were sunk across the length and breadth of the plain. The interior of the Gezira resembled the Butana, an endless expanse of yellow grass where the refraction at midday is such as to delude the traveller into trudging for hours to reach the shelter of a tree which turns out to be only three feet high. The borders of the Niles, however, provided forests of acacia which amply sufficed for building needs and firewood until the re-founding of Khartum at the beginning of the twentieth century spread devastation far around.

It was amongst these forests beside the rivers that the new centres of learning flourished in the first 150 years of Fung rule, but in the second half of the seventeenth century their power began to wane. First the Shilluk came pushing up from the south and after a disastrous famine in 1683, 'the year of meat-eating', destroyed the

---

* el Huoi. Many and ingenious are the theories advanced about the origin of this name — including the suggestion that the ferry boats were always moored on the left bank of the Blue Nile and the right bank of the White so that travellers to the Gezira had to stand and shout 'Hoi!' until they attracted the ferryman's attention. The most interesting, however, was that put forward by Mek Hassan Adlan, heir to the throne of Sennar, that it is in fact the Alwa name for the Gezira. It was still used in the twentieth century by the inhabitants of Tuti Island at the Nile junction, the most independent-minded community in the Sudan, for the river bank opposite, on which the Turks had recently built a city called Khartum.

White Nile villages right down to its junction with the Blue, cutting off Sennar from its colonies in Kordofan and retaining effective possession of the riverland till the end of the nineteenth century.* Then a new enemy appeared in the north. The Fung had established a settlement on the Nile bend south of Dongola. Upstream of it on the fourth cataract lived a small and undistinguished tribe, the Shaigia, which suddenly emerged at the beginning of the eighteenth century as a paramount predatory power, reducing the Abdullab viceroy to impotence and depriving Sennar of any semblance of power in the north. So distinctive have they been ever since, in character, custom and appearance, so prominent as adventurers and soldiers, so un-Arab and un-Nubian, that it has been conjectured that they owe their supremacy to the arrival during the sixteenth century of a party of Mamlukes or Bosnian mercenaries displaced or dispatched from Egypt by the Ottoman Turks.

The reign of King Badi Abu Shelukh (1723–60) brought a temporary recovery for the Fung, thanks partly to the military ability of a Hamag cavalry commander called Muhammad Abu Likeilik. After winning his spurs in a successful campaign against the Abyssinians in 1744, Abu Likeilik rescued the Fung armies from a hitherto disastrous involvement against the Musabaat of Darfur, whom he drove back into the waterless country west of Jebel Kordofan. In 1760 however, he returned to the Nile, deposed King Badi, and put Badi's son on the throne. From then onwards the Fung Sultans were puppets in the hands of Hamag *Wazirs*. By 'Hamag' the Arabs meant 'African' or 'Negro' or 'previous inhabitant' and it is possible that Abu Likeilik, whose family owned land in the central Gezira near Managil, belonged to an old Alwa family. When he died, in 1776, his sons and later his grandsons ruined what was left of the Fung power and the Fung economy by a series of violent fratricidal wars. By the end of the century conditions were anarchic and the Keira Sultans of Darfur had recovered all the territory previously held by their cousins the Musaba'at, and more. The town of Tendelti, between the Jawama country and the river, dates from this period of Fur rule, and even Shendi, the Jaalin capital north of Khartum, is said to owe its name to the Fur.

Darfur was only incorporated in the Sudan at the end of the nineteenth century. It is inhabited mainly by Negroid peoples for whom the high peaks of the Marra range provided fertile and

* A survivor of the force which captured the Mahdi's family in 1898 near Fashishoyya opposite Aba Island, described it in 1931 as having happened 'in the Shilluk country'. The name *'Fachichoyya'* is of course a Shilluk one.

inaccessible sanctuary. North of Marra the country, although still studded with fantastic volcanic cores, like two-thousand-foot standing stones, is open to invasion from the north and west as well as the east. So in addition to the Meroitic and Christian settlements near Kuttum and a Nubian colony at Jebel Meidob there was frequent infiltration by Tibbu and Goraan, Bedeyat and Zaghawa, from Tibesti and beyond. It was presumably in this area that the Garamantes (as Herodotus called the Goraan) used to hunt 'the Ethiopian troglodytes' in chariots of iron.

The first paramount tribe known to us in Darfur was called Tajwa by the Arab historians. It was at war with Christian Dongola in the twelfth century A.D., was later converted to Islam, was driven out of J. Meidob by the Nubian Meidobis, and finally replaced as ruler of the north by the Tunjur, a tribe of Nubian or Berber origin. The Tajwa survive today in Dar Sila (Chad) and southern Darfur as the Daju or Beigo, with colonies farther south and one far to the east on the edge of the Nuba Mountains.

The Tunjur, whose power may have been broken by invaders from Bornu, gave place early in the seventeenth century to a new dynasty, founded amongst the Fur by one Suliman Solong ('the redskin', or Arab). Under his descendants dominion was extended over Kordofan and in 1784–5 the Sultan Teirab led an army as far as the Nile. The Fung were only saved from subjection by the river and the sudden death of Teirab himself. His successor recovered and maintained his hold on Kordofan.

Meanwhile south of J. Marra the Daju principalities had been disturbed by the arrival, probably in the eighteenth century, of Baggara Arabs from the west. Judging by their pedigrees, the Baggara owe their origin as tribes to the great Arab revolt in Egypt in the thirteenth century. The defeated tribesmen escaped to the west and then moved south, coalescing round successful leaders and so forming new tribal units as the centuries went by. Their development into a distinct type took place along the Gazelle river, north of Lake Chad. Here they acquired Negro cattle and Negro blood, a distinctive dialect, distinctive habits, a characteristic long spear with a leaf-shaped blade, and the wide-sleeved 'dervish' *jibba* which distinguishes them from the Jellaba and the *Jummala* (camel-men).

Unlike the Negro, the Baggari uses his bulls for transport and riding. He is usually dark of skin. Like the pastoral Fulani of the Niger, whom he resembles in many ways, he varies in feature from the Negroid to the aquiline. The typical Baggari has hawk-like features and a jutting beard (carefully tended with a short comb, carried on a string round his neck). He is an intrepid horseman, riding by balance with one toe in a stirrup and pursuing the giraffe at full gallop through thick and thorny scrub over ground pock-marked with elephants' footprints. The riverain people, with memories of the Mahdia, accuse him of cruelty and tell lurid stories of the atrocities of the *Emeers*, but he is as hard on himself as on his beasts or his fellow men. His women must be the freest in the Islamic world and in the grazing areas the unmarried girls stride and ride clad only in a strip of cloth passed between the legs over a belt, to fall to the ground fore and aft. They are great dancers and the drums will beat all night, sometimes all day as well for forty-eight hours or more.

They like to spend the summer on the edge of the sandy country or in the lower valleys of the hills. In these latitudes there are still plenty of trees, giant figs and *haraz* acacias. The *haraz* loses its leaves when the ground is soaked so that crops can be grown right up to the great trunks. Later it drops quantities of succulent pods to fatten the animals which pasture under its winter shade. These belong usually to the sedentary local inhabitants or to camel nomads who move down into the area when the Baggara have gone south. In recent years more and more Baggara have taken to planting cotton on the clay pans and ground-nuts on the dunes, staying on to pick their crops and quarrel with the new arrivals. But there is no grazing left for cattle by that time and a move has to be made across the area of thick waterless bush which usually separates them from the watercourses where they spend the summer. There is an inevitable tendency to beat the pistol in this race to the summer grazing and in recent years a tribal assembly used to be held at a suitable date, before which nobody was allowed to leave.

As the Baggara pushed on eastward across southern Kordofan towards the Nile, they came to the Nuba Mountains, a group of scattered granite hills covering about 20,000 square miles between Khor Abu Habl in the north and the swampy plains of the lower Bahr el Ghazal in the south. These hills are inhabited by the people known to the Arabs as Nuba or, a century ago, as Turug, remnants of all the tribes who have been driven up off the plains in the course of the years. Black and brown, Negro and Negroid, naked and unashamed, they defied all comers from their hill tops and were only slowly subjected in the twentieth century. The young men however, descended from races which provided Egypt and Kush with their fighting infantry, were never very reluctant to do the same for their successors. Their most surprising commander was perhaps the Emperor Maximilian of Mexico in the 1860s. At the battle of Omdurman Nuba soldiers were numerous in both armies.

Today, they and the Baggara have settled down in comparative amity to grow American cotton in the fertile plains between the hills. Amongst them will be found representatives of the only foreign ingredient in the population of the northern Sudan, immigrants from northern Nigeria, Wadai and Bornu. There have been west African settlements along the pilgrim route to Mecca for centuries, but three factors combined to make them more numerous in the twentieth. One was the improvement in public security and communications. The second was political. When Lugard defeated the Sultan of Sokoto in 1903 one of the Fulani princes, Mai Wurno, escaped to the eastward and finally settled on the Blue Nile near Sennar with a large following. This formed a nucleus for further immigration. Finally the expansion of cotton growing provided the pilgrims with a means of earning money *en route*. Many who stopped to pick stayed to grow, and when cotton suddenly ceased to pay, during the great depression of 1930–5, a number of Gezira farmers gave up their tenancies, which were taken over by the Fellata, as the Sudanese call them. They are more hard-working than the local cultivators and their women and children were prepared to take a full share in the labour. When cotton recovered, of course, the local people wanted their tenancies back and a political problem arose.

During the nineteen-thirties there was also an influx into Darfur and Kordofan of nomad Fula with great flocks of sheep. There has long been a Fulani element among the Darfur Baggara but this new invasion was resented and the visitors had to be continually escorted back to the frontier, whence they usually returned a few weeks later.

The people and the problems of the three southern provinces of the Sudan will be dealt with in a separate chapter at the end of this book. The livelihood of the northerners, as will be apparent by now, is mainly agricultural and pastoral, although in recent years the proportion of town dwellers has greatly increased. The Nubians are still the most versatile, skilful orchardists and market gardeners whose ability to operate in uncongenial surroundings will be put to the test in the new irrigated area at Khashm el Girba on the Atbara river, where the villagers flooded out by the High Dam have been settled.

The Sennar Dam has converted the Gezira farmer into an expert grower of long-staple cotton, second only in quality to the product of Sea Island and the foundation of the viability of the Sudan.

Elsewhere, though millet, ground-nuts and sesame are widely grown on dune and clay and terraced hillside, the economy is mainly pastoral — camels, sheep and cattle, but always and everywhere the poor man's cow, the all-destroying goat, trailing the desert behind him as he bares the soil to the erosive action of wind and rain.

The Negroid peoples who survive north of the twelfth parallel have been absorbed into the Islamic world and it was the purpose of the republican governments to ensure the stability of their new state by a similar assimilation of the inhabitants of the three southern provinces. The attempt has provided their major problem up to the time of writing, a problem which will be discussed below.

For all their differences* the northern provinces are fairly homogeneous and present a national identity which has played, in Near Eastern and African politics a part which is distinctive and usually salutary. Its main characteristic is common sense. There is an absence of neurotic xenophobia, a congenital reluctance to be stampeded into hasty action, an un-Arabian dislike for bloodshed and assassination, and a cool appraisal of what is and is not obligatory under existing alliances. All this admittedly contrasts with what we are told of the behaviour of the Baggara *Emeers* in the Mahdia and with recent allegations of brutality in the south, but it was none the less a marked feature of the first decade of independence. Amongst themselves the Northern Sudanese are a cheerful, hospitable and friendly people, with little social snobbery or insolence of office. If they could extend this democratic outlook to include their southern compatriots they would be in a fair way to presenting the despondent world with an object lesson of internal stability and external sanity as well as providing a badly needed bridge between Islamic and non-Islamic Africa.

* Culturally for instance, Darfur is closer to the Niger than to the Nile; linguistically the Arabic spoken in Kordofan has more affinities with North Africa than with Kassala Province; spiritually, the west in general reveres Muhammad Ahmed as having been the true Mahdi, the east regards this claim as misconceived.

Chapter 2

The Nineteenth Century

IN JULY 1798 Europe, in the person of Napoleon Bonaparte, burst upon the sleeping Islamic world like a bomb. After he had occupied Cairo the Sultan of Darfur sent him a message of congratulation. Napoleon's reply set the theme tune for the next hundred years. He asked for two thousand able-bodied black slaves.

Of all the 'ifs' of history, few are more fascinating than to speculate on what would have happened if Nelson had not sailed away from the vicinity of Alexandria an hour or two before the French came in sight. The local effect of the French occupation of Egypt was not only to focus European attention on the Nile and give birth to a permanent British concern about communications with India. It also created conditions which prepared the way for a *coup d'état* while Napoleon himself provided a spur and an example to anyone able and ruthless enough to make the attempt.

Muhammad Ali Pasha, the Macedonian soldier who brought it off, was very able and very ruthless. He massacred his Mamluke predecessors, drove the Wahhabis out of the Holy places, conquered the Sudan, and would almost certainly have displaced the Ottoman Turks from control of the Arab world if the European powers had not intervened. The Sudan was invaded in 1821 in order to supply soldiers for his wars and gold to pay for them. When the dream of Asian Empire faded it became, under his grandson, a springboard for expansion southwards into Ethiopia, the Somali coast, and central Africa, an expansion which inevitably overreached itself. From the Sudanese point of view the real trouble was that they were regarded as a means rather than as an end in themselves. At first attempts were made to develop their resources, but these faded out with the death of Muhammad Ali and when they were revived under the Khedive Ismail they were subordinated to imperialist adventures which swallowed up the increased revenue and plunged Egypt and the Sudan alike into bankruptcy. By that time Egypt was galloping a length ahead of the scramblers for Africa. She dared not stop to give her mount a breather.

The Khedives were wise on the whole in their choice of personnel, seldom promoting to high office a man without previous Sudan experience, but from the time of Abbas they changed their staff far too frequently and began to use the country as a reception area for deportees and criminals, a process which hardly contributed to the prestige or the popularity of office.* Sudanese were appointed from time to time to positions of responsibility, but there was a certain basic dissympathy between the two races. This was aggravated in the formative years by the arrogance of a usurping dynasty and by various acts of appalling cruelty. These were to be rivalled in mid-century by the behaviour of the mad Emperor Theodore of Ethiopia (another usurper) but they dumbfounded and revolted the Sudanese.

Nor was there much provocation given to the invaders to begin with. The Shaigia opposed them in two pitched battles, but they submitted and signed on as friendlies as soon as they found their valour useless against firearms.† At Sennar the Wazir Muhammad Adlan Abu Likeilik, who had re-established some sort of order early in the century and might have organised resistance, was murdered by the only cousin he had left alive, as soon as word arrived of the advance of the Turks. In Kordofan the Fur cavalry was no more successful against firearms and discipline than the Shaigia.

Not for the first or last time, the climate proved a more dangerous foe than man. After a disappointing visit to the Eldorado of Fazoghli the army commander Ismail Pasha, a son of Muhammad Ali, had to withdraw his weakened forces northward. When he reached Shendi his overbearing and insulting behaviour goaded the Jaali ruler, Mek Nimr, into assassinating him and his staff by setting fire to bales of fodder which had been commandeered and built in round their tents during a banquet. Revolt flared up all over the country but Ismail's brother-in-law, the Defterdar, who commanded in Kordofan, put it down with a brutality which was remembered in detail a hundred years later. It did, however, ensure that for over half a century resistance to the new Government was localised and half-hearted.

The main reason why acquiescence in Turkish rule never gave place to anything more positive was the persistent demand from Cairo for revenue. The collection of taxes became the paramount objective of officials who wished to retain their places. Inadequate

* Hill (*Egypt in the Sudan*, p. 87) quotes from a Khedivial letter to the Governor-General, 'You say that you wish the three persons to be returned to Egypt on the ground that they are deportees. This is a misapprehension; we sent them to the Sudan not as deportees but as governors'.

† They served the new government loyally and were the only section of the population to whom the Mahdi refused amnesty.

accounting and lack of a regular system of audit meant also continual leakage of revenue into the pockets of collectors. In consequence
the ordinary Sudanese, unaccustomed in any case to the idea of
paying regular taxes, came to regard the government agent as indis-
tinguishable from any other robber. To quote a survivor of that
epoch, 'In the Turkia and the Mahdia the approach of a government
representative was the signal to go into hiding with your wives and
your livestock and all the portable possessions that you could carry'.

The ultimate support of government in these circumstances came
to depend on vested interests — the Shaigia irregulars who collected
the taxes; the heads of favoured religious orders such as the Khatmia;
the members of the new Council of *Ulema*, doctors of the religious
law which is the basis of orthodox Islam; the tribal leaders singled
out for promotion to the post of *Shaikh el Mashaikh* or a position in
the Government hierarchy; and the Danagla and Jaalin merchant
venturers who organised the slave trade in the south. But the support
of all these would not have sufficed without the loyalty of the *Jehadia*,
the black troops who replaced Ismail's Turkish regulars as soon as
it became apparent that they could not stand the climate. This
loyalty was remarkable as we shall see when considering events in
Equatoria during the Mahdia. It is a tribute to their officers, whose
reputation suffered in the disasters of the Mahdist revolt, and it
reflects the innate capacity of the African for total devotion to a
leader. 'These Southern Sudanese troops,' wrote Robert Collins,[*]
'and particularly their Negroid officers, had a profound loyalty to
the Khedive of Egypt whom they looked upon with mystical awe,
and there were countless incidents in Equatoria where their actions
were based solely on a blind devotion to the Khedive.' Only once
in the 1860s was this loyalty undermined by long spells of garrison
duty, arrears of pay and the too-rapid expansion of the army. There
were mutinies in various places at this time, notably in Kassala,
where order was only restored by a regular campaign.

A similar devotion was later given to the Khalifat el Mahdi.
The future Bishop Llewellyn Gwynne in a letter home from Khartum,
written in December 1899, relates how he obtained a servant from
the military hospital, a boy who had been in the Khalifa's body-
guard when he was killed. 'He had been stolen away from the
Shilluk country when he was only three and stuck to his master up
to his death. We asked him whether he liked the Khalifa ... He
answered, "I ate his bread, was I not ready to die with him?" '[†]

The success of early Turkish attempts at economic development

* *The Southern Sudan, 1883–98*, p. 51.
† *Pastor on the Nile*, by H. C. Jackson, S.P.C.K., 1960, p. 21.

was hampered by the lack of public security, due to the activities of the tax gatherers, the resistance of the people to innovation, the inexperience of local officials and the inability of imported experts, whether Egyptian or European, to stand up to the rigours of the climate. There was certainly no lack of initiative from Cairo. Practically every project canvassed or implemented by British administrators a hundred years later had already occurred to Muhammad Ali Pasha. His successes included the revival of riverain irrigated farming and the introduction of fruit trees, the development of boat building and river navigation, tanning, ostrich farming, gum tapping, the manufacture of soap, the growing of sugar cane and indigo, the export of cattle and camels on the hoof, and the beginnings of a cotton industry which was greatly expanded under his grandson, when high-grade tobacco was also grown successfully on the eastern border. His failures were the search for gold, the exploitation of Kordofan iron and of copper from Hufrat el Nahas in southern Darfur (then, as later, too remote from the market), silkworms, the improvement of the local breed of sheep by cross-breeding with merinos to produce wool, and the cultivation of opium and rice.

The division of the country for administrative purposes into *Mudirias* (provinces) and *Gisms* or *Mamurias* (districts) which has survived more or less unaltered to the present day, was the work of the second, and perhaps the ablest, of the Turkish Governors, Ali Khurshid, who took over from the Mamluke general Osman Jarkas in 1826 and held office for thirteen years. 'It was Khurshid,' writes Richard Hill, 'who imposed an intelligible rule and maintained it with administrative skill.'*

Between the death of Muhammad Ali in 1849 and the accession of the Khedive Ismail in 1863 the country relapsed into uneasy stagnation. A succession of Governors and Governors General (the administration was twice de-centralised during this period and ruled as part of Egypt) did little to further development and they were mainly engaged in warfare on the frontiers against the Beja or the Abyssinians in the east, and the Kings of Tegale or the Baggara or the Kababish in the west. During this period Turkish slowly gave way to Arabic as the official language, restriction on the entry of European traders and European missionaries was removed and the slave trade in the south reached its zenith. In December 1854 the Khedive Muhammad Said, under European pressure, took the first steps towards repressing it.

The Khedive Ismail, who succeeded Muhammad Said in 1863,

* op. cit. p. 64.

C

was by far the ablest of his house after Muhammad Ali and was a much more attractive character. But he was nearly as impulsive as his subordinate, General Gordon, and he was ignorant of the first principles of finance.

Under him the Egyptian Empire expanded to include the coasts of the Red Sea as far as the Horn of Africa, the better part of Eritrea and the Beni Shangul country, Uganda north of Lake Albert, parts of what are now the Congo and the Central African Republic, and the whole of Darfur. A military survey of the country was undertaken. A comprehensive postal service was installed with 3,000 miles of telegraph line. Railways were projected and partly constructed from Suakin inland and surveyed from Assuan southwards to Darfur. Fleets of steamers plied regularly on the Nile. The *sudd* channel was kept open. The port of Suakin handled a respectable export trade in gum arabic and cotton. The cultivation of rain crops like millet, sesame and ground-nuts was encouraged and improved.

But Ismail overreached himself administratively as well as financially. The government and its personnel were in a state of continual arbitrary reorganisation and replacement. The army suffered two disastrous defeats in Ethiopia in 1875–6 and ceased to be an efficient fighting force.

In 1877, when Gordon Pasha returned to the Sudan as Governor General after previous service in Equatoria, the survival of the Government really depended on the support of the powerful slave-traders with their private armies, and these Gordon was pledged to destroy. Already, in 1872, it had been found necessary to send a military expedition against the chief of them, Zubeir Rahma Mansur, who had virtually made himself king of the Bahr el Ghazal. The government troops were defeated and Zubeir had to be recognised as Governor. In 1874 he marched north against the Sultan of Darfur, defeated his armies in two pitched battles, and occupied el Fasher five days ahead of the Governor General, Ismail Pasha Ayyub, who had been hurriedly sent to forestall him. Feeling himself aggrieved by the subsequent division of the two provinces, Zubeir went to Cairo to protest and was detained there by the Khedive. His son Suliman and his lieutenants, however, remained and it was against them that Gordon's operations were primarily directed.

This remarkable man was destined to produce, by his life and death in the Sudan, 'A hurricane of controversial literature the like of which the Sudan has never seen before or since'.* He was an exceptionally able, active and unorthodox soldier and during his three years of office he 'broke the Bahhara' and virtually abolished

* R. L. Hill. op. cit. p. 144.

the slave trade. But he had no great gift for administration and a disastrous instability in his judgement of character. The favourite of one month was ruthlessly discarded the next and he was capable of the most astonishing *volte-faces* and compromises with principle. He has been accused of disloyalty to the Khedive but his record in furthering Ismail's interests against those of his own country in Uganda is sufficient evidence of his loyalty, and when Ismail was deposed he resigned his post.

Ismail's deposition was due to the intervention of France and England in 1879 on behalf of the Khedive's angry bondholders. This was to result ultimately in solvency and financial stability for Egypt but it was intensely resented and in 1882 an Army officer, Arabi Pasha, tried to stage a *coup d'état* against the new Khedive, Tawfik. But Arabi was seventy years ahead of his time. The British intervened, assumed control of Egypt, and tightened down on all expenditure.

Gordon's successor, Muhammad Rauf, a Nubian from Upper Egypt, could have been a successful Governor General in less troubled times. He was a man of peace and reform and his economies to meet the financial crisis included a reduction in the armed forces, which created a new disgruntled class of ex-soldiers. He was ill-equipped to cope with the unexpected danger which now arose.

Amongst Zubeir's prisoners at the capture of Shakka, in southern Darfur, in 1874, was a Baggari of the Taeisha tribe called Abdullahi Muhammad el Taki, the son of a holy man, who was pardoned by his captor at the request of local religious notables. According to Zubeir, Abdullahi then approached him secretly, saying that it had been revealed to him in a dream that Zubeir was the Expected Mahdi, the rightly-guided *Imam* who, according to tradition, would complete the work of the Prophet and establish Islam throughout the world. Disappointed in his hopes of Zubeir, Abdullahi accompanied his father eastwards on the pilgrimage, intending to remain in the Holy Land until conditions improved at home. The old man died and was buried at Abu Rukba, near Tendelti, and Abdullahi continued the journey eastward. As a Baggari he was unpopular, and was 'continually molested and hooted at' but he persevered because he now had a nearer objective than Mecca.

Life in the Northern Sudan ever since the days of the Fung has centred upon the religious brotherhoods, the *tariqas* or 'ways' of approaching God through the Sufic ceremony, the *Zikr*. Among the leading holy men in the Gezira at this time were Shaikh Muhammad el Sherif Nur el Daim, local head of the Sammania order and grandson of Shaikh el Tayyib, who introduced it into the Sudan from

Medina at the end of the eighteenth century, and Shaikh el Ghorashi el Zein of the Halawin, one of Shaikh el Tayyib's three *khalifas*.

Some stir had been caused at this time by the defection from the former to the latter of a remarkable disciple, Muhammad Ahmed, the son of a Dongolawi boat-builder on the White Nile. Muhammad Ahmed had denounced the licentious behaviour of the guests at a circumcision party given by Muhammad el Sherif and, although he apologised afterwards with great humility, was roughly dismissed with the old Jaali insult about the Dongolawi being *Shaitan* enclosed in the skin of a man. He then took himself to Shaikh El Ghorashi who lived near Mesellemia, the great market town of the central Gezira. When Abdullahi arrived there the Shaikh had just died and Muhammad Ahmed was engaged in building his tomb. Abdullahi swore eternal fealty and from then on was accepted as a member of the community, which withdrew to Aba Island on the White Nile as soon as the work was finished.

As time went on Abdullahi rose higher in Muhammad Ahmed's favour and it was to him, so he told his prisoner Slatin,* that the leader first confessed that it had been revealed to him that he was the Mahdi. 'But', added Abdullahi, 'I knew from the first moment I beheld his face that he was *El Mahdi el Mantazer*' (the expected deliverer).

By all accounts the Mahdi was a remarkable personality with unusual beauty of face and serenity of manner. From now on Abdullahi, a man of a very different type, whose strength and ability however concealed a genuine religious fervour, constituted himself the '*eminence grise*' which subtly influenced his master's decisions and movements. They went together to Dar Jimaa west of the river, where Abdullahi's brothers still lived, and then to el Obeid where they won over the leading religious shaikh, Sayed el Mekki, and returned to Aba Island via Tegale. Word of this tour by Muhammad Ahmed eventually reached Rauf Pasha, who sent troops, in August 1881, to bring him in.

An incredible and, to Sudanese eyes, miraculous inefficiency characterised this and subsequent military operations against the Mahdi. The troops attacked each other in the dark and fell an easy prey to their opponents. The Mahdi then returned to the Nuba Mountains, after appointing as his *khalifas* Abdullahi, Ali Wad Helu, a member of a local tribe, and his distant cousin Muhammad el Sherif. There he was joined by local malcontents and devotees, the latter mainly westerners. Responsible men still held aloof and

* Rudolph Slatin, late Governor of Darfur; author of *Fire and Sword in the Sudan*. For his life see Richard Hill, *Slatin Pasha*, O.U.P., 1965.

orthodox Islam regarded him as a pretender. It needed a whole series of successes to bring them round. He twice escaped capture on his way west, and was then attacked by a government force with Shilluk auxiliaries led by the *Mudir* of Fashoda, which walked straight into an ambush and was cut to pieces. Next came an expedition by Yusef Pasha el Shellali, an experienced soldier, who none the less neglected the most elementary precautions and was surprised at dawn and his force of 6,000 men annihilated. Now at last the urban Sudanese began to be interested, and Elyas Pasha, the wealthiest and most important merchant in el Obeid, established contact with the victor. Most of the Arabs threw in their lot with him at once and the outlying government posts in Kordofan were reduced in turn.

The Mudir at el Obeid, Muhammad Said, was known con-temptuously to the local people as *Gerab el Ful* Pasha, 'the old bag of beans', but he defeated the dervish assault with great slaughter and was only starved into submission after a five months' siege. The dervish commanders were not always merciful to conquered garrisons but on this occasion the Mahdi showed great clemency. It was only after Muhammad Said had attempted to conceal the hiding place of his money that he and three of his principal officers were executed.

It was now January 1883, and the Italians, with British con-nivance, were already landing troops at Assab on the Red Sea Coast in anticipation of the collapse of Egypt. But Abdel Qadir Hilmi, who had replaced Rauf as Governor-General, was operating quite successfully against Mahdist supporters on the Blue Nile while awaiting reinforcements. His policy was to leave Kordofan to the Mahdi, garrison the White Nile, and hold on until the situa-tion improved. His views were shared by his new chief-of-staff, a British officer called Hicks who had seen service in India and Ethiopia. In spite of the unsatisfactory nature of his troops, mainly recruited from the defeated army of Arabi Pasha and sent south as prisoners of war, Hicks succeeded in clearing the Mahdists out of the Gezira, but was then instructed by Cairo to reoccupy el Obeid.

He and yet another Governor-General, Ala el Din Pasha, left Dueim in September with the gravest misgivings on a march on which everything that could go wrong went wrong until finally they were led into an ambush in thick forest about thirty miles from el Obeid and annihilated. This disaster settled the fate of the Sudan. Darfur capitulated in December and the Bahr el Ghazal in April, but the Mahdi was in no hurry to advance to the river. He preferred to remain in el Obeid and consolidate.

The part played in these events by the British Government has
been severely criticised.

'How came Great Britain', asked Milner in 1892, 'to allow
Egypt to engage upon a course at once so futile and so perilous?'
The answer is a curious piece of political psychology. The
British Government had from the first taken up the position that
it was 'not responsible for the affairs of the Sudan'. It followed as
a logical consequence that, whatever follies the Egyptian
Government might commit in that quarter, Great Britain was
bound not to interfere with them. And to this theory we clung
with extraordinary tenacity during all the time that the Hicks
disaster was in course of preparation. General Hicks was in the
habit of sending despatches to the Egyptian Government
through Sir E. Malet, the British Consul-General. These
despatches, despite the forced hopefulness of certain phrases,
teemed with indications of the desperate nature of the venture
he was about to make. But Sir E. Malet was under the strictest
orders to hand them over to the Egyptian Government
without attempting to influence its decision . . . Over and over
again the Egyptian Government was informed that it could do
just as it liked in all matters connected with the Sudan; that it
might keep it or give it up, withdraw its troops, or reinforce them.
The matter was one about which Great Britain had simply
nothing to say.

'The faith in the power of phrases to alter facts has never been
more strangely manifested than in this idea, that we could shake
off our virtual responsibility for the policy of Egypt in the Sudan
by an official disclaimer . . . We were by our own express admission, as well as by the plain and palpable circumstances of the
case, responsible for the stability of the Egyptian Government.
But the Sudan was still an integral part of the Khedive's domi-
nions. Its retention involved, even under normal conditions, a
loss of £200,000 a year to the Egyptian Treasury. If things got
worse, there was no saying what proportions that loss might
assume . . . It was possible to hold that the best course for Egypt
was to try and cut the Sudan adrift altogether, withdrawing her
troops while it was yet time, and concentrating all her efforts
upon the defence of her own frontier. But it was not possible to
hold that the course she might pursue with regard to the Sudan
was otherwise than of urgent and vital importance to herself.
The very existence of Egypt might depend upon the proper
handling of a question concerning which we, the temporary

guardians of the country, were declaring that we had no responsibility!

'The theory of óur limited liability for the management of the affairs of Egypt is one that has played a great part in the history of the last ten years. Its genesis is not difficult to explain. As has been already shown, we plunged into the business of setting Egypt on her legs without any conception of the extent or the difficulty of the task. As the magnitude of our undertaking began to reveal itself to us, we strove by every means in our power to limit our obligations, and to narrow the field of our interference. We felt that we were bound to see Egypt out of trouble in vital issues, but that in all other things she had better look after herself. And in certain cases this principle has not proved a bad one. When we had our hands too full, and were doing everything badly because we were trying to do everything at once, it was a prudent policy to concentrate our scattered energies, and to direct our whole attention to a few essential points. But the success of such a course depends entirely upon a right judgement as to what is essential at a given time. And our judgement on that question was never more hopelessly at fault, than when we averted our eyes from what was going on in the Sudan and hugged ourselves with the fiction that we were not responsible for the action of the Egyptian Government in that region. It was this fiction which destroyed Hicks and his ten thousand men.'*

A few days after Hicks set out from Dueim there arrived in Cairo to fill the post of British Consul-General a man who was never to be accused of non-interference or of shirking responsibility. Sir Evelyn Baring, as Lord Cromer then was, rapidly came to the conclusion that Egypt must cut her losses and evacuate the Sudan. Public opinion in England decided that Gordon was the man for the job. Gordon as usual had different ideas — successive different ideas. Their most consistent feature was that it might not be necessary to evacuate at all. The Mahdi, like Zubeir before him, could be recognised as Governor in the West. Or (after an interview in Cairo) Zubeir himself could be brought back to re-form the private armies of the slave-traders. When these plans fell through there were alternatives and little action was taken to evacuate the Egyptian garrisons until it was too late. Gladstone in London was convinced that he was being jockeyed into occupying the Sudan and kept refusing to send reinforcements. The subsequent story is familiar. Khartum was besieged from May 1884 until the end of the year.

* *England in Egypt*, Chapter V.

The belated relief expedition scored some striking successes and its approach precipitated a desperate assault which carried the weakened defences on 25 January 1885. A forlorn hope, two steamers with some British troops on board, arrived on the 27th and withdrew northwards under heavy fire. It is doubtful if their presence could, in any case, have enabled the garrison to hold out until the arrival of a larger force to cover an evacuation.

Anybody who supposes that Gordon himself would have withdrawn leaving the garrison to its fate would be gravely in error. His death was an important factor in the reoccupation as he well knew it would be. It was also the basis of his subsequent reputation in the Sudan. 'He died strong in his faith' according to one who claimed to have been present at his death, and the Sudanese contrasted his religious fervour unfavourably with that of young Rudolph Slatin, the Governor of Darfur, who announced his conversion to Islam in a vain endeavour to hearten his Muslim troops against the Mahdists.

Except for garrisons at Wadi Halfa and Suakin, the Sudan was then abandoned to the Mahdi, whose generals reduced the outlying posts at Kassala and Sennar in July and August. The defence of Sennar, cut off from all aid, was a particularly striking achievement. Meanwhile on 22 June the Mahdi died and upon his successor, the Khalifa Abdullahi, fell the task of reorganising the administration of the country.

The Mahdi's system of government had been based on his three *khalifas*, of whom Abdullahi was *primus inter pares*,* and their primarily military administration was exercised through subordinate commanders known as *Emeers* and civil commissioners called *Amils* The hated Egyptian taxes were abolished in favour of the traditional Islamic *zeka*, a tithe whose payment is one of the obligations of every Muslim. This and other dues, in cash and kind, with the booty of war which was at first naturally considerable, were paid into a central treasury, the *Bait el Mal*, presided over by an official called the *Amin*. The administration of justice — perhaps the most important function of a ruler in Arab eyes — was vested in the Mahdi himself and his *khalifas*, but the hearing of routine disputes and petitions was normally delegated to such experts in Islamic personal law as had joined the Mahdist cause, under a chief justice called *Kadi el Islam*. Government was conducted through a personal secretariat, which filed copies of all correspondence, much of which has survived in the archives at Khartum. The Khalifa Abdullahi's

* He came to be known simply as Khalifat el Mahdi, the Mahdi's Successor. The other *khalifas* were distinguished by their personal names.

secretary, Shaikh Mudathir Ibrahim, father of a future Grand Kadi of the Sudan, maintained till his death a firm refusal to talk or write about the Mahdist administration. To do so would, he said, reopen too many old wounds.

Abdullahi, when he succeeded, had to rely on his brother Yagoub to deputise for him. The Khalifa Ali Wad Helu was a quiet and pious person whose chief role lay as a mediator. The young Khalifa Sherif, a disappointed candidate for the succession, could not be trusted. On him were centred the hopes of the Mahdi's family and the '*Awlad el Belad*', the Danagla and Jaalin and riverain people in general, to secure the preponderating share in the government to which they not unnaturally considered themselves to be entitled. Their leading man was the Jaali Emir Abdel Rahman el Nejumi, the conqueror of Sennar, an able soldier of whose loyalty the historian can have little doubt, whatever Abdullahi himself may have thought. Abdullahi's power, at the time of his accession, rested on the armies of the Black Flag, which were under his personal command and which included not only the fickle Baggara but the black Jehadiya, who had produced two able generals in Hamdan Abu Anja and Zaki Tamal.

The Khalifa Abdullahi's character may not have been as dark as it was painted by his prisoner Slatin. He was capable of sudden acts of clemency, as when he struck the chains off Hamid Fatin, the Hamar shaikh, because he found Hamid's little son, one of his attendants, in tears after encountering his father on some menial task about the house. None the less he lingers in Sudanese memory as a capricious despot and his rule was characterised by mass executions and by the cruel and arbitrary putting to death of faithful servants. Such was Ibrahim Muhammad Adlan, the able keeper of the treasury, whose road to the scaffold in Omdurman is still known as the 'path of blood'; and Zaki Tamal, whose successes against the Abyssinians aroused the Khalifa's jealousy so that he was walled up and left to die. Adlan's financial ability was badly needed to cope with famine conditions which prevailed at the time of his death (1890) and the loss of Zaki, following upon the deaths of Nejumi in battle and Abu Anja from natural causes, meant that there was no able commander left when the end came save the old fox Osman Digna, whose main objective in any battle was to bring off his own men intact, and Arabi Dafa'allah, who was away fighting the Belgians in the south.

The famine was due in part to bad rains but also to the Baggara *razzias* which were needed to provision the large armies and the great wen of Omdurman, the new capital across the river from the ruins of Khartum. The Gezira farmers, on whom the grain supply mainly depended, grew more and more reluctant to plant crops which were carried off as soon as they were ripe, and the stored grain which normally comes into the market in times of scarcity had long since been dug up and commandeered.

As time went on too, most of the old Egyptian taxes were re-imposed and the *Awlad el Belad* began to feel that they had exchanged a frying pan for a fire.

In 1891 discontent came to a head and the supporters of the Khalifa Sherif took up a threatening position round the Mahdi's tomb, virtually on Abdullahi's doorstep. A settlement was nego-tiated by Ali Wad Helu, but after they had laid down their arms the Khalifa Sherif was imprisoned and thirteen of his leading supporters, including two uncles of the Mahdi, shipped off to Zaki Tamal at Fashoda to be flogged to death with thorn branches.

For support against the local dissidents Abdullahi had compelled his entire tribe to migrate to Omdurman from southern Darfur. Most of them never returned, as the survivors were settled on the river for security reasons by the Condominium Government. So the Taeisha, who for a smallish tribe had supplied a quite remarkable number of *Emeers*, were reduced at home to a comparatively in-significant position *vis-à-vis* their old rivals the Beni Helba and Rizeigat.*

They were more of a liability than an asset, however, in Omdur-man, where their hand was against everyman's and their loyalty to Abdullahi (who was not of the leading families) questionable. A new praetorian guard had to be recruited and lodged between the Khalifa's house and the river in the quarter called after them *Harat el Mulazimin* and long left uninhabited after their departure, an abode of ghosts.

In addition to these domestic troubles and the invasion of the south, which will be described below, the Khalifa was involved in continuous fighting on his other frontiers.

Between 1884, when he defeated Valentine Baker at el Tebb, and his final repulse in 1896, Osman Digna was busy harassing the garrison of Suakin. From 1887 to 1889 Abu Anja and Zaki Tamal were fighting the Abyssinians, only to find that they had facilitated the advance of the Italians, who defeated a Mahdist army at Agordat in 1893 and occupied Kassala the following year.

---

* They retained, however, a not-untypical survivor in their *Nazir* Ali el Senussi, who died in December 1964. 'I have served under many rulers,' he remarked in 1953, 'Ibrahim Gerad, Zubeir, Slatin, Khalid, Osman Janno, Mahmud and Ali Dinar; but the present government is the first I have ever heard of which resigned without losing a battle. You must be mad.'

Darfur was a permanent thorn in the flesh. First of all the Governor, Muhammad Khalid Zugl, a cousin of the Mahdi's and a supporter of the *Awlad el Belad*, had to be lured eastwards with his army and forced to surrender by Abu Anja at Bara. Then the Fur prince he had left in charge became independent-minded and had to be expelled by Abdullahi's kinsman Osman Janno. Then a fanatic from Dar Masalit called Abu Gemmaiza, claiming to be the Mahdi's fourth *Khalifa*, marched on Fasher, which was only saved by his sudden death from smallpox. This was in 1889, and Osman's successor, the Emir Mahmud Ahmed, another relation of the Khalifa, was hard put to it to maintain his authority against the Masalit and other tribes west of Marra.

But the greatest danger lay in the North. The Nile column had been allowed to withdraw unmolested after the fall of Khartum, having shown itself to be a formidable opponent. But the Mahdi's dream of conquering Egypt had to be fulfilled and, after the fall of Sennar, Wad el Nejumi led a reconnaissance in force, which was repulsed with heavy losses.

For three years his army remained inactive at Dongola, living off the country and soon alienating whatever sympathy the people of Nubia may have felt for the Mahdist cause. Finally, in the summer of 1889 when the weather was at its hottest in one of the world's hottest areas, Nejumi started north along the left bank of the Nile. The enemy held the strong-points on the river and the *Ansar** were forced out into the desert in order to avoid a series of petty sieges. They struggled on to a point near the village known to history as Toski and there they were annihilated. The Baggara Homr, who disliked the Taeisha and suffered heavily in this battle always maintain that their contingent, like Nejumi himself, was deliberately sent on a forlorn hope in order to get rid of them.

The Anglo-Egyptian command made no attempt to follow up their success for some years. In 1895, however, Rudolph Slatin's romantic escape from captivity in Omdurman re-aroused interest in Europe and provided valuable military intelligence. In England public opinion began to renew its demands for vengeance for Gordon. Rumours reached London of a French plan to unite Djibouti with Dakar in a vast empire across the upper Nile. In Halfa the British officers who had been training the Egyptian army had long chafed under the restraining hand of Cromer and the cautious attitude of the British Government, which was at the time contemplating the evacuation of Uganda. In the same year there followed a complete change of policy in London and when, on

* Mahdists.

1 March 1896, the Italians were heavily defeated by the Emperor Menelik at Adowa and looked like being chased out of Kassala and Eritrea, Sir Herbert Kitchener was authorised to reoccupy Dongola.

By this time it was becoming clear that France was profiting in Abyssinia by the discomfiture of Italy and a French expedition from the west was rumoured to be on its way to the Upper Nile. There was therefore no question of halting the invasion at Dongola. The era of inefficiency was now over and the Khalifa was confronted in 1897 by a remorseless machine, advancing slowly and inevitably across the Nubian desert to the Nile and laying a railway as it went.*

Meanwhile the Emir Mahmud had been summoned from Darfur to take command of the defences. He swept the population before him as he came, adding useless mouths to his ration strength and creating hostility everywhere. He fixed his headquarters at Metemma, on the left bank of the Nile opposite Shendi. The Jaalin inhabitants objected to being turned out of their houses and were massacred, so that a stream of refugees and deserters poured northwards to supply intelligence to the invaders, who continued their slow advance. The arrival of Osman Digna with the army of the east, in February 1898, at last got Mahmud moving again† and the Anglo-Egyptian force found him strongly entrenched with his back to the dry bed of the river Atbara. On 8 April Kitchener attacked and after desperate hand-to-hand fighting inside the *zareeba* completely defeated the dervish army and captured Mahmud. As he has been severely criticised by a later generation for leading his captive in triumph through the streets of Berber, it may be of interest to quote two contemporary accounts, one British and one Sudanese. G. H. Steevens, a war-correspondent, wrote:‡ 'Farther behind, in a clear space, came one man alone, his hands tied behind his back. Mahmud, holding his head up and swinging his thighs in a swaggering stride — but Mahmud a prisoner, beaten, powerless. When the people of Berber saw that, they were convinced. . . . You may call the show barbaric if you like: it was meant for barbarians'. The Sudanese account was verbal and referred to the previous evening. 'When we had captured the Emeer', he said, 'we brought

---

* Professor G. N. Sanderson, in the *Journal of African Studies*, Vol. iii, Part 1 (1962), pp. 69–90, has shown that Kitchener after capturing Berber expected a strong dervish attack and was nervous of meeting it without further British reinforcements. Since Lord Salisbury was still, in October 1897, refusing to credit the tales of a French advance from the west, the final decision might easily have gone the other way.

† Sanderson also explains the reasons for Mahmud's long delay at Metemma.

‡ *With Kitchener to Khartum*, Blackwood, Edinburgh, 1898, p. 111.

him before the Sirdar, who was sitting in a rhorkee chair. Mahmud cursed him and reviled him as an infidel. For a time he was silent and then he leaned forward in his chair and roared like a lion. So we took Mahmud away.'

The advance south was resumed after four months' delay for reinforcements from England. On 1 September, after negotiating the Shabluka gorge, Kitchener encamped on the left bank of the Nile at Kereri, a few miles north of Omdurman, in a position surrounded by high ground which concealed the movements of the enemy. A night attack might have been very unpleasant but the Khalifa waited until daylight on the 2nd. After repelling a tremendous charge launched over the ridge between Jebel Sirgham and the river, the Anglo-Egyptian army moved out in pursuit, and was suddenly attacked on its right flank by the main body of the dervish army whose existence had been concealed by the rise in the ground. After a bad quarter of an hour discipline told and the victory was complete.

The Khalifa withdrew to Kordofan, and Omdurman, which had been heavily shelled by the gunboats, was occupied without opposition. Kitchener's first act was to desecrate the Mahdi's tomb. His object was to prevent it from becoming a centre of pilgrimage, and he was in no way deterred by the possibility of adverse criticism. Nor was he unmindful of the fate of Gordon's head and body, commemorated by a special service next day in the palace ruins.

The war was not yet over, but, as after the defeat of Hicks, all but the hard core of loyalists saw that a new power had come to stay and hastened to make their peace. This process was made easy by the presence of Rudolph Slatin, who was personally known to every man of consequence. Less helpful perhaps was the confidential secretary who drafted Kitchener's proclamation. 'What is this word for Amnesty?' he was asked. 'A very pure classical word,' was the proud reply. 'I doubt if any man save myself this side of Cairo knows what it means.'

Conditions during the interim period when the Khalifa and several of his *Emeers* were still at large are reflected in the following account of events which influenced subsequent history.

Immediately after the battle a gun-boat was sent up the Blue Nile to look out for a force under Ahmed Fadil, the *Emeer* at Gedaref, which was reported to be on its way to reinforce the Khalifa. On the morning of 4 September it encountered an advance party near Abu Ushur, shelled them heavily and forced them to retire to Abu Haraz at the mouth of the river Rahad. Their commander, a Hamari called Abdel Rahim Abu Dugl, was personally known to Slatin, who offered him amnesty and a commission. Although his career in the Abyssinian wars had been successful and rewarding Abu Dugl lost no time in changing his *jibba*. He was issued with 300 rifles and sent off in pursuit of a body of Taeisha under one Salih Hammad which was reported to be escorting a party of political suspects towards the Shilluk country. These were duly overtaken and found to include the Khalifa Shereef and the Mahdi's four remaining sons, el Fadil, el Bushra, Ali and Abdel Rahman, all of whom were interned at Shukaba on the Blue Nile. Soon afterwards the officer commanding at Sennar was informed that they were preparing to escape, raise the Kenana Arabs and join up with the Khalifa or the Emir Ahmed Fadil. A small force was sent to arrest them and while discussions were going on there was an attempt to rescue the prisoners. After a drum-head court martial the Khalifa Shereef and the two adult sons, el Fadil and el Bushra, were executed.

This distressing affair reflected the nervousness of the new administration and it influenced subsequent history, because it was upon the Mahdi's heirs that nationalist feeling has tended to concentrate. The Khalifa had designated his son Osman as '*Shaikh el Din*' to succeed him but Osman was killed at Kereri and none of his brothers seems to have been regarded as a claimant to the throne. They were competent men and a credit to their father, but they did not possess the '*baraka*', the odour of sanctity, which attached to the house of the Mahdi. The Khalifa's faction died with him on the battlefield of Gedid in November 1899, a few miles from his father's grave at Abu Rukba. But the cause of the Mahdi has never ceased to engage the earnest attention of the government of the day. The death of el Fadil and el Bushra meant that it had no leader in the early days. Ali, a boy of eighteen, was interned at Rosetta till 1905 when he entered Sudan Government service. He was a genial undistinguished little man who resigned to act as agent for his brother in 1926 and died in 1944. The youngest son, Abdel Rahman, born after his father's death, was brought up at Gezirat el Fil, near Wad Medani, by a relative, the *Omda* Muhammad Taha Shegiddi, and later lived quietly on a government pension in Omdurman. Round this remarkable man Sudan politics were later to circulate and through him modern Sudanese nationalism was to find its focus.

Chapter 3

Rehabilitation

D URING THE MAHDIYA the powers paid little attention to any claims Egypt might have to sovereignty over the Sudan. The various spheres of influence were allocated and re-allocated like those in any other part of Africa and it seems doubtful if Egypt's case — or rather Turkey's — would ever have been put forward had it not been for the accident of Britain being involved. The River War was a joint Anglo-Egyptian undertaking and it was in the name of the Khedive that the French were persuaded to withdraw from Fashoda, the Italians from Kassala and the Belgians from Lado.*

Lord Cromer was however determined not to allow a restoration of the old regime, the *Turkiya*, as the Sudanese called it — or the Old Turkiya to distinguish it from the new one just beginning — to which he saw two grave objections, Egyptian inefficiency and European interference. His solution was a Condominium, which would free the country from the capitulatory shackles which had been attached to the Turkish Empire. The idea may have been suggested to him by a brief experiment with Italo-Egyptian rule at Massawa in 1885. A condominium of a kind had been functioning in the New Hebrides since 1887, with France and Britain as administering powers, and was still functioning three quarters of a century later, but a dyarchy possible on a small island is not so well suited to the government of a large territory. There it could only be made to work when one partner dominated the other. The real power remained with one set of nationals while the other had to be content with the great mass of subordinate posts and a few senior ones. Egypt, of course, did not lack for channels of influence. The *Sharia* Courts,† the *Ulema*, the teaching profession, the commissioned ranks of the army and the administration of the *mamurias* were all or nearly all in Egyptian hands. The English, moreover, while still convinced that the Egyptians were incompetent to run their own country properly, were at this time strongly pro-Egyptian notwith-

* See Chapter 10.
† Islamic personal law courts.

47

standing. They saw themselves extending to the Sudan the same process of beneficent uplift which Cromer had been bestowing upon Egypt. They thought as well as talked in terms of defending Egypt's southern frontier and protecting the headwaters of the Nile. It seemed to them eminently reasonable that Egypt should pay for these privileges out of her new British-bestowed solvency, under-writing the Sudan budget and providing capital for railways and docks. So did many Egyptians at the time, but it was obvious that they would not submit to indefinite subordination in the Sudan any more than in Egypt. As soon as independence at home came in sight there was bound to be trouble. One has only to imagine the impossibility of, say, an Anglo-American Condominium working successfully, to understand the impracticability of the idea in other circumstances.

From the Sudanese point of view, however, this new status presented several advantages. It provided them with a more or less autonomous state of a unique character and with its own govern-ment. As the soldier administrators were replaced by civilians whose allegiance was to the Sudan instead of to Egypt the natural tendency of such officials to identify themselves with the interests of the territory, as they saw them, was accentuated by their peculiar status. In their order of priority British interests ranked second and Egyptian third, but the Sudan's came first. Later still, in the 'thirties, they themselves were inclined to worry about their isolation from the main stream of British colonial policy, but this does not appear in retrospect to have done much harm to the Sudan. Theories applied in Whitehall to the British colonial territories could be watched in action and accepted, modified or rejected, and experi-ments could be made freely — in local government or educational policy or 'Sudanisation', to use its modern title.

Anglo-Egyptian rivalry and friction also had its advantages. The exodus of Egyptian officials after the troubles of 1924 accelerated Sudanese entry into responsible positions in all branches of the administration and the commissioned ranks of the army and police force.* Later on the politicians were able to win concessions by playing off one power against the other. So the achievement of inde-pendence was undoubtedly accelerated, though this was perhaps a doubtful gain. Assuming, as it is not unreasonable to assume, that the post-war decisions to promote democratic self-government at the centre and start welding together the south and the north would have inevitably been made in the current climate of opinion, then

* Sudanese had held commissioned rank in the Army since 1905 and had served as sub-*mamurs* in the administration since 1915.

a delay of ten or even five years might well have been in the long-term interest of the Sudan. Time might also have allowed for experiment with some sort of federation, such as many Sudanese as well as British were advocating as a method of counteracting southern sensitivity and isolation, without necessarily weakening national cohesion.

From the point of view of the British civil servant condominium status was an advantage so long as Whitehall and Westminster were content to leave the Sudan to its own devices, but turned into a liability as soon as the country became a bone of contention between London and Cairo, with the British Embassy intervening as guardian of Egyptian rights and susceptibilities. The tendency in such circumstances is to put a brake on action, and if successive British governments have one chronic tendency it lies in this direction. Regarded dispassionately the imperialist adventures of the United Kingdom in the nineteenth and twentieth centuries seem always to have been initiated and executed by individuals on the spot or by vested interests — by Rhodes or Stamford Raffles or Consul Kirk at Zanzibar, or by a chartered company, cajoling or blackmailing the home government into supporting or ratifying their activities. Always Whitehall is at first nervous of action and hesitant to give offence to some third party. Sometimes in the end Westminster is precipitated into belated and ill-advised action of a kind never contemplated by the adventurer himself and better calculated to offend the third party than any or all of the acts from which the government previously shrank. In no context have the attempts of the home government to control her ducklings from the shore or launch out on her own been more consistently disastrous than in Egypt. The Sudan Government, whose development projects were usually reasonable enough, suffered to a certain degree from this propensity but on the whole it was left to get on with the job and the praise or blame must rest firmly on its own shoulders.

The tune was called by Kitchener at the outset. 'It is not mainly to the framing and publishing of laws,' he wrote in 1900, 'that we must look for the improvement and the good government of this country. The task before us all is to acquire the confidence of the people, to develop their resources, and to raise them to a higher level. ... It is to the individual action of British officers, working independently but with a common purpose on the individual natives whose confidence they have gained that we must look for the moral and industrial regeneration of the Sudan.'

It is difficult for anyone familiar with conditions a decade or two later to realise quite what a task confronted the soldiers in 1899. To

D

quote Steevens again (op. cit. p. 324): 'It is not a country: it has nothing that makes a country. Some brutish institutions it had, and some bloodthirsty chivalry. But it is not a country . . . Its people are naked and dirty, ignorant and besotted. It is a quarter of a continent of sheer squalor.'

Conditions in Omdurman a year after the battle are described in the third chapter of H. C. Jackson's *Pastor on the Nile* from Llewellyn Gwynne's letters home. The town was inhabited chiefly by gangs of masterless slaves who, while prepared to kill a man for a loaf of sugar, refused to work for hire in the rebuilding of Khartum.

The task of restoring order and establishing confidence was shared by the Egyptian *mamurs* and the British officers seconded as Inspectors of *Mamuria*, or as *mudirs*. Some of these remained permanently in the Sudan. H. W. Jackson, for instance, who was left in charge at Fashoda* while London and Paris argued and the issue of peace and war hung in the balance, stayed to govern Dongola from 1902 till 1921, and then retired to live in his old province.

The British were an arrogant set, according to P. M. Holt.† Steevens saw them as 'half savage still on the pinnacle of their civilization' and counted it for virtue. Kipling painted their portrait in *Little Foxes*, the story which includes his biggest howler, the statement that the Mahdi was killed on the battlefield of Kereri. Perhaps because the Sudanese at that time were not tuned in to liberal ideas, perhaps because the arrogance of the new rulers was at least preferable to that of a Taeishi *Emeer*, perhaps because there is a natural affinity between the two races, they succeeded in their double task. They won the confidence of the people and they established a standard of public security which amazed contemporary Sudanese and was a common topic among them a quarter of a century later. That a woman could go unescorted to the well, or return after dark from the market laughing and chattering with her sisters, that a man could travel long distances unarmed, that robbery and house-breaking were rare and the offenders usually caught and punished, that policemen were respected, that the soldier drew rations from the government and kept himself in barracks — all these things were still a positive good in their eyes a quarter of a century later. They came afterwards to be accepted

---

* Kitchener's staff when he arrived at Fashoda to persuade the French to withdraw included, besides Wingate and Lord Edward Cecil and another *Mudir*-to-be in Colonel Stanton, four future Admirals (Keppel, Beatty, Hood and Cowan) three future Generals (Smith Dorien, Maxce and Capper) and Lieut. Roberts, son of the Field-Marshal, who was to earn a posthumous V.C. at Colenso.

† *A Modern History of the Sudan*, p. 118 and *passim*.

as normal, and when breaches of the peace did occur Sudanese public opinion was shocked at incidents which would pass unnoticed in Damascus or Baghdad. This first achievement of the colonisers must be counted to their credit. They brought to the Sudan and to other parts of Africa a peace which was not a desolation and had not yet qualified for the inspired sobriquet 'Pox Britannica', once bestowed by a hurried typist in Kordofan.

The road was not an easy one. Away from the river pacification was a slow and arduous task. Those who believed in the Mahdi were on the watch for his destined successor, the prophet Jesus, and pretenders to the title caused trouble west of the Nile in 1903, at Singa in 1904, and at Tegale in 1912. A more serious affair was [the murder of an inspector and a *mamur* by the Halawin in the Gezira in 1908.

The frontiers too were unsettled and the hitherto unconquered Nuba, like the tribes of the south, were slow to trust or submit to the new breed of Turk. The anti-slavery department in Cairo set up a special branch in the Sudan to deal with raiders on the Abyssinian frontier and elsewhere.

In the west Ali Dinar, a grandson of the Sultan Muhammad el Fadl (1802–39) had made his way home from Kordofan to Darfur in 1898 as soon as he heard of the Khalifa's defeat and succeeded in defeating rival claimants to the throne of his ancestors. He was recognised as Sultan by the new government in 1900 and paid a nominal tribute, but the existence of a virtually independent despot on the western frontier did not facilitate the re-establishment of security in south-west Kordofan or the northern Bahr el Ghazal.

Security and justice, under codes introduced from India, provided a major step towards the achievement of public confidence. Their propaganda value was enhanced and supplemented by the health service established by the British and Syrian officers of the Egyptian Army Medical Corps. Their first task was to provide elementary sanitation in the towns (not in itself a very popular procedure); their second was the creation of small civil hospitals and the prosecution of a vaccination campaign. Once its initial suspicion was overcome the public response was tremendous and the new civil medical service early achieved its chronic condition of being over-worked and understaffed. Its battle honours are campaigns against malaria, bilharzia, cerebro-spinal meningitis, relapsing fever, yellow fever and sleeping sickness. A midwifery service inaugurated after the 1914–18 war by the Misses Wolff was probably appreciated more than any other activity in the whole history of the Condominium.

Next to Health, Education. One of the first acts as Governor-General of the paradoxical Lord Kitchener had been to collect money in Britain for a Gordon Memorial College. Apart from an abortive attempt by the Khedive Abbas to open a school in Khartum in 1850 the old government had left education to the Koran schools and the missionaries. Kitchener's first objective was to provide material for the civil service. His policy, as implemented by the first Director of Education, James Currie, has been criticised for 'poverty of conception and meagreness of execution'.* It started at the bottom with elementary vernacular schools and worked slowly up with its own output, the Gordon College keeping one step ahead from primary to intermediate, intermediate to secondary, until it finally blossomed into a University College in 1951 and a University in 1956.

The limiting factor in all these developments was revenue and the whole procedure in these early years was only made possible by the Government of Egypt subsidising the Sudan Budget until it balanced, at £1,600,000, in 1913.† This meant that the Condominium Government, though subject to strict financial control from Cairo, had the enormous advantage of being able to tax lightly while new sources of revenue were created.

Obviously financial independence for the Sudan must come from the soil and obviously the rain was not going to provide it. Irrigation must be the answer and in the interests of Egypt this could only be allowed if confined to the flood season (July to January) when surplus water was running unused into the Mediterranean. While these problems were under examination the first task was to get the farmers back on to the river lands and have those lands surveyed and registered. The new Governor-General, Sir Reginald Wingate, who succeeded Kitchener at the end of 1899, realised at once that

* P. M. Holt. op. cit. p. 120. *Per contra* Arthur Gaitskell (*Gezira* p. 54) writes that 'James Currie . . . whose reports show an astonishing interest in the economic needs of the country, decided, as soon as Garstin revealed the great potential of the Gezira, that his education department must begin to provide the basis for Sudanese technicians, for the civil and mechanical engineers which the future would demand. There was no money for such a purpose. The only thing was to appeal to philanthropists in Britain. The response came on the engineering side from Sir William Mather, who equipped the Gordon College with its first technical workshops'.

This personal link with the Sudan, Gaitskell points out, had important consequences, since it was upon Mather's initiative that the British Cotton Growing Association resolved, in 1910, 'that the attention of His Majesty's Government be drawn to the extreme importance of encouraging the further cultivation of cotton in the Anglo-Egyptian Sudan'.

† The exact revenue figure was £E1,568,352. Unless otherwise indicated the symbol £=£Egyptian up till 1957 and £Sudanese thereafter. The sterling equivalent of each was £1 0s. 6d.

there was a danger of speculation in land values as soon as the possibilities of an export trade were appreciated. Legislation was introduced to give province governors a strict control of sales both before and after registration and sales to foreigners were virtually prohibited. The immediate advantages of this for the riverain farmers and later on for the landowners of the Gezira were incalculable. Meanwhile the railway was pushed on to Khartum North in 1899. A branch line from Atbara to Suakin was begun in 1904, but the channel there was inadequate and difficult for modern shipping and the harbour of Sheikh Barghut, thirty miles to the north, was substituted as a terminus. The line was opened to traffic in January 1906 and in April 1909 the new harbour works of Port Sudan were formally inaugurated by the Khedive. Meanwhile the Blue Nile had been bridged at Khartum and the line went on south to reach Sennar in 1909, Kosti, by bridge over the White Nile, in 1910, and el Obeid in 1912. After prolonged operations in the *sudd* the natural channel was discovered and cleared in 1902 and regular steamer services established to Mongalla and Meshra el Rek. As a result of these activities, and especially of the revival of the trade in gum arabic from Kordofan, exports had risen by 1913 to a value of over £1,000,000, imports amounting to twice that figure.

The capital for all these enterprises was provided by Egypt, whose interest-free loans were left unpaid until after the Second World War.

Meanwhile experiments were made with flood irrigation in the Northern Province, and cotton cultivation was resumed at Tokar in the Baraka delta. These provided valuable experience of the merits and de-merits of various methods of tenancy and land tenure. Still more valuable was the research carried out on the only concession granted to foreign capital. This was at Zeidab, near the confluence of the Atbara river and the Nile. The concessionaire was an American millionaire called Leigh Hunt, who visited the Sudan in 1903 and convinced Wingate and Cromer of his ability and his good intentions. He formed a Syndicate in London to grow cotton and wheat by pump irrigation on an area of 10,000 acres.* In the succeeding years the Syndicate learned not only the techniques of successful cotton growing and rotation, but the advantages of tenant farming over direct labour.

Meanwhile farther south the vast plain of the Gezira with its gradual tilt from the Blue Nile to the White awaited the results of a survey of Nile waters, of investigation of the possibility of growing

* The local unit of land measurement, the *feddan*, equals 4,200 square metres, or 1·038 acres. Acre is used throughout this book as the equivalent of *feddan*.

cotton on the flood, and the arrival of rail communication to Port Sudan.

The Nile survey was carried out by William Garstin and C. E. Dupuis and established the principles of future planning — that storage works above the *sudd* area were useless until it had been by-passed, and that the water lost in the *sudd* by evaporation amounted to fifty per cent. If it could be conserved it would suffice for Egypt's forseeable needs and so release the Blue Nile surplus for the use of the Sudan. The objective was put by Garstin in 1904 as being 'to rescue the Upper Nile from the marshes in which it has lost half its volume; to control and regulate the great equatorial lakes, making them add to the flow of the river at will; to cause the waters of the Blue Nile to rise and irrigate the fertile tracts through which they pass; to secure to Egypt a constant and sufficient supply for the entire area between the cataracts and the Mediterranean; to free that country from the ever-present danger of a disastrous flood'. These were tasks which he felt to be worthy of comparison with any previously recorded in the world's history.

The possibility of irrigating the Gezira from a dam site near Sennar was established in 1908 and the question arose as to whether it would be possible to grow cotton there as well as wheat in the close period. An experimental pumping station at Tayyiba on Gezira soil was therefore planned and the Syndicate from Zeidab invited to run it on a fee basis. (They had to bring their tenants with them the first year (1911). No local farmers were interested.)

Meanwhile capital had to be found if a dam was to be built and irrigation works installed. The British Government, which had spent a great deal of money on various campaigns in the Sudan, took the line that Condominium development should be financed by Egypt. Egypt, however, could hardly be expected to produce capital for the growing of long-staple cotton in competition with her own major cash crop and with water drawn from her life-line, the Nile. The persistence of Wingate (who met Lloyd George as a fellow guest at Balmoral in 1912 and forced him to listen) and the British Cotton Growing Association, who interviewed the Prime Minister in January 1913, finally extracted the promise of a guarantee of interest on a loan of three million pounds. This was duly ratified by Parliament and a draft partnership agreement was initialled in London in July.

The events leading up to the Gezira agreement are described in detail by Arthur Gaitskell in his book *Gezira*. The points that emerge are first the value of prolonged experiment; second the successful adaptation of local customs of agricultural profit-sharing to the new partnership of Government, Syndicate and tenant farmer; third the solution of the problem of raising capital without alienating local rights by the device of lease-hold concession. In the elaboration of this scheme several names were prominent, but Mr. Gaitskell's account justifies his conclusion that the ultimate voice was that of one man — Lord Kitchener.

Kitchener had returned to Cairo as Consul-General in 1911, and it is characteristic of him that in 1913 he was riding round the cotton plantation in the Gezira.

When the military government removed the statue of the victor of Kereri from its plinth outside the old Secretariat building in Khartum they might perhaps have considered re-erecting it at Tayyiba. What he and his contemporaries did for the Sudan in this one context outweighs any other consideration.

Work began on the main canal on 1 January 1914. There were to be twelve more years of enforced experiment before water flowed in it.

The pause of the 1914–18 war rounds off this initial phase of condominium rule in the Northern Sudan. Two personalities dominate the picture. Reginald Wingate, the Governor-General, had been connected with Sudan affairs ever since 1883, when he was appointed to the staff of Sir Evelyn Wood in Egypt. From 1887 onwards, as Director of Intelligence to the Egyptian Army, he had sifted all the reports that filtered through to Assuan, sent in his agents, contacted anti-Mahdist notables, and arranged escapes. He it was who finally defeated the Khalifa in 1899, and who first thought, in 1900, of the irrigation possibilities of the Gezira. His subsequent part in initiating the Arab Revolt against the Turks and his attempt in 1919 to persuade the British Government to negotiate with Zaghlul Pasha testify to his ability and his imagination. It is difficult to fault Wingate. In the Sudan they thought him a little pompous, unduly proud perhaps of his victory

'which ended the Khalifa's bloody reign,
The finest battle of the whole campaign,'

but there is little evidence of this in his papers, which reveal him as extremely shrewd and able. What he lacked was *panache*, the gift of catching the public eye, like Cecil Rhodes or T. E. Lawrence or Gordon or Kitchener. Few dependencies have been so fortunate as to be governed for a decade and a half by a man with so much ability and so much local experience. If the British Government had realised his value, they would probably have taken him away much sooner.

The second personality was Rudolph Slatin, ex-Governor of

Darfur and prisoner of the Khalifa, now Inspector-General of the Sudan. Wingate governed the country in semi-military fashion through three secretaries, legal, financial and civil. In later years the Civil Secretary approached but never achieved the position of the Chief Secretary in the Colonial Service. In these early years he was mainly concerned with matters of personnel. In administration it was the Inspector-General who held the control. After all he knew personally every important man in the country. If the governor of a province wanted to dismiss a *Nazir*** or appoint an *Omda* it was no use arguing with Slatin. His omniscience naturally caused resentment, and in later days the 'Slatin *nazirs*' were not always regarded very favourably, but during the pacification period his presence was invaluable. With an inexperienced Governor-General this might have been dangerous, but with Wingate in the saddle there was a constant check.

In the end they went at much the same time, removed by the circumstances of war.

They left a country well on the way to economic prosperity, as has been seen. The administration had settled down under the triple secretariat, to which had been added in 1910 an Executive Council, of which the four functionaries already mentioned were *ex-officio* members. The Heads of Department were grouped under the appropriate Secretary and the Province Governors, while answerable to the Governor-General through the Civil Secretary, were subject to inspection by Slatin. Departmental heads in the provinces were answerable to their chief but were expected to operate generally under direction of the Governor. The Inspectors were originally, as their title indicates, intended to supervise the work of the *Mamurs*, or district officers, but inevitably became District Commissioners in fact long before they were given this title officially.

As time went on the soldiers were progressively replaced in the northern provinces by civilians recruited from university graduates in Britain. In the south soldiers or ex-soldiers were retained on contract as it was soon realised that the four-year period in a station normal for pensionable staff was too short for the acquisition of

---

* The title *nazir* literally means overseer, and was used not only for the head of a tribe but for a station-master and the headmaster of a school. The Arabic title *Mufattish* (Inspector) was always used for the District Commissioner and as all British officials, except the engineers, were inspectors of one kind or another newcomers used to assume it to be the Arabic for an Englishman. The ordinary word for a foreigner, *Khawaja* (mister), for some reason acquired a vaguely derogatory meaning in the Sudan.

southern confidence. The average strength of the service was 140. Its total intake during the whole period of 54 years was 391.

In this period of direct rule the District Commissioner did practically everything. Chauncey Stigand's handbook on *Administration in Tropical Africa** includes chapters on Selection of a Station, Building a House and Office, and How to keep accounts and start a filing system, as well as The Establishment of Order. Later developments include such remarks as 'At each station the official hopes to have a doctor, hospital and veterinary arrangements'. 'It would be an immense benefit if there was a sanitary board of the central government to give advice.' His 'eventual ambition' would be the establishment of a school, with an agricultural class and technical instruction as well as the three 'Rs'. For the sons of chiefs Stigand recommends a course of four years at a station, two as a soldier (or policeman) to learn discipline, one year at school and having agricultural training, and one year attending courts and learning 'simple judicial and official work'.

The chiefs — or in the northern Sudan the shaikhs — continued of course to administer their tribes and villages and retained sufficient traditional power and prestige to enable them in later years to be given statutory judicial and administrative powers without difficulty.

In the south this Sanders of the River period lasted well on into the 'thirties. In the north it began to disappear soon after the war.

* Constable, 1914.

Chapter 4

Years of Strife—1914–24

THE WAR did no real harm to the Sudan. It postponed the building of the dam at Sennar and sent the costs up, but the delay enabled the Syndicate to get useful experience of cotton-growing in Gezira conditions and it was not difficult to raise capital in the post-war boom. Sudan products had their share in the boom too, and exports rose to a value of over two million pounds in 1921. Revenue reached the £4 million mark at the same time.

In 1914 there had been a period of extreme scarcity after bad rains and it was remembered in the Sudan not as the year of the war but as the year of the flour, because the Government imported flour from India to prevent a famine, a step which had an unlooked-for propaganda value.

Administratively the war involved a period of marking time. Slatin Pasha as an Austrian subject had to resign and the post of Inspector-General was abolished, with the result that the Civil Secretary's office became more important. Turkey's entry on the German side complicated the political picture because Egypt was still subject to Turkish suzerainty and the Khedive Abbas Hilmi, unlike his predecessors, was on excellent terms with the Turks. The British Government cut this Gordian knot by proclaiming a protectorate over Egypt, deposing the Khedive, and appointing his uncle, Prince Hussain Kamil, to be Sultan. Abbas had visited the Sudan in 1909 and was not unpopular; but there was no great enthusiasm for the Turkish connection and Wingate in effect removed any danger of sympathetic action when he engineered the Arab Revolt in the Hejaz. In Sudanese eyes the Shareef of Mecca was a better Muslim and a better-known Muslim than the Turkish Sultan and the possibility of a *Jehad* against the infidels became remote.

The deportation of the Khedive did however very much annoy the Sultan Ali Dinar of Darfur. During the first decade of the century the new Sultan had succeeded in consolidating his position. Rival candidates to the throne had been disposed of, the Baggara reduced to unwilling submission, and the Masalit in the west forced to recognise his suzerainty. But the frontier with Wadai was undefined and in spite of repeated requests Slatin was unable to give him any detailed information about it. Nor did Khartum appear to be very helpful in defending his claims against the French, who had captured Abeché in 1909 and occupied a number of territories over which the Sultans of Wadai and Darfur had both claimed dominion at one time or another.

The Sudan Government was in fact doing its best on the diplomatic level, and various assurances were received from the French and passed on to the Sultan; but the French ideas of boundaries were very different to Slatin's* and each promise was betrayed in turn. The Masalit resisted fiercely but were forced in 1911 to cede one third of their territory to France. Still the fighting continued and when French and British took the field as allies in Europe in 1914 the Sultan had had enough. In 1915 he formally renounced his allegiance to the Sudan and in May he wrote to the shaikhs of Kordofan calling upon them to revolt. Rumours also reached Khartum of correspondence between him and Nuri Bey, the Turkish agent with the Senussi at Kufra. It was obvious that something would have to be done, but Kitchener (now Minister of War) could not sanction anything in the way of military operations with the Dardanelles campaign in full swing. Wingate had to wait, while the Sultan despatched to the Inspector of Western Kordofan at Nahud threatening messages, and formal challenges fastened to the hafts of spears. Finally, hearing in February 1916 that a force was being got together in Kordofan, he despatched a final cartel addressed to the Governor of Hell in el Obeid and the Inspector of Flames at Nahud.

By this time preparations had been completed for crossing the waterless dunes and the body of 2,000 troops moved off on an unopposed† advance to a point twelve miles north of Fasher, where, on 22 May the Fur attacked and were defeated. Ali Dinar withdrew to Jebel Marra. As soon as the rains were over a flying column under Hubert Huddleston, a future Governor-General, went out to look for him. The royal camp was surprised at dawn and the Sultan killed by a chance shot in the act of mounting his horse. So Darfur was again absorbed into the Sudan.

* There is an interesting French version of these events in *Du Congo au Nil* by General Hilaire, Marseilles, Ed. A.S.C.G. 1930. See also *Ali Dinar, last Sultan of Darfur* by A. B. Theobald, Longmans, 1965.

† Arabi Dafallah (see Chapter 10) tried vainly to persuade the Sultan to attack the invaders in the sandy country and use harassing tactics. Ali Dinar executed Arabi instead, and had a curse put on the wells at Abyad, which unfortunately only came into force after the invaders had passed, but has been remarkably effective ever since.

More important to the future of the country than the recovery of Darfur was the emergence of el Sayed Abdel Rahman el Mahdi as a potential political leader. He had been living quietly in Omdurman but was recognised by his father's followers as the heir to his *baraka*. His elder brother receded into the background, for primogeniture does not bestow an unquestioned claim to succession in the Arab world. It is personality that counts; and of that Abdel Rahman had a large share.

He was a man of considerable height and presence, western Sudanese in appearance (his mother came from the west), emotional, sometimes petulant, with a keen sense of the dramatic. He never failed to rise to the occasion or seize an opportunity. Irked to ask as a favour what he felt to be his of right; prone at times to listen to unsound advice, yet always basically shrewd; moving in public with a studied grace and dignity, yet capable of throwing the whole thing aside with his ceremonial head-dress and going down on his knees to play with a three-year-old child. Like his Machiavellian henchman, Muhammad Khalifa Sherif, the Sayed had a very endearing quality.

His opportunity came when it was suggested that he might contribute to the allaying of anxiety by reminding his father's followers that the Turk was after all their traditional enemy. He went out on tour with this objective and left an agent in every district he visited. After the war he was given the wood contract for the Sennar dam construction, and with the capital so acquired laid the foundations of a considerable fortune from pump-irrigated cotton grown on Aba Island, his father's old refuge.

Had the population of the Sudan been predominantly Mahdist the Sayed might have ended up as a constitutional monarch, but the bulk of the Jellaba and the tribes east of the Nile did not recognise his father's claim. Their leader was el Sayed Sir Ali el Mirghani, head of the Khatmia order, who had returned from exile at the *Futūh** and had since been regarded as the unquestioned religious leader of the country. It was to Sayed Ali that Ali Dinar addressed a grand remonstrance in 1915, prior to declaring his independence. It was Sayed Ali who took precedence as first citizen at all official functions. His *khalifas* enjoyed a similar priority in the provinces, but from now on the Government tent and the Khatmia tent at the Mulid celebrations were confronted by a Mahdist enclosure. As Sayed Abdel Rahman's wealth increased so did the splendour of his entertainment. Sayed Ali was increasingly resentful.

He could hardly have differed more from his new rival. He is a

* *Futūh*, the 'Opening' of the new regime.

little man; in complete control of his emotions; essentially conservative ('He would like the world to have stood still about the
year 1911', Sayed Abdel Rahman once remarked), grave and
courteous and blandly inflexible, refusing to be drawn on matters of
politics, playing his cards with consummate skill, never forgetting
a friend or forgiving an enemy, the extent of the web he weaves will
be appreciated only when he is no longer there to weave it.*

From now on politics begin to play an increasingly important
part in Sudan affairs and if the new political groupings provided the
woof of the pattern of Sudanese nationalism the Sayeds and their
followers furnished the warp. Many hands plied the shuttle. As often
as not they were Egyptian.

Wingate had gone to Cairo at the end of 1916, to succeed Sir
Henry McMahon as High Commissioner. (The new title dated
from the new Protectorate). The death of Lord Kitchener had
deprived the British Government of its expert on Egyptian affairs
and Wingate's experience was needed there, provided a competent
successor was available for the post of Sirdar.† Wingate's choice
was the Civil Secretary, Lee Stack, one of the original Egyptian
Army officers seconded for service in the Sudan. He had served in
the south in 1902 and acted as Sudan Agent and Director of
Intelligence in Cairo from 1908 to 1913.

These two appointments involved a return to the old personal
relationship of the days of Cromer and Kitchener. Unfortunately
Sir Edward Grey, whose telegram of 12 October 1916‡ offering
Wingate the post reveals a sympathetic understanding, was removed from office almost at once, and as the war progressed there
was less and less realisation by the harassed authorities in London
of the need to pay some attention to Egyptian susceptibilities. In
spite of Wingate's efforts the *fellahin* were virtually conscripted into
labour battalions and by the time the war came to an end resentment at the British occupation, hitherto confined to the educated
classes, had become universal. When, in November 1918, an Anglo-
French manifesto was published offering self-determination to the
peoples freed from Turkish rule the Egyptians felt that they were
entitled at least to similar treatment. So did Wingate, but his

* In conversation on Wednesday of Munich week, when all seemed lost and the
Sudan lay open to Italian invasion, he discoursed on world affairs with dispas-
sionate erudition. A quarter of a century later, in December 1963, he seemed quite
unchanged and spoke in similar fashion, revealing a keen interest in all kinds of
extra-mural events and activities. What a remarkable pair of men they were!

† The Command of the Egyptian Army and the Governor-Generalship of the
Sudan were combined until 1924.

‡ Quoted on p. 201 of Ronald Wingate's biography of his father, *Wingate of the
Sudan.*

request that the nationalist leader, Zaghlul Pasha, be allowed to accompany an official delegation to the U.K. was rejected and he had finally to stand impotently by in London while Zaghlul was arrested and deported to Malta. The resultant explosion of violence in Egypt brought the British Government to the belated realisation that they had more than a seditious minority to deal with, General Allenby to Cairo to restore order and Wingate into undeserved eclipse.*

Lord Milner was then sent out to inquire into the origin of the disturbances, which had caused considerable loss of life in the now familiar setting of mob violence.

They had two unfortunate consequences — they led Zaghlul and his successors to conclude that England would not listen to reason but could be shocked into acquiescence, and they had upon the English attitude to Egyptians an effect similar to that of the Indian Mutiny on the English attitude to Hindus.

The Milner Report had a rider on the Sudan, rejecting most of Egypt's claims to a voice in the administration but recognising her vital interest in the distribution of Nile Waters. It proposed to set up an international Nile Waters Commission, with representatives of Egypt, the Sudan and Uganda. It added that 'the contiguity of Egypt and the Sudan and their common interest in the Nile make it desirable that some political nexus between the two countries should always be maintained but it is out of the question that this connection should take the form of the subjection of the Sudan to Egypt. The former country is capable of and entitled to independent development in accordance with its own character and requirements. It is much too early to attempt to determine its ultimate political status'. The Condominium should therefore continue as before, but the administration 'should be left as far as possible in the hands of native authorities, wherever they exist, under British supervision'. Sudanese should also be introduced into official posts as they became available. The office of Governor-General should be disassociated from the command of the Egyptian Army and given to a civilian.

Needless to say these proposals were quite unacceptable to the Egyptians. Negotiations dragged on until 1922. Zaghlul and five of his colleagues were deported again, but no other Prime Minister was either willing or able to take a more conciliatory line. Finally, in February 1922, the British Government made a unilateral declaration which in effect gave away all their bargaining points. It recognised Egypt as an independent sovereign state but reserved

* The sorry story is related by Ronald Wingate. op. cit., Chapter 9.

for subsequent discussion four crucial matters — the Suez Canal, Defence, the Minorities and the Sudan.

In spite of this gesture and of measures taken to implement it the wave of violence continued. In September 1922 Zaghlul, now back in office, held discussions with Ramsay Macdonald in London, but he was not prepared to agree to anything short of complete independence for Egypt with the Sudan, and the evacuation of British troops. In October the Conservatives returned to power in the United Kingdom. In November Sir Lee Stack was assassinated in the streets of Cairo. This brought the conciliatory period to an end.

Naturally all these happenings had a direct impact on the Sudan. Most of the army officers, the *Mamurs* administering districts, the civil servants and schoolmasters and artisans were Egyptians. They were in full control of the Irrigation Service and the Muhammedan Law Courts. All of them were in full sympathy with their countrymen and vociferous in support of them. They, and 'private persons operating from Cairo' rapidly made the Condominium almost unworkable.*

The younger generation of educated Sudanese had grown up with these men and was strongly influenced by their ideas. A White Flag Society was formed in Khartum to work for the unity of the Nile Valley in collaboration with a 'National Egyptian League for the Defence of the Sudan'. Its leader, an officer of Dinka origin called Ali Abdel Latif, led a demonstration in June 1924 and was sentenced to three years' imprisonment. The cadets at the military school, Egyptian and Sudanese, demonstrated in protest and on the same day (9 August) members of an Egyptian Railway battalion at Atbara mutinied and ran amok for three days. There were similar disorders at Port Sudan and Malakal (H.Q. of the Irrigation Department).

All this provoked a stream of protests and counter-protests between London and Cairo. British public opinion, made aware for the first time since 1899 that the Sudan existed, grew more and more uncompromising and anti-Egyptian.

When Stack was assassinated Lord Allenby went to the Council of Ministers escorted by an entire British cavalry regiment and delivered an ultimatum which included a demand for the withdrawal from the Sudan of all Egyptian officers and units, after which the Sudanese battalions would be reconstituted into a Sudan Defence Force, and a notification that the Sudan Government would be authorised to increase the irrigated area in the Gezira from 300,000 acres to an unlimited figure.

* *Survey of International Affairs* (1925) Vol. I, p. 241.

The military provisions were put into effect immediately, but not without bloodshed. On 27 November two platoons of the 11th Sudanese Battalion in Khartum mutinied and marched on the Palace, where they intended to join up with the unit on guard duty and, in conjunction with Egyptian artillerymen in Khartum North, bring off a *coup d'état*. The Palace Guard, however, were marched off in another direction by a resourceful officer and the Egyptian artillery remained quiet. The Sudanese moved off towards the Blue Nile bridge and were met by the G.O.C., Huddleston Pasha, who ordered them to return to barracks. They refused, and on continuing their march were fired on by British troops. They then broke into the military hospital alongside the road and went to ground there, resisting to the last man with great heroism.

So ended Egypt's first real attempt to reassert her rule over the Sudan. Mature Sudanese opinion was not yet ready for a change and was indeed surprised at the retention of the Condominium façade, and the Egyptian flag. At the end of the year the Council of *Ulema* substituted the title of the Caliph of Islam for that of the King of Egypt in the Friday prayers, and the country settled down to twelve years of virtual British protectorate.

Chapter 5

Irrigation and Devolution

T HE INCLUSION in the Allenby ultimatum of a threat to increase the area irrigated in the Gezira was ill-advised. In Egypt it destroyed faith in the one definite pledge the British Government had always insisted on, the guarantee of her paramount right to the waters of the Nile. To the world at large it sounded like an empty threat. After all the dam was still a-building and the possibility of irrigating more than 300,000 acres a long way off.

The clause arose out of negotiations which had been going on for some time. The Gezira Scheme had long since been approved in principle and formed part of a comprehensive plan put forward in 1919 by Murdoch Macdonald for the Egyptian Ministry of Public Works. This included the Jebel Auliya Dam on the White Nile, a dam at Roseires on the Blue, and the Nag Hammadi Barrage in Egypt itself. But the proposals got bogged down in the morass of political strife and in 1920 the figure of 300,000 acres was put forward as a voluntary limitation to allay Egyptian anxiety. It was the area contemplated in an agreement drawn up between the Sudan Government and the Syndicate in October 1919, providing for a ten-year concession in the first instance. When, in May 1921, the Egyptian Government decided to suspend all its own irrigation works in the Sudan until such time as the political status had been determined, no objection was raised to the Sudan Government carrying on in the Gezira subject to the 300,000 limit.

The British Government was strongly criticised at home over this threat and in January 1925 undertook to cancel it on condition that a commission be set up to discuss how irrigation could best be conducted in the Gezira without detriment to Egypt's rights and interests. This commission was successful in finding a solution which was embodied in the Nile Waters Agreement of 1929 and has governed all subsequent Nile Control.

The plan was that in future the allocation to the Sudan should not be calculated by acreage but by consumption. This meant that the area irrigated could be increased by economy in the use of water. Existing privately-owned pump schemes were included in the resultant rather complicated assessment and provision was made for a gradual increase in the Sudan allotment as extra water became available to Egypt, from her new dam at Jebel Auliya and successive improvements in the storage capacity at Assuan.

Meanwhile in July 1925 the first water from Sennar flowed on to Gezira soil. By this time so many experiments had been carried out and so many safeguards introduced that the most bigoted of anti-capitalists has failed to find any serious objection to the Scheme. The land was surveyed, registered and rented (or purchased) from the owner at the rates prevailing for first-class rainland. Controls were instituted to provide against absentee landlords and the accumulation of too much land (now a good interest-bearing security) in one pair of hands. Possibilities of cropping in the limited period available had been exhaustively studied and tried out on the various experimental pumping stations.

Tenancies of thirty acres were allotted in the first place to owners of land in the vicinity, up to their farming capacity. The remainder were held for good farmers from elsewhere. Profits were divided on a traditional system of 60 per cent/40 per cent. The Government, as proprietor, hired the Syndicate to work the Scheme, for ten years in the first instance, by allocating part of its 60 per cent share.*

The Syndicate had been carrying the risks during the experimental period, when prices rocketed to 45 pence per pound in 1920 and slumped in 1921 to eightpence halfpenny.

The tenants' privileges included exemption from taxation on his animals and his personal food crops (part of the ten-acre rotation). This exemption caused considerable bitterness amongst the rain-farmers outside the Scheme and incidentally made it difficult for subsequent local government authorities to find a method of raising revenue. (Most L.G.A.s in the Sudan levied a rate on the main taxes or else retained the bulk of the tax itself, passing on a proportion to the central government.)

But the neighbouring population soon began to share in the general prosperity by providing manual labour for weeding, clearing canals and picking the cotton. Later on this mobile force was augmented by immigrants from farther afield, the White Nile, Kordofan, Darfur, Wadai and West Africa, making their slow way to and from Mecca on the pilgrimage. An unforeseen result of the new labour market was that it accelerated the final elimination of domestic slavery. Hitherto the freedman had had to live in a special settlement or go to work in the towns. (The situation of the freed-

---

* 25 per cent of the total, later reduced to 20 per cent as part of a revised set of conditions which included the prolongation of the concession to 25 years.

woman was not so simply solved. She lost her guaranteed maintenance in old age and unless she could find a freedman to marry was apt to drift into prostitution.)

The first extension under the new plan was allotted in 1929 to a sister syndicate, the Kassala Cotton Company, which had been vainly trying to grow cotton economically in the Gash Delta since the railway reached Kassala in 1924. The trouble was that the land belonged to the Hadendoa, a Beja tribe with little aptitude or inclination for farming, but the Government considered that they should be persevered with as tenants. This task had finally been assumed by a Government Board and the Company moved to more congenial surroundings in the Gezira.*

The Scheme was now beginning to show signs of paying its way, covering the interest on the added capital costs of the extension and providing the Government at long last with surplus revenue for much-needed expansion of the social services.

The general economy also was flourishing. Revenue had recovered from the trough of 1921–3 and climbed steadily to nearly £7 million in 1929. In the same period the value of external trade nearly doubled itself. Standards of living were rising, particularly in the Gezira of course. The railway extension had reached Gedaref and was moving on to Sennar. The southern provinces seemed at last to be sufficiently pacified to be ready for development. To quote The Gentleman in the Small-clothes — 'All was gas and gaiters'.

But a double disaster lay ahead. At the very time when the bottom fell out of the American economy and prices slumped all over the world the twin diseases of blackarm and leaf-curl, which had been engaging the worried attention of the Government Research Farm since soon after its foundation in 1918, struck at the Gezira crop. In 1931 the yield fell to 1·4 kantars to the acre (against 4·8 in 1926) and the price from eighteenpence to sevenpence halfpenny.

The whole future of the Scheme was in the balance and so was the solvency of the Sudan. External trade fell from thirteen million to five and the revenue for 1931 was short of the budget estimate by a million pounds (about one fifth). Drastic measures were obviously required. Expansion programmes were eliminated, 20 per cent of all government staff retrenched, allowances cut or abolished, salaries

---

* In spite of its unreliable floods and unsatisfactory farmers, the Gash continued for some reason to produce the finest long-staple cotton in the world and to provide the seed for the Gezira Scheme down to the nineteen-sixties when a combination of factors, including, apparently, irrigation works upstream in Eritrea, combined to interfere so seriously with production that consideration was given to letting the whole delta revert to grazing.

reduced, and charges increased.* The country was back in pre-Gezira days but with the weight of the Gezira overheads to carry. One more bad season would mean bankruptcy. In the circumstances the Syndicate gambled on a change of rotation. They cut out the leguminous fodder crop, switched the grain to a separate area, and gave the land adjacent to the cotton two years fallow to dry out. In addition new seed was imported from Egypt and sowing delayed as long as possible to avoid the worst of the rains. The gamble succeeded and production in 1932 rose to 4 *kantars*, but 1933 saw another failure and so did 1934. The causes, however, were not always the same, much was learned on each occasion, and 1935 saw not only a yield of 4·5 *kantars*, due to the digestion and application of these lessons, but the appearance of a new variety of cotton, resistant to both leaf-curl and blackarm, which produced an average of 5·3. This variety was the product of experiments conducted by a botanist at the Research Farm, A. R. Lambert. If Kitchener's statue deserves re-erection in Tayyiba Lambert's might go up in Khartum. He made an independent Sudan possible. Prices had recovered slightly to eightpence in 1933, but remained consistently low during the 'thirties, dropping below sixpence in 1938. The Gezira Scheme succeeded in spite of the price of cotton and in spite of the load of debt it now carried. But succeed it did, from then on.

The Government's measures to compete with the great depression were facilitated by the existence of machinery for the closing down of sub-district headquarters and the transfer of watch-and-ward duties and control of petty crime to local authorities. This system of Indirect Administration has been much criticised, but it cannot be denied that it is far more inexpensive than a bureaucracy.

The Milner Report, it will be remembered, advocated what was later to be called 'Sudanisation' of the Civil Service and utilisation of indigenous institutions as well. The old administrative service has in fact continued to function in India, and the Sudan, but British Colonial theory in the 'twenties and 'thirties regarded direct administration as unsuitable for a self-governing state. 'Sudanise' the state services as fast as you like, ran the argument, but remember that the District Commissioner as such will cease to exist when independence comes. 'Regional Commissioners' had not yet made their appearance in England and those who suspected that the French prefect or the Turkish Kaimakam might provide a more

---

* A treasury expert, H. E. Fass, was sent out from England to act as Financial Secretary from 1931 to 1934. *Fās* is the Arabic for an axe and the wry amusement which the Sudanese got out of this helped to tide them over the period of adversity.

useful pattern for Sudan local government than the English county council were in a minority.

The Sudan approach, however, was in its inception purely pragmatic. Sir Lee Stack and his colleagues, looking back over the first twenty years of Condominium Government, found it to have changed its aspect. There appeared to be an unnecessary proliferation of government agencies: too much centralisation, too many petty imposts and market rules, too much correspondence, too many functionaries. In 1921 Stack was feeling his way towards a readjustment by judicious use of the native authorities quoted in the Milner Report.* The idea was not new.† It had been tried out successfully by Sandeman in Baluchistan, by the Brookes in Sarawak, and in Nigeria under Lugard, whose 'Dual Mandate' was to appear in 1922 and become the *vade mecum* of a generation of colonial servants. It was also to have striking success in Tanganyika under Sir Donald Cameron.

The principle was that there is nothing about Western institutions, instruments of government, legal procedure, police or penal methods, which makes then universally right *de natura*. Some of them may be regarded as having proved their general applicability. Others may be suited only to the local society which gave them birth. It is wiser therefore to rely at first on indigenous instruments where they exist, rejecting them only when they are manifestly inefficient or undesirable and otherwise adapting them for the work in hand.

On the face of it this principle sounds reasonable enough and likely to commend itself to local patriotism. From a utilitarian point of view it has obvious advantages. Take, for example, a case of camel stealing in Kordofan, normally punishable by a sentence of two years' imprisonment. Is justice likely to be better served by a visiting magistrate with clerk and interpreter, recording evidence on oath and in full detail, and dependent upon expert testimony concerning tribal grazing custom and the brands on camels — or by a panel of elders with all this information at their finger-tips?

Sir John Maffey, who came from India to be Governor-General in 1926, had no doubts on the subject and made Indirect Rule a main plank in his policy. But the educated classes in the Sudan regarded it as a deliberate attempt to set back the clock and retard development.‡

---

* See his Annual Report for 1921 with quotation from Rajah Brooke of Sarawak.
† The rebellion of Boadicea in East Anglia in A.D. 61 was the result of the mishandling of an important native authority by officials who failed to appreciate the niceties of indirect rule.
‡ For a fierce attack on the whole policy see P. M. Holt, op. cit., pp. 132 seq.

The chief reason for this opposition had very little to do with local government as such. Nobody in the Sudan today seriously questions the value of the native authority as an instrument of conciliar administration. Criticism is concentrated on the shaikh's age-old combination of judicial with administrative authority, and the Sudanese District Commissioner, whose interests the new policy was supposed to threaten, has become its strongest advocate. He foresees that any attempt to split these powers is likely to lead to administrative chaos and that further substitution of stipendiary magistrates for the local J.P.s who in 1963 disposed of 130,000 cases will not only be very expensive but will lead to endless delays in justice and to the proliferation of the type of local lawyer whose main objective is the suppression or fabrication of evidence, with the result that in Egypt and India conviction on honest evidence has become virtually impossible.*

The original objection to the policy was political, not administrative. The whole set of the times was away from tribalism, squirearchy, aristocracy and constitutional monarchy towards universal suffrage, national socialism, one-party government, and dictatorship. The later stages of this trend were not, however, as yet discernible in the 'twenties and the administrative advantages bulked large. Was it not also welcomed by the Government as a counterpoise to urban nationalism? Undoubtedly. Maffey's generation had grave doubts about the suitability of twentieth-century parliamentary democracy to Africa. They thought of the future more in terms of the eighteenth, a country governed by clever men from towns and rotten boroughs held in check by the Tory squires in the back benches, solid and stolid but by no means squalid, keeping their eyes open for any infringement of rural rights.

The express train of African development never stopped at this station, but the attempts of tribal chiefs and rural populations everywhere to pull the communication cord earned for them and for the policy that upheld them a permanent unpopularity with all right-thinking and progressive persons.

It is, however, as incorrect to suppose that the entire system of indirect rule was invented by the Sudan Government out of spite against the educated classes for the events of 1924 as it is to imagine that the Gezira Scheme was inaugurated for the same reason with the intention of putting a spoke in the wheel of the Egyptian

---

* There is a vivid account of conditions in Egypt in a book called *Maze of Justice*, by Tawfik el Hakim, published in English by the Harvill Press, London, 1947.

economy, as I was told by a young Sudanese in Nyala in 1964.*

Implementation began in 1922 with an ordinance regularising the authority which the nomad shaikhs had in fact never ceased to exercise. Three years later village headmen were empowered when sitting with elders to inflict a fine not exceeding £2. This was the beginning of judicial devolution. The same year the Sultan of the Masalit, who had been left in semi-independence after his incorporation in Darfur province in 1919, was granted a 'native administration budget'. This was the beginning of financial devolution. In 1927 the powers of nomad shaikhs were extended by an ordinance empowering the Governor-General to issue a warrant to any shaikh, nomad or sedentary, specifying the powers conferred. In 1928 grants were legalised to cover the pay of court retainers and officials, night watchmen, and similar functionaries hitherto belonging to what were called 'local provincial services'. The town *omda* and his dog-berries took over watch-and-ward from the province police, sometimes holding disorderly persons in a lock-up overnight and bringing them before a panel of justices of the peace functioning with the powers of a magistrate of the third class under the code of criminal procedure. The rural shaikh and his elders judged by local custom and tradition, subject of course to appeal, and a body of case law and precedent was rapidly built up in each area, co-ordinated by the supervising authority,† and executed by retainers who soon came to include in their ranks not only messengers, bailiffs, and policemen, but forest guards, quarantine men, veterinary and agricultural overseers.

In this rather haphazard way a degree of administrative authority and financial autonomy grew up in town and country round the original judicial unit.

At first there were obvious possibilities of friction — the government policeman directed to take an accused before the *omda* instead of the *mamur*, the police officer arriving on the scene of the murder to find that the shaikh and his clerk had been interrogating witnesses, the departmental official told to apply to the *nazir* for personnel to establish his quarantine or fence his forest reserve — all these in their several ways were at first irritated or resentful. The government *kadi* was particularly suspicious of those courts which, by virtue of

* Another criticism advanced was that money was diverted to rural schools which should have been spent on higher education. This would have laid the Government open to the same charges later levelled in respect of the south, that it deliberately left the undeveloped areas in a state of ignorance and backwardness.

† Questioned as to the propriety of sentencing an offender under the Public Order Ordinance, a court president remarked, 'Not local custom? Of course it is local custom. It has been in force for twelve years hasn't it?'

possession of an *alim*, or certificated Doctor of Law, had power to deal with Muslim personal law inside the tribe or unit. Women litigants would play off one against the other. But all these anomalies were ironed out without much difficulty as the years went by and criticism became restricted to theory rather than practice. It was, for instance, commonly believed for years in Omdurman that shaikhs' courts could impose the death sentence,* that there was no right of appeal, that nobody ever checked the books or interviewed the prisoners.

Those upon whom this duty fell were the District Commissioners and, later on, *Mamurs*, the men whose future the policy was designed to threaten. No administrative officer could regret, however, a policy which freed him from the eternal tasks of tax assessment and collection, the investigation and punishment of petty crime, the drudgery of market control and herd checking, and all the tedious paraphernalia of bureaucratic administration.

Local government, of course, had to be regularised and legalised and provision made for village and district councils. This was catered for by a corpus of legislation passed in 1937, which divided up the whole country into Municipalities, Townships, and Rural Districts and prescribed the range of powers which could be transferred to the Local Government Authority in each. From this time onwards all administrative power was vested in an L.G.A. and where no native authority existed the District Commissioner was formally designated as such, thereby acquiring for the first time a statutory authority for such powers as he had hitherto exercised either under a specific ordinance or undefined.

The next important legislative step was not taken until 1943 and will be described in the context of devolution at the centre, but the following review of local government made at the time is a convenient summary of the progress achieved in spite of financial stringency.

'In 1943 the Native Courts tried 49,327 criminal and 14,084 recorded civil actions, compared with 25,492 criminal and 4,049 civil cases dealt with by the state courts. The administrative form accompanying the judicial responsibilities has varied considerably. The nomad shaikh with his tribal organisation was naturally given a larger measure of control in the early stages, whereas the duties of a small *omda* in a sedentary district may still be confined to settling minor disputes and collecting taxes under the authority

---

* Native courts were rarely allowed to impose a sentence exceeding two years imprisonment.

of the District Commissioner. Between these two a variety of conditions prevail. . . . Financial responsibility, entrusted to rural authorities only after they have proved their worth in justice and administration, is normally delegated at once to the town councils and other urban bodies which have existed in a consultative capacity for some years. In the rural areas twenty administrations, entrusted first with the disbursement of block grants and later with expenditure on works and services and the collection of revenue, now have budgets of their own. . . . One of them has controlled for several years a complicated system of local markets, the fees from which constitute a large proportion of its revenue, and has successfully avoided friction with the representatives of the big native and foreign commercial firms bidding at the auctions. For the most part, however, the rural areas do not, like the townships, draw their revenue from local rates, but retain a portion of the taxes collected on behalf of the Central Government.

'. . . The next step was to extend to rural areas the system of councils which had been applied to the towns. . . . Councils are being inaugurated in village, pump-scheme, *khut* (a local division comprising a group of *'omodias'*), district and, in fact, any suitable existing unit. They may be co-terminous with an entire administrative district, combining several local authorities, including a town committee. They may be subordinate to a local government authority or they may constitute such an authority. They may be advisory or executive or a little of both. Their members may be nominated or elected or some of each.'

This account* goes on to describe the inauguration of Province Councils in 1944 and to discuss the attitude of the educated Sudanese and the possibility of providing a career for him in local as well as central government service. The system described above has in fact provided the basis for the local government system in the new Republic.

Meanwhile as the nineteen-thirties proceeded the economy slowly began to recover and in 1939 revenue and volume of trade were again standing at five and six million pounds respectively.

Economic development and social services had meanwhile been gravely handicapped. The export trade in cattle was however encouraged by the sinking of deep bores along the trails from Darfur to the railhead at el Obeid and the growing of rain cotton successfully fostered in the Nuba Mountains (finally pacified in

*Extracted from *Survey of the Anglo-Egyptian Sudan*, Longmans, 1946.

1929). The drilling rigs were few and the ginneries far between, but by 1941* the export of cattle had expanded in a decade from 5,324 cattle to 29,131 and of sheep from 858 to 62,474. The gum trade was flourishing and the institution of auction markets at the main centres in Kordofan facilitated in addition the building-up of an export trade in ground-nuts, sesame and melonseed.

Restriction of medical services is a very grievous thing. The ideal for a country like the Sudan is to concentrate the skilled surgeons and physicians in central hospitals fed from a circle of dispensaries with accommodation for in-patients, staffed by less qualified medical officers. Each of these in turn provides a nucleus for a series of dressing-stations. If every potential patient is within twenty miles of a dressing-station and every dressing-station has a weekly ambulance service, curative medicine can be regarded as functioning reasonably well. There was still a very long way to go before this ideal could be achieved but the Sudan had one asset, in the Sudanese doctor.†

On his last visit to Khartum, in 1914, Lord Kitchener had remarked on the need for a medical training centre there, and when he was drowned two years later a subscription list was opened in England for the foundation of a school in his memory. The Kitchener School of Medicine, built and endowed with this money, was opened by Sir Lee Stack in 1924 just before his assassination.‡ For many years it attracted the best brains in the Gordon College, and its products were not just good examinees. They were usually extremely good doctors.

These efforts were supplemented by a hierarchy of medical assistants and male nurses and by traditional midwives trained in modern methods at the School of which mention has already been made.

In spite of the depression these men between them attended in the year 1934 some 86,000 in-patients and six million out-patients§ against 1924 figures of just under 20,000 and just under 400,000 respectively. Operations performed also increased during this decade from two to ten thousand.

On the preventive side a Public Health Ordinance had achieved, with the aid of the vulture and the sun, a fair standard of sanitation throughout the country. Endemic diseases such as malaria and

---

* Accelerated by war conditions.

† Tribute must be paid to the pioneer work of the Syrian doctors who provided a large proportion of the military and civil medical staff in the early days.

‡ Stack himself was commemorated by the Stack Laboratory, which with the pre-existing Wellcome Tropical Research Laboratories, financed by Sir Harry Wellcome, has earned the Sudan a reputable place in the field of tropical medicine.

§ The population at the outbreak of war was estimated at seven millions.

bilharzia and tuberculosis were subject to permanent preventive measures and constant propaganda. Two unwelcome immigrants from the west, sleeping-sickness and relapsing fever, had been met by prolonged campaigns. Cerebro-spinal meningitis, the Axe-Wielder, as the Sudanese called it, stood always at the door, ready to 'strike once and strike no more' because no second blow was needed.

Various new drugs and pesticides have now lightened the task of combating these afflictions. In January 1939 experimental injections of sulphonamides reduced the mortality in a C.S.M. epidemic from 80 per cent to 10 per cent. Dusting with D.D.T. now kills the relapsing fever louse with alacrity, whereas in 1930 villagers and pilgrims had to be cajoled into taking a bath while their garments were handed out and boiled. The sleeping sickness campaign will be described later.

All these activities had a benison upon them. They were unquestionably doing good. In the Sudan the process of saving life can be pursued for years to come without the emaciated spectre of over-population peering over the shoulder of the doer. Meanwhile he can see the reward of his labour in the eyes as well as the bodies of the healed, and the knowledge that he is only touching the fringe of the dark cloak preserves his humility.

But it is Education which bulks largest in contemporary esteem, perhaps because Health is beginning to be taken for granted. Here success cannot be measured by statistics. The Sudan Education Department's case for the defence of its achievement before the war cannot be based upon the numbers but upon the quality of its product — the civil servant, the doctor, the judge and *kadi* and schoolmaster. It had at first to contend with prejudice and suspicion. A proposal in 1928 that a Koran school for little girls be opened in Wad Medani, the capital of the Gezira, was accepted by the citizens on condition that the teacher be over seventy and the pupils under seven! A society in which young men were seen and not heard, in which a grey-haired son did not take a seat in the presence of his father and abstained from lighting a cigarette when travelling in company with his elder brother, viewed with dismay a system under which a boy was constantly told to think for himself and encouraged to voice his views:

'Take but Degree away, untune that string
And hark! what discord follows.'

The conversion of conservative opinion took a long time and political disturbances in the schools after the war revived much of the old criticism. The demand for girls' education finally came after years of patient propaganda, with dramatic suddenness, expecting the Government to produce teachers by the wave of a wand. British administrators and British educationalists seldom saw eye to eye on this subject, but the product is a good product. The rude son has not struck his father dead. Nor does he engage in pitched battles on the Omdurman waterfront.* The reputation of the Sudanese student in English university towns today stands high, with land-ladies as well as with tutors.

Currie had defined his objectives in 1900 as three. First, the provision of vernacular schools to spread elementary education among the masses by training teachers and converting a few of the existing Koran schools into models. Secondly, the supply of educated Sudanese for the Army and the Civil Service by means of inter-mediate schools at Khartum and Omdurman, where English would be taught. Finally, the provision of skilled artisans by the creation of a technical school.

By 1910 there were 39 elementary schools and six intermediate, with the Gordon College now providing secondary education. A woman controller of girls' education was appointed in 1920 and twenty years later had 65 elementary schools in action, with one intermediate and a teachers' training college. By 1936 the strength of the Gordon College (which included a Law class) had risen to over 500. In 1943 there were 117 government elementary schools for boys, 11 intermediate and two junior secondary, in addition to a number of non-government educational institutions and 144 village schools. Between them they provided a measure of education for about 50 per cent of the town boys and 15–20 per cent in the country.

Technical training was confined till 1924 to one department of the Gordon College (founded in 1903) and a school for stone-masons at Omdurman, founded in 1907. In 1924 a school for railway artisans opened at Atbara and in 1932 the Omdurman school was extended to include all the building trades. (The year being 1932, in the trough of the depression, they built all their own workshops, class-rooms and offices.) In 1933 the Railway School achieved a higher course for chargemen, and schools for enginemen, marine engineers, electrical engineers, and traffic officers followed. The product of these schools experienced little difficulty in taking over the running and staffing of the government railways and steamers when the time came for them to do so.

In 1937, when money was at last becoming available again from the Gezira, the De La Warr Commission was invited to visit the

* For an opposing view see p. 122–3.

Sudan on its way from East Africa and draw up a plan for future development which bore fruit in spite of the war in the opening of a series of higher schools, Veterinary Science and Agriculture in 1938, Science and Engineering in 1939, Arts in January, 1940. When the Gordon College itself was raised to post-secondary level in 1944 these colleges, with the Kitchener School of Medicine, formed the nucleus of the University College of Khartum.

But the most important advance in the period under review was made in 1934, when a Teachers' Training College for elementary schools was opened at the village of Bakht el Ruda on the White Nile. Here the whole teaching system and syllabus were revised and revivified from the bottom upwards and a model created for African education in general. In 1939 the process was extended to the inter-mediate level and experiments inaugurated in adult education, the after-care of former pupils, and the provision of text-books and literary material.

This review has inevitably outrun the account of political events, to which is it now necessary to return. Progress was retarded but not halted by the Italian invasion of 1940. The Sudan was in good shape and good heart when the crisis came.

Chapter 6

External Affairs
and Political Development

THE YEAR 1934 saw the return to the Sudan as Governor-General of Sir Stewart Symes, who had served before the war as private secretary to Wingate and Assistant Director of Military Intelligence.

The two chief planks of his platform were economic development and the state services. He was convinced that the D.C. and the *Mamur* would be an anachronism in an independent Sudan and that the sooner their functions were handed over to revenue officers, a centralised police force, a professional judiciary and the like the better. He viewed with a lack-lustre eye the enthusiasm of the Arcadians who had come to regard the shaikh as suspect if he sat on a chair behind a table instead of on a rug under a tree. His astringent criticisms served as a useful corrective in many aspects of administration and although he revived the old controversy over immigrant cotton-growers — this time in the Nuba Mountains — it was undoubtedly due in large measure to him that economic development there* and elsewhere was pushed on as soon as financial conditions allowed.

It was also fortunate that he was so well qualified by service under Wingate and later experience in Palestine and Aden to take an expert part in the negotiations between Britain and Egypt which at long last looked like bearing fruit. Relations had improved slowly since 1924 and a common apprehension was now bringing the two countries together in opposition to Mussolini. Symes arrived in the middle of a crisis caused by an Italian attempt to occupy the oasis of Uweinat in the top left-hand corner of the Sudan, which resulted eventually in the cession to Italy of the Sarra Triangle, west of the oasis. The invasion of Abyssinia followed in 1935, with sanctions and repercussions and refugees, and appeals to the Sudan Government

* Douglas Newbold, Governor of Kordofan, initiated in 1935 an annual conference at Delami of heads of departments from Khartum to study and further the possibilities of development in the Nuba area. This project was very much in tune with Symes's policy and had his enthusiastic backing.

to move in from the west. Sudanese opinion was strongly anti-Italian and anxious for military intervention. The foundation of subsequent friendly relations between the Sudan and Ethiopia after centuries of hostility were laid at this time and consolidated when the Emperor came to Khartum in 1940 and fought his way back to Addis Ababa with the aid of the Sudan Defence Force.*

Meanwhile Anglo-Egyptian conversations had taken place in 1927 (Sarwat-Chamberlain), 1929 (Mahmoud-Henderson) and 1930 (Nahas-Henderson). All reached a measure of agreement. All broke down over the Canal and the Sudan. But the general atmosphere improved with each visit to London, and the construction of the Jebel Auliya Dam in the early 'thirties brought Egyptians back into contact with British officials in the Sudan.

At the end of 1935 negotiations were resumed, this time in Cairo and with a delegation more widely representative of Egyptian opinion than any of its predecessors. In spite of delays due to the death of King Fuad in April and a general election shortly afterwards a twenty-year treaty was finally achieved in August 1936 which recognised Egypt as a fully sovereign state and restricted military occupation to the Canal Zone. The Condominium Agreement was reaffirmed and the *status quo ante* 1924 restored without prejudice to the question of sovereignty over the Sudan.

Although the High Contracting Parties agreed that the primary aim of their administration must be the welfare of the Sudanese, the Sudanese themselves took no part in the negotiations. A considerable body of opinion in the country determined not to let this happen again. Since 1924 a new national consciousness had developed. Kipling's prophecy of 1913 that the demand would soon go up 'Soudan for the Soudanese'† had been fulfilled in just over a decade, though the rider, 'devoted enmity' has not. The most prominent feature of the movement was the new Mahdism. Sayed Abdel Rahman had accompanied a delegation to England in 1919, and had unexpectedly presented his father's sword to King George, who handed it back with the request that it be used in the defence of his realm. Various versions of this story spread across Africa and were reported to be causing repercussions at one time as far afield as Nigeria, but the Sayed had no intention of putting himself at the head of a body of fanatical *Ansar* from the west. Instead he insti-

---

* Since the war Abyssinian raids into Sudan territory, a commonplace in pre-war days, have virtually ceased. 'Between 1916 and 1927 there were 41 incursions into Kassala and the Fung (Blue Nile) Province and 23 into Mongalla, in addition to organised slave-raiding and arms-running all along the border.' — Macmichael, *The Sudan*, p. 96.

† *Letters of Travel*, last page.

tuted in Khartum a sort of salon where most of the future political leaders were to be found discussing the events of the day. Inevitably a rival group developed round Sayed Ali, so that from the beginning nationalist feeling was split into two groups. On Divide and Rule principles this should have been satisfactory to the Government, but in fact it was an irritating handicap to progress, and involved responsible officials in a continual tight-roping act. To please one Sayed meant offending the other and the usual result was to satisfy neither.*

Thinking Sudanese looked round for neutral ground and found it in the Sudan Schools Club in Omdurman, an institution twenty years old which now emerged as the headquarters of a Graduates' General Congress, constituted on non-sectarian lines in February 1938 with a Committee of Sixty and a Council of Fifteen.

Its object was defined as being 'to promote the general welfare of the country and its graduates' (former pupils of intermediate and secondary schools) and the Government was asked to give consideration to its views and suggestions on matters of public interest.

The men responsible for this venture have never really understood why they fell foul of the Government, especially as the new Civil Secretary, Douglas Newbold, who succeeded Sir Angus Gillan in 1939, was not only sympathetic in the English sense but also in the French. The demands they put forward in 1942 were, they felt, reasonable enough and yet they received a violent rebuff. Why?

The real reason had nothing to do with their demands. It lay in their claim to represent the whole country, which the Government could not admit, as it repeatedly emphasised. In its first recognition it debarred the Congress specifically from claiming to represent the views of any but its own members and even its acceptance of a declaration of loyal support on the outbreak of war with Italy had to be qualified by a similar *caveat*. A further contention arose over the Government's right to individual consultation with Congress members, which Congress sought to prevent.

The trouble was that the Government's own plans for setting up representative institutions had taken too long. The basic idea was not dissimilar from the pyramid system later introduced by the military government on a Pakistan precedent. Village councils would return members to district councils, district to province and province to central. For this to work in practice it was necessary to get the district councils functioning properly first, and it was not

* In his *Personal and Historical Memoirs of an East African Administrator* (Oliver and Boyd, 1963) Sir Geoffrey Archer (Governor-General 1925–6) ascribed the difference of opinion with Council which led to his resignation to Mirghanist resentment at his partiality for Sayed Abdel Rahman.

until 1937 that the necessary enabling legislation was passed. The first town council in control of its own budget did not open until 1942 and the province councils (advisory) did not come into existence until 1944.

Looking back from a period in which the current of events is quickening in geometric progression, the leisurely nature of this approach is obvious. It is significant that both Symes, in his 'Note on Administrative Purposes in the Anglo-Egyptian Sudan', dated May 1938, and Newbold in a broadcast about the Advisory Council dated January 1944, quoted an Arabic proverb about acting in haste and repenting at leisure. Both these men were well aware of the need to keep a step ahead of public opinion. Newbold in fact, writing to J. W. Robertson (his successor) in June 1944, quoted W. K. Hancock's *Argument of Empire* in criticism of British administrators for 'quietly ambling along, very just, very humane, very patient — when they ought to have been . . . in the dickens of a hurry'.*

Both would certainly have felt, confronted by the speed of post-war political development, that it could not help being disastrous, condemning Africa to a century or more of Latin-American anarchy. Yet need they have taken quite so long to get moving?

The answer is that by pre-war standards they did move quite fast after 1937, considering the imminent threat of war and, in 1939–40, the possibility of having to evacuate the country altogether. The delay lies farther back than that. How long did it take to get the 1937 legislation through the drafting office? Several years, one would guess, judging by experience with other legislation. The Advisory Council, however, need not have waited. Proposals were in draft in 1939. The delay was really due to doubt as to whether an advisory council would function properly and whether the pyramid system was suitable for long-term development. Newbold approved for publication as late as 1945 a statement that 'the local government unit might double the role of parliamentary constituency with success for a sufficiently long period'.† In September 1941 he had admitted that the question of a method of associating the Sudanese with the Central Government was unanswered and must be settled 'in the next few years'. Legislative councils on the Colonial Service model, he wrote in March 1944, were not ideal, according to the experts, and parliamentary institutions unsuitable. 'Something new must be decided, but what that something is they don't know.'‡

Meanwhile he was unhappy about the Advisory Council, which

---

* *The Making of the Modern Sudan*, p. 380.
† *Survey of the Anglo-Egyptian Sudan 1898–1944*, p. 50.
‡ *The Making of the Modern Sudan*, p. 357.

F

met for the first time in May 1944 and, in spite of a Congress boy-cott, was remarkably successful within the limits of its functions. The Congress boycott was the result of a series of disagreements. Relations had been fair until 1940, when everyone's nerves were on edge and the Prime Minister of Egypt, on an official visit to Khartum, was approached by Congress for a grant-in-aid. The Sudan Govern-ment's assumption of umbrage at this appeal for an outside subsidy at least disabused Egypt of the notion that Congress was the creation of British intrigue. It led to another tiff later in the year and the resignation of the Committee of Fifteen. This procedure was re-peated in 1942 and seems to be part of the predestined pattern of recent colonial history — the moderates present a request deemed unacceptable, are rebuffed, and give place to extremists, so that in retrospect the original request seems so mild that nobody can remember why it was turned down.

The election of the new Committee was conducted for the first time on Mahdist-Mirghanist lines and it forthwith imposed a ban on members taking part in the broadcasting service (the current bone of contention), discussed a similar ban on military service, and considered the admission of non-graduate merchants and farmers to broaden the basis of Congress representation and increase its membership. (Then about 1,000 strong.) Peace was restored in October after conversations between Newbold and the future Prime Minister, Ismail el Azhari. The year 1941, which saw the defeat of the Italians in Ethiopia and the recession of immediate danger to the Sudan ,was uneventful as far as internal politics were concerned.

The 1942 President, Ibrahim Ahmed, was a known moderate, and cannot have expected that the Government would accept the twelve demands which Congress put to it in April of that year. What he did expect, however, was that the Government would discuss them, and this the Government could not do without admitting that the Congress was entitled to speak for the nation. The demands themselves cover practically every point of controversy then and later, and provide a useful summary thereof:

(1) The issue, on the first possible opportunity, by the British and Egyptian governments, of a joint declaration granting the Sudan, in its geographical boundaries, the right of self-determination, directly after this war; this right to be safe-guarded by guarantees assuring full liberty of expression in connection therewith; as well as guarantees assuring the Sudanese the right of determining their natural rights with Egypt in a special agreement between the Egyptian and Sudanese nations.

(2) The formation of a representative body of Sudanese to approve the Budget and the Ordinances.

(3) The formation of a Higher Educational Council, composed of a Sudanese majority, and the devoting of a minimum of 12% of the Budget to education.

(4) The separation of the Judiciary from the Executive.

(5) The abolition of ordinances on 'closed areas' and the lifting of restrictions placed on trade and on the movements of the Sudanese within the Sudan.

(6) The promulgation of legislation defining Sudanese nationality.

(7) The stopping of immigration, except within the limits agreed upon in the Anglo-Egyptian Treaty.

(8) The termination of the Sudan Plantations Syndicate contract at its expiration.

(9) The carrying out of the principle of welfare of the Sudanese and their priority to government posts as follows:

(a) By giving the Sudanese an opportunity to share effectively in ruling the country; this is to be attained by the appointment of Sudanese in posts of political responsibility in all the main branches of government.

(b) By limiting the appointments to government posts to Sudanese.

(10) The Sudanese to be enabled to exploit the commercial, agricultural and industrial resources of the country.

(11) The promulgation of an ordinance imposing on companies and commercial firms the obligation of reserving a reasonable proportion of their posts for the Sudanese.

(12) The cancellation of subventions to missionary schools and the unification of syllabuses in the northern and southern Sudan.

The subsequent correspondence and government action up to the opening of the Advisory Council are given in detail on pp. 542–70 of *The Making of the Modern Sudan*. Newbold died suddenly in March 1945 and his successor, J. W. Robertson, decided that leading political figures must somehow be brought into consultation over the next step. For this purpose he called in 1946 a constitutional conference to discuss measures to further the association of Sudanese with the machinery of central and local government.

Before considering the recommendations of this conference, however, it is necessary to go back to 1938 and review the distracting events of the years between.

The Munich crisis caught the Sudan Government in the middle

of the leave season. It had practically no arms or reserves and neither had they in Cairo. There was no reason to suppose that Italy would remain neutral if Germany went to war or that she would prove so ineffectual an enemy. Nor was the Sudan's own position clear supposing Britain was at war and Egypt was not. No one really knew the answer to this in June 1940 and there was a story of a senior Naval officer sailing unchallenged into Port Sudan by night after Mussolini declared war and being reduced to apoplexy by the retort that, 'So far as I know, Sir, this is a neutral country'.

It soon ceased to be neutral *de facto*, because the R.A.F. took off the same night from their base in the Red Sea Hills and bombed Massawa and Asmara; but the position of the Egyptian troops in the Sudan remained a mystery. They used to fire at air-raiders and their artillery was ready to defend Port Sudan against Italian destroyers, but when a defence line was being worked out round the city of Khartum it was not known exactly what part the Egyptian battalion in Abbas Pasha barracks on the perimeter was supposed to play in the event of attack.

Since the entire defence of the country depended at this time on the Sudan Defence Force and three British battalions, a total strength of less than 10,000 men, with the police force* and a few aircraft, the responsibility for the defence of the city was relegated to the Auxiliary Defence Force, a body whose history will never be written, but which had its comic side.† Being based originally on departmental anti-aircraft teams, each with a Lewis gun mounted on the office roof, it included private soldiers who were Members of Council and corporals who were office messengers. British and Egyptians and Sudanese, Greeks and Cypriots, Orthodox, Protestant, a Coptic Presbyterian, a Moravian and even a belligerent Quaker were on the role of religious allegiance. The constitution of the force proved convenient also for granting combatant status to various categories of civilian — District Commissioners or Syndicate Inspectors commanding police or irregulars on the frontiers,‡ telegraphists and engine drivers in the forward areas, minesweepers

---

* The police were embodied *en bloc* in the armed forces as soon as the Sudan was declared to be at war.

† As when Corporal Roseveare was unable to give evidence before a mystified military court because he was attending a meeting of Council, or when Private Flaxman applied for his discharge because as Chief Justice he had to have non-belligerent status. A recurring *contretemps* was when a newly posted D.A.Q.M. at Area H.Q. would discover the existence of several hundred British Other Ranks who never drew any pay or rations.

‡ Notably in the defence of Kurmuk and the Eritrean operations of Frosty Force and Meadow Force, Banda Bukr and Banda Fung.

at Port Sudan, interpreters attached to non-Arabic-speaking military forces, ambulance units recruited from the Sudan Medical Service, listening-post personnel between Khartum and the frontier, anti-paratroop patrols in outlying villages, all found harbourage in its all-embracing ranks.

There had been some talk of the desirability of keeping Africans out of the war and undoubtedly the Duke of Aosta hoped that the capitulation of Britain to Germany would involve the cession of the Sudan to Italy without any fighting, but when it came to the point there was no question of any similar attitude on the Sudanese side. They regarded it as their war and in the light of subsequent history they were right. So incidentally were the Afrikaner organisations which supported Hitler. If Germany and Italy had won the war the wind of change would have blown through Africa in a very different direction. Some of the South Africans and Rhodesians who contributed so largely to the conquest of Italian East Africa must look rather wryly on the result of their efforts.

For the Sudanese the war provided a tremendous incentive to national pride. Their troops held off vastly superior forces for six long months and their police kept six hundred miles of frontier more or less intact. They put the Sudan back on the map as a co-belligerent with the rest of the allies, and rubbed shoulders with troops from many parts of the world on equal terms and with mutual respect.

For the Government it was at first a period of intense anxiety. The Munich Agreement had enabled them to carry out some invaluable stock-piling against the loss of direct communication with Europe. Planning and controls prevented any serious shortages and delayed the inevitable rise in prices. It was only after nine months of waiting that Mussolini finally declared war, at a time when French Africa was not only powerless to give the promised aid but looked at one time like interposing a hostile territory between the Sudan and Nigeria. Felix Eboué, the Negro Governor of Chad, saved the situation by joining De Gaulle, but from June 1940 until late in the autumn a determined attack from the east could hardly have failed to take Khartum and sever Britain's line of communication with the Near, or as it now came to be called, the Middle East. There were over 300,000 men under arms in Italian East Africa and after the conquest of British Somaliland the Sudan and Kenya had their undivided attention. But the revolting Abyssinians, as the B.B.C. once called them, provided a considerable distraction and in the event the Italians contented themselves with the occupation of Kassala and Gallabat and a few minor forages down the Blue Nile.

In 1941 they were rolled up between two armies, advancing through Kassala and Keren in the north and Mogadishu and Addis Ababa in the south. This campaign was a classic of its kind and deserves a better place in public memory, if only because it was the first substantial and permanent success of Allied arms in the war.*

By the end of 1941 Gondar had fallen and the Sudan was part of the African Line of Communication,† but as long as Rommel threatened Alexandria there was always a danger of evacuation southwards or westwards.

After 1942 things settled down again and more attention could be devoted to post-war planning, and in particular to the development of the south (see Chapter 10 below) and the formation of Province Councils and the Advisory Council, which met in May 1944. There were still, however, many exterior distractions — the future of the Italian colonies being foremost among them. The possibility of the Sudan taking over the Muslim part of Eritrea was one of the points under discussion and there was much to be said in its favour. At least however the final decision has not left a running sore on post-independent relations‡ like Kashmir or the Somali district of Kenya. On the whole the closing years of the war were the lull before the storm: tired administrators waiting for a chance to revisit their homes and families in Britain; Sudanese politicians and civil servants awaiting the outcome of the peace settlement and the possibility of self-determination; and the rural population content to live as they had always lived and find a good market for their products.

---

* At least one of the school histories of the war doesn't even mention it.

† AFLOC — By boat to Matadi, rail to Leopoldville, river steamer up the Congo, rail again, road to Juba, boat to Kosti, rail to Halfa, boat to Assuan, and rail to Cairo. The aircraft flew in convoys from Takoradi and the first of these, five Hurricanes with a Blenheim mother-craft, was a very welcome sight when it arrived in Khartum late in 1940.

For a picture of Khartum during the war years through the eyes of the Civil Secretary, Sir Douglas Newbold, see *The Making of the Modern Sudan*, Faber, 1953.

‡ At least not until 1965.

Chapter 7

First Democratic Experiment

HE STAGE was now set for a political drama in which the actors were to play their various roles rather like marionettes controlled by some ironic President of the Immortals, or perhaps by the law of *Karma*. Everything moved remorselessly on through a decade of mounting excitement to self-government and self-determination. The Sudan's good genius forced the hands of Egypt and Britain by a whole series of twists of fortune. The Sudan's evil genius, unable to hamper the process, accelerated it a little too fast for safety;* laid up trouble for the future through the first rebuff to Congress and the consequent Congress refusal to co-operate, so that a government without experience of parliamentary procedure came to power at a crucial period; introduced political strife into schools and colleges, the bane of the Arab world; bedevilled labour relations in Atbara and economic responsibility in the Gezira; finally, and most important of all, deluded the politicians into ignoring or scorning the Greek chorus before whom they strutted, the great inarticulate body of rural opinion which was still the ultimate voice of the Sudan and which we shall find at the end of the chapter welcoming the entry of Fortinbras.†

Could Fortinbras have justly commented that 'He was likely, had he been put on, to've proved most royally'? I think he could. There was no real reason, whatever contemporary opinion may hold about African ideas of democracy, why the Westminster system should not have worked in the Sudan had the circumstances been normal. It suited the national temperament well enough. The Sudanese are not so volatile as the Arabs or the Egyptians. The disadvantages of decision by majority vote as against argument and compromise are no more apparent to the Sudanese eye than to the

---

* In preparing a country for self-government the ideal is to time the take-over to take place at the moment when the demand has spread from the towns to the countryside. The new government must have popular backing and adequate trained personnel to ensure public security from the moment it takes over. If the process goes too slowly there is a danger of revolution; if too fast, of anarchy.

† The south (see Chapter 10) provided a drama within a drama, where the evil genius has been busy and successful for a hundred years.

English. The leading politicians of both parties had been at school together. Personal dislikes and jealousies, tribal and sectarian differences, naturally existed but personal recrimination was rarer in Sudan politics than in Britain, and when all was over the gladiators consorted together with great goodwill in club or internment camp. Certain rules of conduct were observed throughout, even against the common enemy, and only when the south was in question did 'the soul sour and gradual rancour grow, embitter'd more from peevish day to day'.*

There was often an engaging air of flippancy about the political game as played in the north during those years of struggle. The author of a particularly violent personal attack could wander into his victim's office next morning in search of copy and reply to an expression of surprise at his keeping such low company with the remark that 'you shouldn't believe what you read in the newspapers'. It delighted the firebrand whose advent was expected to set the town alight to devote himself at a political reception to a long discussion with an official guest on the desirability of regional government. It was natural for the *Ashiqqa* leaders to postpone a demonstration when they learned that it would interfere with a wedding party; for the *Umma* delegates presenting a protest against British perfidy 'even at the base of Pompey's *statua*' to murmur *sotto voce* 'Nothing personal, of course'; for the committee of a province labour organisation, at the end of a week of disturbances with undertones of religious fanaticism, to substitute for the expected strike notices a message of sympathy to the British community 'on the death of their beloved monarch'.

Flippant is the wrong word. Perhaps a sense of humour would be better. Its constant presence surely means that the English party system might have worked in the Sudan, with the southerners playing a role similar to that of the Irish party at Westminster before Home Rule.† The necessary floating vote existed in the provinces, a vote increasingly non-sectarian as time went on. Failure was no foregone conclusion and those who, in 1940, favoured a pyramid structure of councils were soon aware that it would not have been acceptable. The procession of the 'forties and 'fifties was necessary and inevitable, but the failure of the democratic institutions was not. The immediate cause, in 1958, was the manipulation by vested

* The Khartum C.O.I. Pamphlet *Basic Facts about the Southern Provinces* published in 1964, is far more bitter about the Condominium Government than anything one remembers a decade earlier.

† The south resembled the Highlands in 1716 or 1746. Would it be assimilated, like the Highlands, after much migration? Or could it win through, like the Irish, to Home Rule and penurious independence?

interests of members without strong political conviction, but the long term cause was the presence of an interested outside power, Egypt. The shadow of sponsored revolution lay across the floor of the House from the beginning.

The curtain rises at the conclusion, in December 1944, of the second session of the Advisory Council. The Council was proving quite a success in a quiet sort of way. Its nominated and urban members included three future ministers, and the elected members (eighteen chosen by the six northern province councils and two by the Sudan Chamber of Commerce) were far from being the collection of hayseeds and yesmen portrayed in the popular press.* It resembled the Lords more than the Commons — a collection of experts in various fields of experience and professional skill with a predominantly bucolic atmosphere not inappropriate to an agricultural community with as yet no landlord-tenant conflict of interests. The Government, generally speaking, acted on Council's advice and the country, generally speaking, approved of it. Like everything else about colonial government, however, it was unexciting; it provided wholemeal bread, but no circuses.

When the play begins the stage is occupied by rural members of this Council, who express their dissatisfaction at having no mouthpiece to put their case to the public. (The press was uniformly pro-Congress and anti-provincial.) Before dispersing to their homes, they appoint certain of their number to pursue the matter of starting a newspaper. Finance is the first requirement and it soon becomes clear that the only source of capital is Sayed Abdel Rahman el Mahdi. The newspaper project recedes into the background and there emerges in March 1945 a new political party calling itself the *Umma*, the Community Party† with the slogan of 'the Sudan for the Sudanese'.

El Miralai Abdullah Bey Khalil, lately senior Sudanese officer in the S.D.F., and nominated as such to be a member of the Council, is leader of the party. A major protagonist has entered the lists against Congress. The chorus is not quite sure that this is exactly what it wanted. Most of the Mirghanist shaikhs drop out. Sayed Ali inevitably moves into opposition. The grouping is not after all to be Town *v.* Country, but something much more complicated.

* Abdullah Bey Khalil, future Prime Minister; Ali Bedri, first Minister of Health; Abdullah Bakr, first Under Secretary for Defence; Mekki Abbas, first Sudanese Managing Director of the Gezira Board; and Mirghani Hamza, later Deputy P.M.; all were members of the Advisory Council.

† The Mahdists were experts at taking over titles of Islamic significance. The *Ansar* were the original companions of the Prophet of God—the *Umma* is the Brotherhood of Islam, the Community of the Faithful which will one day include all mankind.

Things might have developed differently, with Sayed Ali rallying rural opinion against rapid change and Sayed Abdel Rahman backing Congress demands for early self-government. That they did not was due mainly to the strength of rural Mahdism but also to developments associated with the Congress elections of 1943. Among the members of the Sudan Schools Club was a group of young men united by such close ties of friendship that they were nicknamed the Blood Brothers, the *Ashiqqa*. Dissatisfied with the acquiescence of the Committee of Fifteen in the 1942 rebuff, they saw an opportunity of replacing it when a decision was reached to extend Congress membership not only to ex-elementary schoolboys but to 'their equivalent'. When the time for the 1943 elections approached Congress was inundated with applications for membership from *Ashiqqa* contacts with a bare literacy qualification. As a result the new Committee of Sixty (from which the executive Fifteen was chosen) contained a majority of their supporters. An elder statesman was needed to head them and an approach was made to Ismail el Azhari, a member of the old Committee, who had been a member of Sayed Abdel Rahman's *salon*. Azhari accepted and when the Sayed hesitated about bestowing his blessing on the new set-up decided to go ahead without it.

So there came into existence the *Ashiqqa* Party, which inevitably became the chief opponent of the *Umma*.

Behind these two parties the political life of the Sudan ranged itself for the coming struggle. The *Umma* provided the core of what became the Independence Front, the various bodies of opinion which wanted complete independence, and were prepared to co-operate in any constitutional measure calculated to facilitate that objective or provide useful experience in self-government. It was, as has been said, Mahdist in colour so that non-Mahdists were usually forced into some sort of alignment with the opposition, the *Ashiqqa* and the *Ittihadiyin*.*

This group, later known as the National Unionists, included every variety of anti-Mahdist opinion, from those who simply wanted a secular republic to those who wanted complete union with Egypt, the Unity of the Nile Valley men. There was a fairly large middle section who thought some sort of loose association with Egypt would be a good thing, and others who regarded Egypt as a useful instrument for getting the British out, an instrument which could then be

* Nine parties contested the Congress elections of 1946–7 — the *Umma*, the *Ashiqqa*, *Ittihad*, Liberals, Liberal Unionists, Nationalists, two Republican parties, and the supporters of Unity of the Nile Valley. The *Ittihad*, or Unionist Party, originated in a literary society, known as the *Awlad el Bahr*, the Riverside Boys. In spite of its title it favoured federation with Egypt, not full union.

discarded. The group enjoyed the general rather vague support of the Khatmia and Sayed Ali, who would personally have preferred the *status quo ante bella*, but regarded anything as preferable to an independent Sudan under Mahdist rule.

In the background throughout was the chorus, the inarticulate body of opinion which thought everyone was in too much of a hurry. It later included the Southern Liberal party, born full-grown but very much unarmed from the head of a Juba Conference in 1947. From time to time the chorus tried unsuccessfully to take the centre of the stage.* It even spoke at one time of Dominion status in the British Commonwealth, for which it was given scant encouragement by a visiting British minister, who said the Commonwealth was an exclusive club.

The layout of the various shades of political opinion during the 1940s and their pre-conditioned reaction to current events was skilfully portrayed by an anonymous satirist in March 1949 in the *Mustaqbil* magazine. Entitled 'The Disappearance of Lemons, according to the style of writing in the different papers', the article ascribed the reason for the current shortage, in the opinion of the three Independence papers, to the evils of Condominium rule (despite the efforts of the British); the gluttony of the Egyptian army of occupation; and an infamous plot to corner the Sudan market for Egyptian produce. But the orchards of Aba Island were coming to the rescue. The opposition press were represented as placing the blame (*a*) upon Divine Retribution for the new Legislative Assembly; (*b*) on an *Umma*-British plot to spoil a forthcoming reception for the Congress leader; and (*c*) on the desire of the British to undermine the health of the population. This time the plot was to be foiled by the O.C. Egyptian Troops, who had wired for two thousand Egyptian lemons. The more objective papers were represented as contenting themselves with an open letter to the Director of Economics and Trade, and a sarcastic telegram to the Minister of Agriculture. The correspondent of the *Mustaqbil* itself reported having seen 'a certain important personage' carrying a lemon to the Palace and deduced that the visit was not unconcerned with the possibility of Khatmia participation in a reformed legislative assembly. The extracts concluded with a bromide from the government weekly, reminding its readers that 'a thousand years ago lemons disappeared for two complete months from the island of Madagascar' and affirming its confidence that with their customary good sense they would wait undisturbed until the Government took the necessary steps.

* See below, the Socialist Republican Party.

This production is typical of the sense of humour to which reference has been made and which so often preserved sanity in times of high emotion.

A time of high emotion this period was. The threat of subjugation to Hitler or Mussolini had been removed and in the mood of relief any form of subjugation had become intolerable.

The following is a summary of Sudanese grievances, real or fancied, and reasons for unrest, compiled at the end of 1946 for the information of the Civil Secretary:

Procrastination and Parsimony

The Government should be spending, not saving. We have no trunk roads, no proper soil survey, little attempt to prospect for minerals. Health and education services lag behind Iraq, which is no wealthier but much farther advanced.

The Government machine works more and more slowly (e.g. the promised new scales of pay).

Nothing is ever approved until an ideal solution is found, and there never is an ideal solution (e.g. rent allowance for officials who can't get a government quarter).

Insincerity

Sudanisation is just a façade. Senior Sudanese officials are not trusted with secret files. Local Government Authorities are authorities only in name; the D.C. retains the real power. Members of ADCO are government stooges.

Unnecessary Secrecy with which Government surrounds its work and policy (e.g. Cotton Price Stabilisation Account and especially Southern Policy).

Exploitation

Secrecy has resulted in widespread belief that war-time sale of cotton on contract to U.K. Commission was a British ramp to get cotton cheap and that the difference was not, as alleged, paid into the Stabilisation Account.

Aloofness of British officials contrasted with Egyptian cameraderie. (Same language and religion.)

Scandals concerning certain British in Khartum. Association with cabaret girls. Recent cases of corruption over trade licences.

Discrimination

by licensing authorities in favour of foreign traders,

by P.W.D. in favour of foreign contractors,

by Southern Governors in favour of Christians.

Segregation of Sudanese first-class passengers on railways and steamers.

Egyptian propaganda with no effective answer. Hand-outs, British Council etc. ineffective.

Treatment of Press

The Press does reflect public opinion but is always treated as irresponsible. The Government in general and British officials in particular resent any criticism. It is difficult to get at the facts. P.R.O.s never seem to know, and by the time they've found out the news is cold. There is no direct access to the top. Directors hate being rung up and are usually rude. 'Open letters' in the Press seldom get an answer.

The *Star* is believed to get preferential treatment. The Editor being British can get his stuff over the phone. Are English copies of press hand-outs kept back till the Arabic version is ready?

Press Notices are allocated arbitrarily by Departments who have their favourite papers.

The Vernacular Press Summaries bowdlerise the originals.

It was against this background that negotiations began in Cairo in 1946 for a revision of the 1936 Treaty. Officially it had ten more years to run but the new Labour Government in Britain was anxious not to emulate its predecessors and moreover realised that it would be neither desirable nor possible to stand on the letter of its rights. Prospects of agreement were considered reasonably good but there were adverse factors. The army took an unconscionable time to move back on to the Canal Zone — its peace-time station under the Treaty — so that the old suspicions were aroused: Egyptian public opinion was no longer prepared to let the question of sovereignty over the Sudan lie fallow; and Egypt was no longer alone. Behind her stood a new ally in the United States, and in the distance, a formidable bogey, was Russia.

American policy during this decade was based upon the belief that the old discredited colonising powers, England and France (and of course Italy), were a liability to the cause of freedom which they affected to support. The sooner England was deprived of her 'sphere of influence' in the Middle East the better for the Arab world, the Western cause and the United States. The U.S. Embassy in Cairo was therefore prepared to encourage Egypt to take a firm line while Washington brought the maximum pressure to bear upon London to yield to it. Egypt had two main objectives — to get the British out of the Canal Zone and to recover possession of the Sudan. In May 1946 the British Government agreed to evacuate the Canal, but the Sudan's right to self-determination was not theirs to dispose of. The Cairo negotiations broke down on this issue, the Foreign

Secretary having, on 26 March, given a pledge to the House of Commons that 'no change should be made in the status of the Sudan as a result of treaty revision until the Sudanese had been consulted through constitutional channels.'*

In October, however, the Egyptian Prime Minister, Ismail Sidky, went to London in search of some sort of compromise. Tension in the Sudan was high. An all-party delegation had gone to Cairo in the summer to ensure that the Sudan case did not again go by default; but since no basic agreement existed between them on what the Sudan case was, the Independence delegates were soon recalled and the opposition remained to convince the American Embassy and a large section of public opinion in Britain that what the Sudanese unanimously wanted was union with Egypt. When the news came of Sidky's arrival in London Sayed Abdel Rahman el Mahdi was seriously alarmed, especially when the Egyptian Press began to reflect increased confidence that Britain would be brought to recognise Egyptian sovereignty. Finally he sent a personal telegram to Ernest Bevin demanding an opportunity to put the Sudanese case before him. He claimed to have 75 per cent of the northern Sudanese behind him and was ready to leave by air at an hour's notice. British opinion in Khartum felt that he was unduly alarmed and raised no strong protest when the proposed visit was discouraged by London. On 27 October, however, Sidky returned to Cairo with a draft treaty in his pocket which, he announced, recognised Egyptian sovereignty over the Sudan.

The relevant protocol ran as follows:

'The policy which the High Contracting Parties undertake to follow in the Sudan within the framework of the unity between the Sudan and Egypt under the common crown of Egypt will have for its essential objectives to assure the well-being of the Sudanese, the development of their interests and their active preparation for self-government and consequently the exercise of the right to choose the future status of the Sudan. Until the High Contracting Parties can in full common agreement realise this latter objective after consultation with the Sudanese the Agreement of 1899 will continue and Article II of the Treaty of 1936.'

Bevin maintained that this protocol meant no change in status for the Sudan† and that it secured Egyptian agreement at long last

---

* 'Papers regarding the Negotiations for a Revision of the Anglo-Egyptian Treaty of 1936.' White Paper Egypt No. 2 (1947) p. 5.
† See his apologia in the White Paper under reference.

to the right of self-determination. Egypt interpreted 'status' as meaning 'status under the common crown'. Sayed Abdel Rahman and the *Umma* party and Sudanese in general interpreted the protocol as recognition, for the first time since the reconquest, of Egyptian sovereignty over the Sudan.

On 31 October several thousand demonstrators, carrying the red, black and green tricolour* of the Mahdist Sudan, paraded through the streets of Khartum and handed over a protest on behalf of the *Umma* party, saying that they would not permit 'verbal juggling', and the present Government, if allowed to continue, would be resisted by all possible means. It condemned Mr. Bevin's reported concession to Egypt's claim to sovereignty, and expressed Sudanese aspirations for freedom and independence.† A counter-demonstration by the Nile Valley parties followed, but enough had been done to show the strength of the opposition. The Governor-General, Sir Hubert Huddleston, had behind him in opposing the protocol every British civil servant in the Sudan. It was consigned to the waste-paper basket, Sidky resigned, and after fruitless attempts at salvaging the draft treaty, his successor Nokrashy Pasha lodged, on 13 July 1947, an official complaint to the Security Council, alleging that the continued presence of British troops in Egypt and British administration in the Sudan was (although still sanctioned by the 1936 Treaty) contrary to the letter and spirit of the United Nations Charter.

The position of the Condominium Government in Khartum was not enviable at this time. To begin with its days were obviously numbered and no government can afford to stand long upon the order of its going once the lights have changed. The protocol had temporarily lost it most of its support in the Sudan. Its resistance to the protocol made it none too popular in London. The Americans and the Egyptians distrusted it profoundly. It was not a happy time to be a member of the Secretariat.‡

---

* The colours of the flags of the Mahdi's three *khalifas*. The Sudan Republic later adopted a less controversial banner, blue for the Nile, yellow for the desert and green for the crops. There is a certain conscious or unconscious symbolism about this choice. Pour blue into yellow and green results.

† See *The Times* of 1 November 1946.

‡ To quote from a contemporary lament:

'Let Lion and Cuckold struggle for the Crown,
Within whose framework we must sit us down.
Forget that Freedom's fiercest foes are we,
Cursed with thy dying breath, O Liberty;
Hostile to Egypt: anti-H.M.G.'

Another excerpt from the contemporary columns of the Secretariat *Anti-Jacobin* likened the Condominium Government to a tutor who has brought up his orphan charge without interference because the senior guardian, a busy city lawyer,

A special committee had been set up in 1946 to work out as quickly as possible a new constitution which would enable the Sudanese to be consulted on the self-determination issue and provide the next step on the road to self-government. The *Ashiqqa* had refused to co-operate and if the *Umma* were now going to do the same the whole project would be wrecked. Fortunately they did not carry out their threat. The hubbub over the protocol had in fact cleared the air considerably from their point of view. It dispelled a lurking suspicion that the British wanted to take the country over, and it provided a reassurance that however perfidious the British Government might be it was not prepared when it came to the pinch to barter away the Sudan in order to achieve its much desired treaty with Egypt. So co-operation continued, even when the Governor-General was replaced, in April 1947, by a Foreign Office man, Sir Robert Howe. There were inevitable forebodings over this appointment, but in the event Sir Robert fought as valiantly as his predecessor for the Sudan's right to decide its own fate.*

Nokrashi Pasha's letter was duly debated by the Security Council in August. Three Sudanese delegations were at Lake Success, representing the Government and the rival Fronts. The Government representatives were instructed to put their services at the disposal of both *co-domini* but the Egyptians, understandably if rather disappointingly, refrained from calling upon them.

The proceedings, which involved historical claims and denials going back to the year 2000 B.C. were enlivened by the behaviour of one Ahmed Kotb, leader of the Egyptian *Fellah* Party, who rose up in the auditorium crying with a fine impartiality, 'Down with Nokrashi! Down with Imperialism! Down with the Security Council!' and bit one of the attendants in the ear. The attitude of some of the members was pre-determined.† Egypt could count on

supported him against the boy's maternal uncle, a local landowner who encouraged him to extravagant and in tutorial eyes immoral habits. The boy is now approaching his majority, increasingly irked by discipline and responsive to avuncular blandishments. The lawyer, with less and less time to spare and anxious to be freed of the charge, decides that the boy is old enough to fend for himself. The Trust is wound up and the tutor leaves for the railway station, unwept but by no means unconcerned.

* Notably in January 1948, when discussions had been renewed in Cairo and attempts were being made to 'find a formula'. The opposing argument was that friendship between Egypt and Britain was in the best interests of the Sudan and it was not unreasonable to ask her to make some sort of temporary concession in order to achieve that end.

† During the preliminary discussions it was pointed out that the Council had had their fill of 'supporting literature' and never listened to a speech if it exceeded 10–15 minutes. This was understandable enough when one considers what they

Syria and expect Russia and Poland to block any adverse motion. Britain thought she could count on France, Belgium and Australia. That left the U.S.A., China, Brazil, and Colombia more or less uncommitted. The case of Indonesia *v.* Holland was being conducted at the same time — day and day about, which complicated matters. The final result was remarkable. It will be remembered that under the draft treaty Britain had agreed to evacuate the Canal Zone by 1 September 1949. The treaty foundered on the Sudan clause. Yet nearly all the draft resolutions which came to the vote expressed in one way or another the view that if only agreement could be reached on evacuation the Sudan question would solve itself. The exceptions were moved by Brazil and Colombia, the latter of which called upon the two governments to resume negotiations with a view to completing evacuation and 'terminating the joint administration of the Sudan with due regard to the principle of self-determination of peoples and their right to self-government'.

This was unacceptable to Egypt because it 'conveyed the idea that we shall have to discuss with the British the future of the Sudan. We maintain that it is a domestic issue and that we shall solve it to the mutual satisfaction of the Sudanese and the Egyptians with full regard to the democratic principles of the Charter'. It was also opposed by Russia and was only accepted by Britain on the understanding that termination could not take place until the Sudan had been brought to an advanced stage in which she was capable of independent self-government. 'The point of the negotiations would be to provide measures for accelerating the process of making the Sudanese capable of effectively governing themselves.'*

So the motion was talked out, and in September the three delegations returned, sadder and wiser, to Khartum. They found that in the interval a storm had blown up over Southern policy. This is discussed in Chapter 10.

But the new constitution was now approaching final form, and in May 1948 a draft Ordinance was taken to Cairo for submission to the Egyptian Government. A series of discussions followed in an atmosphere of specious secrecy at a suburban palace outside Cairo

---

had to digest, but it was disillusioning to the starry-eyed, and provoked the following, addressed *To All Sudanese Parties*:

'Is it for justice that your hands outreach?
To bring your case to UNO's quite absurd:
The Council's far too bored to hear a speech,
And far too tired to read the printed word.' R.J.H.

* Verbatim Records of the discussions of the 175th, 176th, 179th, 182nd, 189th, 193rd, 198th, 200th and 201st Meetings of the Security Council, 1947. Reprinted for the Sudan Government by McCorquodale & Co., Khartum.

G

between the Foreign Minister, Khashaba Pasha, and the British Ambassador, Sir Ronald Campbell. These resulted in an agreed draft incorporating Egyptian representation on the new Executive Council, but public opinion in Egypt was opposed to any sort of compromise over the Sudan and the Egyptian Cabinet dared not present the agreement for ratification.

After some hesitation the Governor-General decided that the need for a Sudanese representative body was now paramount and the British Government authorised him to go ahead on his own. The new ordinance provided for a Legislative Assembly of 75* plus certain *ex-officio* members.

The pro-Egyptian parties boycotted the elections, though the rural members included several Mirghanist notables. After choosing a Speaker the Assembly elected Abdullah Bey as Leader of the House. He then appointed a Minister of Health, a Minister of Education, and ten parliamentary Under-Secretaries, all of whom were *ex-officio* members of the Assembly. Abdullah Bey himself took the portfolio of Agriculture. The Heads of Department now became the equivalent of permanent Under-Secretaries.

The Governor-General's Council was replaced by a new Executive Council consisting of the three Ministers, the three Secretaries, the Commandant of the Sudan Defence Force, the Under-Secretary for Economics and Trade, the Under Secretary for Irrigation, and three nominated members, one Sudanese and two British. One of the British was replaced in 1949 by a Sudanese, giving the latter a majority on the Council of seven to five.

The Council and Assembly met for the first time in December 1948 and governed the country not unsuccessfully for four troubled years — years of unrest in the towns and in the Gezira, riots in Rufaa and Atbara and Fasher and Port Sudan, violent political friction in Khartum, strikes in the schools, mounting suspicion in the south, and, for the first time, trouble with organised labour.

Industrial labour in the Sudan was until after the war virtually confined to the railway workshops in Atbara. Here the Sudanese artisan had acquired over the years a professional skill unparalleled elsewhere in the country, a skill which had not as yet been recognised by the necessary revision of his rates of pay. A first-class craftsman

---

* 10 elected directly by the towns, 42 by electoral colleges in rural areas, 13 by the southern province councils, and 10 nominated by the Governor-General. These consisted of Abdullah Bey Khalil, a southern notable, the editor of a Labour paper, a merchant, a pharmacist, a school-master, a neutral religious leader, a Gezira Court President who was also ex-President of the *Maahad* (Islamic Seminary), an ex-judge (elected Speaker) and an advocate, Muhammad Ahmad Mahjub, who emerged as Leader of the Opposition.

working to measurements of a thousandth of an inch was therefore confronted by a situation in which he was earning less pay after twenty years' service than his young white-collared son in the clerical cadre. The position was most anomalous and the management were not slow to draw attention to it. The Finance Department unfortunately postponed action until a comprehensive review of all scales of government pay should have been carried out and proper Trade Union legislation enacted. Long before this consummation was achieved the storm burst. A strike was followed by the inevitable concession and the lesson was learned that action pays better than protest. To quote from a note written in 1952:

'A whole corpus of Trade Union Legislation,* drawn up on the British model under expert British advice, was put through the Legislative Assembly in 1949–51. Coming at a time of labour unrest due to rising costs of living, and presented on a plate instead of being striven for through the years, it has gone to the heads of the new unions like wine. Experience elsewhere in Africa has shown how easily the illiterate worker can be exploited by unscrupulous union officials. In the Sudan a series of strikes which by careful timing or unhappy coincidence were followed in succession by increases in government wage rates strengthened the hold of the extremists on the big unions (the Sudan Railways Employees Union is far the most important) and on the Federation of Trade Unions in Khartum. The Federation was, at the end of 1951, completely dominated by communists and openly proclaimed a policy of overthrowing the administration and paralysing the economic life of the country by a series of carefully timed strikes.'

Communism had been introduced into the country during the war by foreign intellectuals and more widely disseminated later by students returning from Egyptian universities. As in England it made little progress as a political force but its exponents showed their usual capacity for obtaining key positions in the Unions. In 1953, as we shall see, this activity was extended to the Gezira.

In spite of these troubles the Legislative Assembly pursued a successful and decorous course and it began to be regarded as likely that Westminster institutions were going to prove both suitable and effective. A new constitutional commission had been created early in 1951 in response to a motion in the Assembly calling for a re-examination of the 1948 Ordinance 'to increase the value and enhance the efficiency of the Assembly and Council as a practical instrument of democratic government, with a full measure of

---

* It consisted of a Trade Union Ordinance, an ordinance for Regulation of Trade Disputes, and a Trade Union (Arbitration and Enquiry) Ordinance.

parliamentary control within the framework of existing constitutional agreements'.

By altering this wording in the commission of appointment to read 'to recommend the next step to be taken in the constitutional advance to full self-government' it was possible to secure the participation of those of the opposition who aimed at dominion status under the Egyptian crown. It thus included all shades of opinion short of the *Ashiqqa*. The Chairman and Secretary were British, the rest of the members Sudanese.

Meanwhile negotiations between Britain and Egypt had petered out in 1948, been resumed in 1950 and continued in a desultory fashion. In 1951 a proposal for a Middle East Defence Pact was adumbrated between Egypt, Turkey, France, Britain and the U.S.A. Obviously this could not be discussed as practical politics until the Sudan question had been solved, and the British Government was still hopeful of finding a solution* when, on the night of 8 October 1951 the Egyptian Prime Minister — once again the familiar figure of Mustafa Nahas Pasha — suddenly announced to an enthusiastic House the unilateral abrogation of the 1936 Treaty and the Condominium Agreement. Farouk was proclaimed King of the Sudan and a Bill was introduced creating a new Sudanese Constituent Assembly with a cabinet of ministers to be appointed by the King and Foreign Affairs, Defence, and Currency as reserved subjects.

This action aroused no enthusiasm in the Sudan, where even the *Ashiqqa* regarded it as arbitrary, but it did in the opinion of many destroy the juridical basis of the Condominium Government. The members of the Constitution Commission invited the Secretary-General of the United Nations to appoint an International Supervisory Body on the lines of the British proposals, and when no reply was forthcoming the opposition members walked out, fortunately not before the Commission had completed the first draft of the proposed bill.

Meanwhile on 25 October the Legislative Assembly had passed almost unanimously a motion deploring the attempt to impose Egyptian sovereignty and expressing warm appreciation of the attitude of the British Government.†

On 15 November Mr. Eden responded in the House of Commons

---

* Proposals had been drafted, and were actually presented to the Egyptian Government on 3 October for an International Commission to be appointed to supervise Sudanese progress to self-government. Sudanese agreement was preconditional. The proposals were no more acceptable to Egypt than their predecessors.

† This pat on the back for H.M.G. was unprecedented and unique.

by promising to back the recommendations of the Commission. He ended by expressing the satisfaction of His Majesty's Government in knowing that a constitution providing for self-government would be in operation by the end of 1952 and promising self-determination in complete freedom to follow.

This was fair enough and the politicians wanted to add the word 'immediately'. But the southerners asked for time to see how the new parliament worked and the chorus of rural representatives agreed with them. They had, it will be remembered, provided the involuntary foundation of the *Umma* Party, and they had since worked in joint but rather uneasy harness with its militant wing. A premature attempt in December 1950 to force a motion in favour of immediate independence through the assembly* had alarmed these conservatives, and now they surprised the political world by calling a press conference the day after Eden's speech and announcing that although they were not a political party they claimed, as elected representatives of the people, to speak for the whole of the three southern provinces and Darfur, for 83 per cent of the population of Kordofan, 50 per cent of Kassala Province, 45 per cent of the Blue Nile, and all Khartum Province outside the Three Towns. Only the Northern Province was unrepresented, but they were confident that a large section of its people would share their views. These were that the Condominium no longer existed, but that an International Commission was undesirable. Instead the Governor-General should 'continue to exercise the ultimate responsibility as head of State' until a constitution had been worked out 'in this country, fitted to our own particular needs, the practical details of which are hammered out by those who will have to work them. Whenever the advice and experience of foreigners is required we should make use of the foreign officials who have spent their working lives in this country and understand our problems'. They summed up their policy as one of full co-operation with the existing government 'until such time as the country is in a position to decide its own future'.

Out of this meeting emerged a new party calling itself the Socialist Republicans. It had some influential backing, including the covert support of Sayed Ali, but it had no funds and it came up against the whole weight of Sayed Abdel Rahman's hostility. The Sayed was convinced that the new party was directly inspired by the political branch of the Secretariat with the object of depriving the *Umma* party of its support in the provinces. What actually appears to have

* It was finally passed by 39 votes to 38, too narrow a majority for the Governor-General to act upon.

happened was that the malcontents came seeking advice and were told that if that was the way they felt, they had better form themselves into a party. Attempts to convince the Sayed that a non-Mahdist pro-independence party would be a valuable ally against absorption by Egypt failed completely. He never really trusted the British officials again, and saw little advantage in retaining their services after independence.

In January 1952 the Report of the Constitution Commission was laid before the Assembly and after prolonged debate substantially approved for drafting. It returned to the Assembly in April and was passed into law in May.

It provided for a House of Representatives with 97 seats and a Senate with 50, 30 of whom were to be elected by province constituencies and 20 nominated by the Governor-General. The decision to provide an Upper House was made rather belatedly and the opportunity missed of creating something which did not simply duplicate the Lower House.*

Meanwhile in Egypt the government of Nahas Pasha had gone down in a welter of blood and fire in the Cairo riots of 26 January. His successor, Najib el Hilali, had a new idea. Britain was now committed to any solution provided the Sudanese agreed to it. Of the Sudanese only the Mahdists were still opposed to Egypt's demands. If Sayed Abdel Rahman could be persuaded to agree to a formula compatible with Egyptian sovereignty, the problem was solved.

The Sayed, not without ironic amusement, allowed his representatives to discuss the matter in May, and was proposing to take it up in person later in the year with Hilali's replacement, Husayn Sirri, when, on 23 July, the entire situation was altered and the climax of the drama introduced by the appearance of the god from the machine, General Muhammad Najib.

The Sudanese knew and liked Najib, who had been born in the

---

* The Civil Secretary, writing in November 1950, said, 'The whole question of a second chamber was under consideration at one time but . . . we decided that there were not sufficient people to fill both an Assembly and a House of Lords, and we thought we had best leave it in cold storage for the present. I cannot remember myself ever saying or hearing much about it and no Sudanese has ever talked to me about it.'

What one would have liked to see was an Upper House recruited from retired governors, judges of the High Court, heads of department and officers of field rank, together with ex-ministers and representatives of the medical and educational professions, the Muhammedan Law Courts, the Bar, the Press, the Trade Unions, Congress, the Gezira Tenants, and a few representative peers chosen by the local government authorities. Ex-ambassadors would be an obvious addition today. With a limited delaying power and the right to refer back legislation for amendment a specialist body of this kind could have been very useful.

Sudan and went to school there with leading politicians. The British in Khartum knew and liked his brother Ali, who had been Military Secretary to the Governor-General. Nobody shed tears for King Farouk, and the July Revolution had none of the revolting features since made familiar in Baghdad. When the General formally abandoned Egypt's claim to sovereignty things seemed too good to be true. They were. The British, who had assumed that they would be allowed to go on serving the new Government, at any rate in the south, for some years to come, got a rude shock when the *Umma* party delegates, incensed at the formation of the S.R.P., signed an agreement with the General providing for the evacuation within three years of every British administrator and officer. (This was to prevent them influencing the electorate.) The southerners got a shock when the same agreement left out all their cherished and hard-fought-for safeguards, and the party leaders didn't bother to explain the reasons for omission. The Socialist Republicans got a shock when their representatives signed a similar undertaking in Cairo, which killed the party stone dead. All the parties signed agreements in the end, in very much the same terms, and the British Government had no real choice about doing the same. It fought hard for the inclusion of safeguards for the south, and incurred northern hostility by so doing, but had to give way and sign an agreement in its turn, in February 1953.

The southerners considered that they had been let down first by the *Umma* and secondly by the British. Not being familiar with the provisions of Isaiah 36: 6, they now pinned their hopes upon Egypt.

The Anglo-Egyptian Agreement provided for a Special Commission (instituted April 1953) to review arrangements for the elections and ensure that they were conducted in a free and neutral atmosphere. It consisted of two Sudanese, one Egyptian and one British member under a Chairman from Pakistan. The elections themselves were supervised by a separate international commission with an Indian expert, Dr. Sukumar Sen, in the chair.

The Legislative Assembly had completed its constitutional life at the end of 1952 so that the country was governed throughout 1953 by the Executive Council, which now consisted of seven Sudanese members and three British. The various parties and the Egyptian Government settled down to an election campaign during which the most extravagant promises were made, especially in the south. The *Umma* should have been in a strong position, after winning their main objective, but their strength had always lain in the provinces and the provinces were far from happy about the turn of events. The *Umma* Youth was responsible for exacerbating this feeling. In the west, where Mahdism is strong but not universal, youth formations began to carry out semi-military manoeuvres in the villages and their leaders claimed to be the agents of Sayed Abdel Rahman. The Mahdist shaikhs resented this alternative channel of approach to their *Imam*, and the non-Mahdists feared a revival of the bad old days. With Britain out of the running Egyptian rule at least presented a fifty-fifty chance of retaining their authority.

The *Umma* were also, of course, tainted by 'collaboration' in the eyes of some and their rivals had the advantage of being able to criticise their record while in power. All the same, the National Unionist Party's absolute majority over all the other parties was not foreseen* and gave rise to much talk of the uses of Egyptian money.

So in January 1954 a new Government took over, with Ismail el Azhari as Prime Minister. On 9 January the Governor-General signed the 'Appointed Day' document which under the Self-Government Act set a period of three years during which the Sudanese had to reach a decision between Independence and Egypt. No time was wasted. In February a Sudanisation Committee started to get rid of the British officials. In April 1955 its work was completed. The same month Parliament asked for the self-determination machinery to be set in motion. By November the British and Egyptian troops had gone. In December Parliament resolved unanimously for independence. On 1 January 1956 the flags of England and Egypt were hauled down and the new Sudanese tricolour hoisted in their place. It was all over as quickly as that, and in spite of serious trouble in the south.

The sense of drama is heightened during this period. Events hurried to a climax — almost regardless of the various initiatives. In March General Najib had arrived to attend the state opening of parliament. (Winston Churchill had also been invited.) There had been some anxiety in the Sudan over Najib's position in Egypt and a certain enthusiasm at his apparent recovery of power, an en-

---

* The final figures were:

	House of Representatives	Senate			
N.U.P.	50	21 elected	+ 10 nominated	=	31
Umma	23	4	+ 4	=	8
Southern Party	9	3	+ 3	=	6
Soc. Republican	3	1			1
Independents etc.	12 (including 7 Southern Independents)				4
	—				—
	97				50

thusiasm not shared by the *Umma* party, which determined on a demonstration. Supporters poured into Khartum, the intention being to welcome the visitors with shouts of opposition along the route from the aerodrome to the Palace. The Government decided to avoid this embarrassment by bringing them in by a detour through the back streets. The angry and disappointed demonstrators swarmed round the Palace and a section of the crowd got out of hand with the result that the British Commandant of Police, and a young Sudanese officer, who came ironically enough of a Mahdist family, were killed. These events were a considerable shock to public opinion, not least to the *Umma* supporters themselves, but they did impress the Government with the idea that too close a connection with Egypt might well mean civil war. Nor was a connection with Egypt so popular in the event. As the British disappeared a lot of Egypt's popularity went with them. A large section of the N.U.P., the Khatmia group led by Mirghani Hamza, had never wished for anything more definite than 'strong ties'. Egyptian visitors were tending to assume a great deal more than this. The dangers of Mahdist domination loomed less large than of old. The Prime Minister began to think twice about close association, though he remained on the best of terms with General Najib and took a prominent part in the Cairo celebrations of Britain's agreement (in October 1954) to evacuate the Canal Zone.

Then, in November, Najib was superseded and Egypt was no longer ruled by a man the Sudanese knew and trusted. The Khatmia group was all for an immediate change of front, but Azhari had not yet made up his mind. Mirghani Hamza and two other henchmen of Sayed Ali's left office in consequence and formed a new party, the Republican Independents.

In Egypt the Government was engaged in extirpating the Muslim Brothers, an organisation which was respected by many in the Sudan but members of which had attempted to assassinate Colonel Jumal Abdel Nasir after the Suez evacuation agreement. It began to look as though Egypt under 'Nasser' and the Sudan of the political parties would find it difficult to run together in any sort of harness.

In April 1955 both leaders attended the Bandung Conference and did not hit it off. On his way home Azhari was mobbed in Cairo for his alleged betrayal of Egyptian interests. He returned to Khartum with his mind made up and in May it was publicly announced that the Government aimed at complete independence. The pro-Egyptian wing objected to this, and its leaders also seceded. From now on the Government's position was precarious. Azhari went to Cairo again in July for Revolution Day and was again dissatisfied with his reception. Violent attacks on him in the Egyptian Press followed. On 16 August the House of Representatives passed a resolution for self-determination. During the debate Muhammad Nur el Din, a leader of the pro-Egyptian party, remarked that the country ought to be grateful to Egypt for her help. Muhammad Ahmed Mahjub, leader of the opposition, replied that the best way to show gratitude would be to help the Egyptian people to achieve democratic freedom.

The first step required by the self-determination clause of the Anglo-Egyptian Agreement was to set up an international body to supervise the referendum and the election of a constituent assembly. There was argument between Britain and Egypt about the composition of this body and in October the Sudan Government suggested dropping the whole idea and letting the existing parliament decide the issue. Britain was disposed to accept this but Egypt objected and the project was abandoned for the moment. Sayed Ali was known to be opposed to a precipitate decision, and so of course were the southern members. The south was in the aftermath of the August mutiny and its representatives preferred postponement for reasons explained in Chapter 10.

On 11 November the Government was defeated in a snap division on the Budget proposals and it looked as though Mirghani Hamza would become Prime Minister, but after four days of prodigious activity Azhari scraped home by 48 votes to 46, when the House met again on 15 November. So critical did the situation seem for the future of the Sudan that the two Sayeds* met for the first time (apart from official functions) and were understood to have agreed upon a joint plan of action.

On 3 December Britain and Egypt at last signed an agreement over the referendum and defined the terms of reference for the proposed International Commission. But nobody in the northern Sudan was prepared to wait any longer. On 11 December the Government issued a statement to that effect; the decision had been reached over its head and the terms of reference were unacceptable. On 15 December the Governor-General, Sir Knox Helm, went on leave.† He had already notified the British Government that he was unwilling to stay on after April, and his absence facilitated

* The title *Sayed* (=Master) had been applied in the Sudan only to religious leaders. After independence it was generally adopted in the Syrian sense of 'Mister' as a substitute for the Egyptian '*effendi*' (=esquire).
† He had been recalled from leave that summer to deal with the mutiny in the south, and was anxious to spend Christmas with his family.

Azhari's plans for the transfer. On the 19th, parliament declared the Sudan to be independent and appointed a Commission of Five to exercise the authority of Head of State. Britain and Egypt raised no objection and on 1 January 1956 the Sudan woke up to find itself autonomous.

Parliamentary government had two more years to run. At the end of January the dismissed Ministers were reinstated, together with Abdullah Bey Khalil, and Azhari's old rival for the presidency of Congress, Ibrahim Ahmed. It was a ministry of all the talents but talents are not easy to control and, when the two Mirghanist groups reorganised themselves into a new People's Democratic Party, Azhari resigned. A coalition of P.D.P. and *Umma* succeeded, with Abdullah Bey Khalil as Prime Minister, and Mirghani Hamza as his deputy. The Mahdist-Mirghanist feud sank beneath the surface, though as long as the question of a President remained open it was always liable to raise its head again.

This coalition government earned prestige for the Sudan abroad. Muhammad Ahmed Mahjoub, the lawyer who had led the opposition, was Foreign Minister and it was he who built up the reputation for sanity at the successive conferences of Arab, African and Asian states which have been such a feature of post-war diplomacy.* The Sudan was now a member of the Arab League (which the *Umma* had distrusted in former days because it refused to listen to their case against Egypt), and, since November 1956, of the United Nations. The Suez affair at the end of 1956 had dealt a heavy blow to British prestige and restored that of Egypt, but even so the Government refused to be stampeded out of its position of benevolent detachment.†

The statutory life of the 1954 parliament had been extended until June 1957 to allow for the completion of the new electoral law and the passage of the Nationality Bill. The electoral law adjusted constituencies to conform to the figures of a census taken in 1956,‡ and increased their number from 97 to 173.

As a result of the *Umma*-P.D.P. pact Mahdists voted for Mirghanist candidates in these elections and Mirghanists for Mahdists for the first time in history. Between them they acquired 89 seats (*Umma* 63, P.D.P. 26) and a working majority, but it is significant that Azhari's N.U.P. fighting on a non-sectarian, or rather anti-sectarian ticket,

* Nothing could have been less like a charging rhinoceros than the foreign policy of the Sudan Republic at this time.
† A traveller reported at the time having watched a Frenchman and an Egyptian contesting the final of the Sudan tennis championship on the lawns of the British club in Khartum.
‡ Total population 10,262,674, of whom 2,784,420 were southerners.

polled more votes than any other party, though it only won 44 seats.*
His programme did not differ markedly from those of his rivals. It
aimed at a socialist Islamic republic on good terms with its African
as well as its Arab neighbours, but especially with Egypt. The
domestic programme outlined reasonable proposals for economic
and social development. The *Umma* prospectus was more militantly
Muslim, more definitely opposed to the new Southern Federal
Party, less restrained in promises of industrial and agricultural
development, in plans for settlement of nomads, and in denunciation
of any form of military commitment to East or West. The P.D.P.
line was much the same. All endorsed the Bandung resolutions and
denounced colonialism and 'neo-colonialism'. The Federalists, who
also wanted parity for Christianity with Islam and for English with
Arabic, plus an amnesty for the 1955 mutineers, were supported by
the Anti-Imperialist Front, which favoured alliance with Egypt and
Syria against the West. Its ambitions in this direction, like those of
the Arab Socialist wing of the P.D.P., were seriously hampered by
the sudden decision of the Egyptian Government on the eve of the
election to re-claim the areas north of the 22nd parallel which had
been administered as part of the Sudan ever since the reoccupation.
Troops were rushed to Halaib, and the Egyptians finally agreed to
leave their claim in abeyance, but intense resentment had been
aroused all over the northern Sudan.

The new coalition Government set sail, therefore, with a fair
wind, and since it enjoyed the support of both the Sayeds it seemed
likely to fare better than its predecessors. Conditions were improving
in the south. There was no outstanding bone of contention with the
opposition. Pro-Egyptian propaganda had been silenced.

The stability was, however, more apparent than real. Parliament
was specifically empowered to act as a constitutional assembly, and
the new constitution had a second controversial feature in addition
to the southern claim to regional autonomy. This was the question
of the Presidency. There were differences of opinion as to whether
the President should be elected by parliament or by referendum and
whether he should be a titular or an executive head of the state. In
any event sectarian rivalry was bound to revive unless a neutral
candidate was forthcoming.

A national commission had been studying these questions since
1956 and the southerners had only supported the independence
resolution on condition that federation be given careful consideration. The sub-committee concerned had, however, decided in
December 1957 that since any regional government for the south

* The remaining forty seats were won by the new Southern Federal Party.

would have to draw heavily on the north for men and money it would simply be an expensive façade. Expensive façades are sometimes worth the money all the same, and some forty members of the new parliament were pledged to resist the committee's decision.

Apart from these political divisions the economy of the country had been weakened by the failure of the Gezira Board to dispose of its cotton.*

Abdullah Bey was not the man to rally public opinion in a crisis of this kind. He was as aloof as Asquith and as contemptuous of demagogy. His enthusiasm for Egypt and the Arab League was tempered by the memory of successive rebuffs during the struggle for independence. He was apt to blurt out an expression of approval for unpopular Western activities like the despatch of Anglo-American military assistance to Lebanon and Jordan. His plans for a rapprochement with Ethiopia, Saudi Arabia and the Yemen against the advancing tide of Nasserite nationalism were unlikely to commend themselves to many of his supporters. He seems too to have been unduly suspicious of the Unionist party and over-confident of the measure of support likely to be forthcoming from Sayed Ali.

The cracks in the structure became evident in June, when the American Aid agreement was ready for ratification. By this time the N.U.P. had withdrawn from the constitutional discussions because of the presidential issue,† and the southerners when their proposals were finally turned down. The question of American Aid cut across party differences and ratification was only secured after adjournment for the energetic canvassing of individual votes.‡ This provided a precedent for similar bargaining by other pressure groups, facilitated by the lack of clear-cut differences of principle.

In this adjustment of political balances sectarian influence again appeared. The *Umma* party was still in a position to push through a constitution providing for the election of a non-executive President by parliament. It was known that Sayed Abdel Rahman's doctors gave him less than a year to live, and that a strong body of opinion, not confined to the *Ansar*, felt that it would be a pleasant gesture to crown his long battle for independence by bestowing the Presidency on him before he died. This Sayed Ali could not be expected to stomach, and his followers in the P.D.P. began to absent themselves more and more frequently from the meetings of the constitutional body. The pro-Egyptian or pan-Arab wing of the party

* See next chapter.
† The N.U.P. wanted an American-type President elected by the nation.
‡ P. M. Holt, op. cit. p. 178, implies that southern votes had to be secured by promises of concession over the regional government issue. This Abdullah Bey strongly denies.

began to take heart. There were rumours of secret negotiations with Egypt by the P.D.P., the N.U.P. and even, incredibly, by Abdullah Bey himself.* The obvious alternative to the existing government was an *Umma*-N.U.P. coalition but neither leader was enthusiastic. In July rumours of an Egyptian plot provoked discussion of preventive action by the Army and thereafter the possibility remained in the back of Ministers' minds. Sayed Abdel Rahman, as is clear from his subsequent behaviour, was very dubious about any such intervention. He was mortally ill and his son, Sayed Saddiq, was strongly opposed to unconstitutional action. Saddiq left the country in September disgusted at the futility of negotiations and the venality of current political bargaining. On 5 November he wrote to his father from Geneva urging him to make one final effort to align support for a national government before parliament reassembled. If necessary Abdullah Bey should be asked to resign.

Negotiations were resumed in an atmosphere thick with rumour. A Paris newspaper had just published an account by its Cairo correspondent of a secret pact between N.U.P., P.D.P. and General Nasser for a National Socialist revolution in Khartum. The story was a fabrication but many people in the Sudan, including the Prime Minister and the Commander-in-Chief, appear to have believed it. According to another story Abdullah Bey was about to proclaim Sayed Abdel Rahman as Head of State. Then it was learned that a P.D.P. Minister, Ali Abdel Rahman, had taken off for Cairo or Baghdad without notifying the Prime Minister.

It was obvious to the negotiators that unless they could hammer out an eleventh hour agreement some sort of *coup d'état* was inevitable. At long last, late in the evening of 16 November, agreement was reached to form an *Umma*-N.U.P. coalition Government. Details were to be announced next morning, but when the listeners switched on their sets they heard instead that General Ibrahim Abboud had moved his troops into the city and taken over the government.

'We shall never know what really happened,' said a Sudanese commentator a year or two later, 'until the Army have been ejected. Some say Abboud was simply fed up with all politicians; others that he genuinely feared an Egyptian take-over. He can't have feared a coup by Abdullah Bey, and although Abdullah Bey denies complicity and has been violently anti-Army ever since, he must have known it was coming. After all his son-in-law Abdel Wahhab was the prime mover.'

So the first Republic came to a bloodless end. Outside the ranks

---

* This queer tale apparently found acceptance in certain American circles.

of those who had political fish to fry not many tears were shed. The chorus of *Gerontes*, and most people in the provinces, asked only for a strong and stable government; even in the towns excitement had given place to fear. Public opinion was disposed to let the Army see what it could do for a month or two, or even six. It was not however prepared for a long period of autocratic government.

Chapter 8

The Bread and the Butter

INDEPENDENCE IS valueless without viability and it remains to consider what assets, economic, administrative, social and cultural, the new republic took over in the middle 'fifties, and how it used them till the soldiers took over. Financial solvency, a sound civil service under an authority answerable only to the Head of State, an independent judiciary and audit similarly privileged, a working system of local government, an imaginative theory of education with a free university to crown and inspire it — these are some of the conditions that emerge as essential or at least desirable for the success of a new state.

For the Sudan something in the nature of a public authority in charge of the Gezira Scheme was an obvious pre-conditional requirement.

Once the decision had been reached in 1944 not to renew the Syndicate's concession when it expired in 1950,* the question of how the Scheme was to be run thereafter gave rise to much discussion. A special committee of the Advisory Council suggested administration by the Department of Agriculture through a Board of Management which would include representatives of the tenant and the taxpayer. The Legislative Assembly, *per contra*, insisted through another special committee that any board of control must be completely independent of government and tenants alike. Everybody felt that a percentage of the profits hitherto payable to shareholders ought to be devoted to social development. The Advisory Council thought that a project of this kind should 'cater for the welfare of the country as a whole and in particular of that community which lies within the boundaries of the Scheme'. The province authorities and the Syndicate favoured something on the lines of the Tennessee Valley Authority, concentrating on the Gezira itself. The Financial Secretary argued that the Sudan in

* The Syndicate's demise merits an Antony, to praise as well as bury. Nothing that state or private enterprise can boast of in the field of successful and practical beneficence rivals its record. Its field staff, like the administrators of Dongola (Chapter 3) and the barons of the Bahr el Ghazal (Chapter 10), whom they resembled, would ask to be judged only by their alleged victims.

general had financed the Scheme and since the Sudan taxpayer was still paying interest on the money borrowed he was entitled to put in a claim for consideration as heir to the shareholders' revenue. The tenants themselves were all in favour of social service in the Gezira, but thought that it ought to be paid for out of the Government's existing 40 per cent share of the profits. If money was going to be available out of the Syndicate's 20 per cent, then it should be added to the tenants' share.

They made this clear in 1946 when they were consulted about expenditure against their Welfare Fund. This had been accumulating since the depression, when the Government had had to provide working capital for the tenant. Recoveries had been credited to the new fund and the time had arrived when something could be done with the money. The usual air of secrecy, however, hung about these financial transactions. The tenants were aware that some sort of reserve was being built up against future disaster. (A fund of this kind had proved invaluable as a stabiliser of prices paid for American cotton in the Nuba mountains.) They at once assumed that the welfare money was being filched from this reserve, and registered strong objection. When informed that all was well with the reserve fund, which stood unimpaired at £1,300,000, they declared that this too had been unfairly deducted from their legitimate profits in order to benefit some farmer of the future and decided, with the encouragement of *Ashiqqa* politicians from Omdurman, that they would not sow the 1947 crop until the whole £1,300,000 had been distributed amongst them.

The Gezira Committee of the Advisory Council was asked to mediate and recommended a handout of £400,000. Although the price in 1946 had risen again to just over 10*d.* and the tenants were reasonably well-off the Government was unwilling to rebuff the committee and finally agreed. It was good money thrown away, for there was by now a temporary world shortage of cotton. The 1947 crop sold for 19*d.* In 1948 and again in 1949 it fetched double that figure. Then came the Korean War and the price rocketed in 1951 to eighty pence a pound.

Meanwhile in July 1949 the Executive Council had finally approved for submission to the Legislative Assembly an ordinance setting up a Gezira Board of seven members, to be appointed by the Governor-General. Its duties were defined as:

(1) The management of the Scheme;
(2) Social development in the Gezira area; and
(3) Research.

The Board's share of the profits was subject to certain fixed charges

H

and its administrative expenses were limited to a maximum of £3·500 per acre. These figures were rendered quite unreal by subsequent inflation.

The ordinance also provided for a social development committee of the Board and for an advisory committee under the chairmanship of the province governor, representing tenants, local government authorities, and government departments. The tenants had had a representative council of their own since 1947 but this and the advisory committee were not an adequate substitute for representation on the Board itself. However, the new arrangement was generally regarded as a reasonable compromise at the time.

A regular but none the less paradoxical feature of Gezira economics was that production seemed always to vary with price. Both withered together in 1931; both shot up in 1951. The yield in 1946 was 3·4 *kantars*, in 1950 4·6, in the boom year 6·8. As a result the whole country was faced by an inflation problem nearly as grave as that of the depression twenty years before. Efforts to spread payments over a long period and to build up ample reserves were thwarted or hampered by the opposition of the tenants' representative council, and the policy of sale in bulk to the U.K. Raw Cotton Commission, which had stabilised prices and afforded security during the war years, was called into anxious question every year until the Commission itself was dissolved by the British Government in 1953.

The average tenant earned a clear profit of £800 in 1951. This he proceeded to spend. He acquired expensive tastes and extravagant hire purchase debts, forgot his old frugal economy and settled down to be a gentleman farmer, hiring labour to work the land.* When, in 1952, the boom ended as suddenly as it had begun and the yield returned with the price to normal levels the tenant's profits were quartered and he was saved from complete disaster only by the law forbidding loans secured on crops or land. The resultant discontent coincided with labour troubles in other parts of the country. In 1953 the tenants' representative council was registered as a trades union and its first president was a professing communist who had acquired a half share in a tenancy.† Under his regime the union ceased to be representative in any normal sense of the word and a

---

* This is the period satirised by a local poet in 'Masefield in the Gezira', the middle verse of which ran:

'Half-starved tenant in his Standard Vanguard
Mowing down a passing herd of tick-thick goats,
With a cargo of scent bottles, tooth sticks, prayer-mats,
Petitions to the Governor and Ten Pound Notes.'

† Shaikh el Amin Muhammad el Amin, who re-appears on the political scene in October, 1964.

pattern of behaviour familiar in other parts of the world developed. Demands were pitched higher and higher and at sowing time in 1955 another strike was threatened. The Board in reply offered a grant from the reserve to any tenant who signed an undertaking to be more co-operative in future. The gamble succeeded. The union committee's popularity had been on the wane since the arrest of its secretary on a charge of peculation the previous November. In 1956 a new and more representative committee took over and thereafter relations were much more amicable.*

Meanwhile, however, the Board had got into difficulties over marketing the crop. Dark suspicions that the U.K. buyer was getting Sudan cotton at bargain prices led to a decision to sell the crop by auction with a reserve price which was more often than not above the market. †As a result a permanent lag in sales developed while the two prices adjusted themselves and the Board was usually left with part of the old crop still on its hands when the new crop was coming on to the market. At the end of 1955 there were 120,000 bales unsold; at the end of 1957, a quarter of a million; at the end of 1958, 263,000.‡

Unfortunately the whole Sudan economy was geared to the fluctuating price of cotton. It was not only the Gezira crop that was involved. It was estimated in 1956 that private pump schemes and water wheels were now producing at least half as much long staple cotton as the big irrigation schemes. The expansion is reflected in the bank advances for cotton-growing which had risen from £69,000 in 1951 to more than £11,000,000 in 1956. The Gezira was producing 4·85 *kantars* again, prices were reasonable, and inflation was again in sight. A mild credit squeeze and a temporary ban on luxury imports deferred the crisis, which was in any case comparatively local in its effect. (In the other provinces cost-of-living figures remained fairly constant for the ordinary Sudanese and figures for meat consumption had shown little variation since 1951.)

But any permanent or effective restriction on imports was ruled out by the fact that the Government was now the chief importer itself. It will be remembered that one Sudanese criticism of the old government was that it saved instead of spending. 'Niggardly Scottish finance' was what some of its own officials termed it.

---

* The above is taken mainly from Gaitskell's *Gezira*, pp. 311 seq.

† Sample reserve prices fixed for X64ˢ cotton over this period were as follows:

March 1956	18·20	May 1956	19·50		
March 1957	22·80	May 1957	19·10	November 1957	16·30
March 1958	14·40	August 1958	12·90	November 1958	10·85

‡ This after another bad crop (259,000 bales). A bale weighs approximately 420 lb.

Expenditure always comes hard when you have been brought up the hard way, and the Finance Department of the Sudan Government could look back on very parsimonious days indeed. So every year the budget was balanced and the money tucked away in reserves for debt-redemption or sinking funds. In 1947 however a Five Year Development Plan was launched, and in 1952 a second. Both tended to concentrate on social services — new schools and hospitals and the like, and were criticised as being little more than a convenient method of financing long-overdue capital expenditure. None the less they drew steadily on the accumulated reserves and they involved considerable purchases abroad. The country had reason to be grateful, therefore, for the £25 million windfall of the 1951–2 budget.

The post-Korean slump was weathered successfully and by 1956 the balance of payments had recovered and liquid reserves built up again to £44 million. Fortunately there were few inherited liabilities, thanks to a judicious conversion operation carried out on the eve of war by the then Financial Secretary, Sir Francis Rugman. Just over five millions were still owing to Britain and just under five millions to Egypt, but a seven million pound budget surplus had come to be regarded as not abnormal* and of course the pound had already depreciated more than a little.

The country now had £50 million invested in development schemes of one kind and another, £15 million in railways, £5 million in Light and Power, and £4 million on loan to the Gezira Board. A public utility company was formed in 1957 to take over all power and light undertakings, the long term plan being to harness hydro-electric power at various suitable cataracts and channel new industries into their neighbourhood.

The new five-year plan due to begin in 1957 was more ambitious than either of its predecessors. The decision to ignore the Nile Waters Agreement, which was responsible for the great increase in private irrigation schemes, also enabled the Government to go ahead with long cherished plans to extend the irrigated area westward over the Managil ridge by building a new barrage at Roseires on the Blue Nile to top up the Sennar Reservoir. Having a capacity three times as great (5 billion tons) as Sennar, the new dam would also make it possible to irrigate a million acres in the Kenana area farther up-stream. In spite of protests from Egypt work on both

* 1954/5 Revenue 38,110,530 Expenditure 30,588,624
　1955/6　　　　42,322,551　　　　　　32,097,705
　1956/7　　　　45,869,401　　　　　　32,698,657
　1957/8　　　　45,585,415　　　　　　40,380,044
　1958/9　　　　41,983,000　　　　　　41,409,000

projects was well in train by 1957. The plan also included a dam on the Atbara river at Khashm el Girba, the Jonglei Canal,* by-passing the *sudd*, a development scheme for Jebel Marra in Darfur and various mining and manufacturing projects.

Obviously all this was going to involve borrowing money on a considerable scale. The Sudan now had its own currency† and was soon to have a central bank. It was a member of the International Monetary Fund and the International Bank. Aid without strings attached was difficult to come by however,‡ and a large section of political opinion was, as we have seen, suspicious of America; but the plan was going to cost £137 million and the Government could not afford to pick and choose. Discussions with the U.S. began in May 1957 and an agreement was concluded the following March for aid amounting to 5·6 million dollars.

Meanwhile cotton was at its old game — production up to 6·76 in 1956–7 and down to 1·50 in 1957–8; prices steadily lower. In April 1958 it was found necessary to impose severe restrictions on private imports. The value of exports fell by £10 million and there was fear of a budget deficit, the first for a quarter of a century.

The financial situation in November when the soldiers took over was that the Egyptian loan had been paid off, a balance of £3,649,395 was outstanding in London, and the Sudan had drawn £1,741,214 of its quota from the International Monetary Fund, repayable in 3–5 years. A 20-year loan of 39 million dollars at 5⅜ per cent had also been negotiated with the International Bank for railway extension, together with a 5-year credit of £5 million from the British Government and another of 25 million marks from West Germany. None of these loans had yet been drawn upon.

Although the fears of a budget deficit were not realised the precarious economic situation in 1958 contributed both directly and indirectly, as has been seen, to the collapse of parliamentary government.

Just, however, as France has contrived to weather all her political vicissitudes at the centre by virtue of a sound civil service and local

* A special committee had been set up in 1946 to investigate the wide-spread social and economic implications of this canal on the livelihood of the Nilotic tribes of the Upper Nile.
† The new currency was introduced in the summer of 1957. The Sudan pound, like the old Egyptian 'guinea', was tied to sterling at a value of £1 0s. 6d. 50 per cent of the issue was backed by sterling balances transferred to a special account and 50 per cent by Government Treasury Bills.
The symbol £ in the text=£S from 1957 on.
‡ A wealthy uninvolved state such as Kuwait has since been invaluable to neutralist countries anxious to lay their hands on a few millions for development purposes.

government system, so in the Sudan the administration and the local government authorities carried on unimpaired.

A Sudanisation Committee had formed part of the Administration Conference of 1946 and had submitted detailed proposals for the progressive replacement of expatriates in senior posts, reducing them from 694 in 1948 to a target figure of 232 in 1962.* Recruitment of foreigners to pension was stopped in 1947 and in 1951 a special commission reorganised the government cadres on a Sudanese pay-scale basis. Thereafter non-Sudanese were recruited on contract and paid an expatriation allowance. A Civil Service Commission was set up under the Self Government statute, but could not give absolute protection because its functions were consultative and the Minister could overrule its recommendations.†

When the new Sudanisation Committee started work in 1954 under the provisions of the Anglo-Egyptian Agreement its immediate task was to eliminate the British from the army, the police, and the administration. Their presence in senior departmental posts was not thought to be so undesirable as to require urgent action. It soon became clear however that this would not work out in practice. A highly skilled and competent doctor cannot be expected to stay on contentedly in a comparatively subordinate post when a man ten years his junior has suddenly been promoted to govern a province. So the senior departmental expatriate had to go too, and vacancies thereby created at a lower level were filled where necessary by non-British foreigners on short-term contract. This is not a satisfactory arrangement because a man needs to spend at least ten years in a country if he is to learn the language and customs and problems, and see something of the results of his work. There is a need for a United Nations service to provide facilities for this, with the prospect of promotion in due course to a post where his experience can be used for the benefit of people elsewhere. The old British colonial service provided a precedent which could be useful, but promotion would of course have to be based on merit and length of service, not on a national quota. The British Government has recently provided for secondment of teachers and local government employees without loss of promotion and superannuation rights, which is a step in the right direction, but inevitably the period of secondment is too short for a man to give his heart to the field of his labour. These arguments also apply, *mutatis mutandis*, in the field of local government. Here it is desirable to leave an executive for a

---

* See p. 106 of *The Sudan Question* by Mekki Abbas.
† See p. 91 of the Report of the Commission of Enquiry into the Southern Sudan Disturbances of 1955.

reasonably long period in the employ of a council, but to ensure his promotion prospects and his independence of mind by enrolling him on a general roster. The Sudan has no *zemindar* class to exert political pressure on province staff through province legislatures but any such possibility had been obviated by a system of secondment from a national local government service.*

Experiments had been made after the war with the English 'two-tier' system of district and shire councils, but it had proved unsuitable to Sudan conditions. The services performed in the United Kingdom by the county council — education, sanitation, upkeep of major roads and the like — were in the Sudan still mainly controlled by the Central Government and as a result the district council was apt to find itself with far less responsibility than the subordinate town committee. In 1948 the Government had invited Dr. A. M. Marshall, City Treasurer of Coventry, to draw up recommendations for future development. He began by assimilating local tradition and recent practice so successfully that his proposals appeared to grow naturally out of them, or in them, by a process of evolution. They were accepted almost as they stood by the Executive Council and the Legislative Assembly and were embodied in a Local Government Ordinance under which existing councils were re-warranted for a five-year period. Flexibility was the key note. The main features were the progressive withdrawal of the District Commissioner and the establishment of a Directorate of Local Government with Inspectors attached to province headquarters, and the abandonment of the two-tier system in favour of independent authorities empowered to create an *ad hoc* association for the administration of a common service where desirable. The financial system was overhauled in 1950–1. Councils now received the bulk of the direct taxes on crops and livestock and were subsidised to cover certain functions performed on behalf of the Central Government, which contributed half the cost of maintaining trunk roads. Councils budgeted for a surplus payable to the Central Treasury, with deficit budgets subsidised temporarily until they could stand on their own feet.

The chief criticism of the new system was that it failed to make use of the traditional loyalty to the province as an intervening unit between the local council and the central bureaucracy. Some of the provinces, like Darfur and Kordofan in the west, had a history going back through the centuries. The comparatively new Northern Province was roughly co-terminous with the Kingdom of Kush,

* Members of this service wear the same uniform as the Local Government Inspector, which is confusing.

the Gezira Province with Alwa and Sennar. Even the newer provinces dated back to the nineteenth century and many felt that they
would provide a natural defence against over-centralisation. They
had always acted as useful regional extensions of the Central Government and would obviously continue to do so as responsibility for
services like elementary education and preventive medicine was
devolved upon them. Surely they could also provide a more satisfactory alternative to the *ad hoc* committee for the administration of
these services and of the police force.* Moreover the governor and
the departmental representatives in the province already functioned
as a unit of local government through the executive committee of
the province council. These councils had been created in an advisory
capacity in 1944 and were composed of representatives elected by
the L.G.A.s together with members nominated to represent commercial, professional and minority interests. They survived because
they were useful and necessary for the discussion of problems common to the province and for adjudication on rival claims to the
province allocation under the development schemes, the services
of a construction team or a boring rig, the siting of new dispensaries
and schools; but in spite of this, and of the retention of the province
as a convenient budgetary unit by the Central Government, the lack
of statutory status left the councils in an anomalous position, their
function purely advisory and their future doubtful.

Apart from this there was little objection raised to the system,
which continued to function unchanged through the period of
parliamentary government.

The District Commissioner was also giving up his remaining legal
functions to the state judiciary. These consisted of direct criminal
jurisdiction and the supervision of the shaikhs' courts. Civil justice
had been handed over at a much earlier period, since it required
professional knowledge to a greater degree than the average D.C.
could hope to acquire. Criminal procedure was less complicated,
and the advantages of the combination of 'Inspector' and Magistrate
still outweighed any minor irregularity which might occur.

* The police force, of which the Sudan had always been justifiably proud, was
centralised by direction of the Governor-General in April 1953, apparently to meet
the objection of Sudanese commandants to being subordinated to the authority of
newly promoted Sudanese governors. The British governors were strongly
opposed to the change, which was blamed for the success of the rebels in the
south two years afterwards. The Commission of Inquiry into the disturbances was
not, however, disposed to admit the validity of the Sudanese governors' arguments
on this point. (See the Commission's Report, Section IV, Administration and
Police.)

Under the military Government further centralisation of powers, from commandant to commissioner, took place.

A great deal of theoretic prejudice has been directed against administrative magistrates. In fact in nearly thirty years of experience in the Sudan I can only remember one case in which I suspected that the public security aspect had been allowed to influence the sentence. Doubtless there were plenty of examples which never came my way, but the compensating advantages were great.

To be a magistrate or a justice of the peace in the United Kingdom is a comparatively simple matter. Centuries of endeavour have made the judiciary proof against political pressure from above or interested approaches from below. Procedure is indigenous and well established. All that is necessary is a good brain, a balanced judgement and a knowledge of the law.

In the new states things are not so easy. Ghana has provided recent examples of what happens when justice conflicts with the interest of the strong. The Sudan's chief problem has been to ensure that Justice in the abstract, justice in the eyes of British legal procedure, and justice as interpreted by local tradition and custom do not fall hopelessly at variance.

It is strange how belief in the absolute validity of Western legal procedure has survived the collapse of so many other institutional idols. So long as the Western lawyer remains convinced it seems that his pupils will do the same. Yet the success and reputation of the Sudan courts was based on compromise. In tribal society it may be just as much a duty to take arms against a local enemy as it is for the soldier in time of war. The father of a mentally or physically deformed infant may be constrained by humanitarian motives as well as tribal custom to expose it. To sentence either offender to death or a long period of imprisonment might be good in law but it would be grave injustice.

There was a legal commission which went out to East Africa between the wars and was shocked to learn that somewhere in Uganda the theft of a cockerel was tantamount to murder. It gave the thief power to cast spells over the owner. But, said the Commission, British Justice could not take cognisance of such superstition! Similarly in Kordofan the Baggara courts punished cattle-theft with two years' imprisonment and camel-theft with six months. The camel-owning Hamar in the same district reversed these penalties.

It is only by understanding these variations that justice can properly be done, and the D.C.s — British or Sudanese — had been brought up in an atmosphere of such understanding. It was therefore vitally important that the new judges and resident magistrates should not be hypnotised by their text-books. The Commission of

Inquiry into the 1955 disturbances in the south (see Ch. 10), whose report reflects the high standard of the professional judiciary, was careful to emphasise that justice must not only be done but must be seen to be done. This is possible only if it conforms to the basic ethical principles recognised by the common man.

Less important, but important none the less, are questions of procedure. The shaikhs' courts are protected by a statutory tie-up with native custom but this will not always prevent interference with, for instance, their excellent practice of letting the witness tell his story and then swearing him specifically on the crucial point in his evidence. Most men find that direct confrontation with a point of perjury in this way is very difficult to slide past.

The Resident Magistrate has therefore to be possessed of an open mind, and must, if the local courts are to function properly, get out and visit them. It is no use simply to call in the clerks once a year with their registers for audit.

The main complaint against the State courts has not been directed (save by the southern exiles) against their standard of justice but against the delay in its administration. This will presumably be remedied as the judicial cadre expands.

In the realm of Islamic Law there was built up over the years by a series of able Grand Kadis* a working system of personal law combining features of the locally observed Malikite and the official (Egyptian) Hanifite Code. Kadis from Khartum were seconded in the 'thirties to the Emirates of northern Nigeria for the religious and legal training of their personnel, and were so successful and congenial that the last of them, Shaikh Awad Muhammad Ahmed, Principal of the School of Arabic at Kano, was appointed in 1960 to be the first Grand Kadi of the Northern Region.

Mention has been made in Chapter 5 of the conflict in the Sudan between modern theories of education and traditional ideas of discipline. The case for the former is now accepted so universally in the west that Solomon's prescription for giving the young man knowledge and discretion has been equated with the crackling of thorns and associated only with sadists.

There was of old in the Sudan a headmaster who agreed with Solomon, and exercised over young Englishmen who came to him for instruction in Arabic the same iron discipline which obtained in his class-room. Forty years on, his views were unchanged.

* The Grand Kadis for many years came from Egypt. They included a number of distinguished men, among them Shaikh Muhammad Mustafa el Maraghi, later Rector of el Azhar, a prominent participator in the 1936 World Congress of Faiths in London.

'I read a great deal of nonsense about the terrifying atmosphere of the schools in this country (and in yours) in the days when I was a boy,'* he remarked. 'Surely the proof of the pudding is in the eating. Were the men turned out by this system neurotics, or lick-spittles? On the contrary. Look at X, Y and Z, men of integrity and moral courage. And what of the product of your brave new world, of the "All-Boys-Together" regime introduced into Gordon College in the 'thirties? Rebels against everything; not rebels of principle, but rebels in principle. Nothing but hot air in the Union and strikes in the lecture room. No respect for anybody or anything. A fine mess you have made of your own country. Every boy a hooligan and every girl a tart. Juvenile delinquency and teenage rioting. This is not due to the war, or to fear of the bomb. It is your soft educational system. You musn't teach a child tables because they are too difficult, or grammar because he may not like it. You must cajole him into learning, beguile him into being interested. In this fashion he may acquire some knowledge almost unconsciously but he goes out into life with his mind untrained and undisciplined.'

He concluded with a plea for traditional Islamic punishments. 'If the old penalty for adultery were reimposed many of our leading citizens would soon be lying under a heap of stones, but you would see a sharp improvement in public morals.'

He is a square, the schoolmaster — surely the squarest man alive, a young listener remarked after his departure. But it was a safe bet thirty years ago when interviewing candidates for a responsible post to choose a boy who had done time under him.

All this is à propos of Khartum University, whose independence was buttressed by a million-pound endowment from the British Government only to be endangered by the political activities of its students. Political activity by university students is undoubtedly a great nuisance, and was scorned by the Oxbridge undergraduate prior to the nineteen-thirties, though it has won more than one battle honour in its time as valuable as academic laurels foregone.† When, however, the unrest soaks down to school level the harm completely outweighs the good; and when the procedure is transferred from politics to academics, and students go on strike, as has happened so often in the Arab world, because their examination papers are too stiff, the whole educational system becomes a farce and the value of a degree negligible.

It was as a safeguard against this depreciation of academic

---

* e.g. Edward Atiya on the Gordon College on p. 138 of *An Arab Tells His Story*, John Murray, 1946.

† Notably in October 1964, after the above was written.

coinage that the link between Khartum and the Commonwealth universities was valuable. There was nothing in principle to prevent its retention. As the Pakistan representative pointed out, if Irish universities are included why not Sudanese? But for purposes of tidy registration it was found necessary to transfer Khartum from the Commonwealth Yearbook to some other work of reference. Links survive in the endowment trusts of the two constituent bodies, the Gordon College and the Kitchener School.

Full university status was still pending when independence came. It was conferred by act of parliament in 1956. The new University enjoyed a government subsidy in addition to its endowments. It was governed by a Council of thirty members, twelve of whom held university offices, eight were elected by the Senate, and two by faculty members. The Senate consisted of the heads of the various departments and representatives of the Faculty Boards. The Faculties were Arts, Agriculture, Engineering, Law, Medicine, Science, Veterinary Science, Economics and Social Studies. English was the language of instruction except in Arabic and Islamic Studies. The ordinary B.A. or M.Sc. course took four years, the honours course five. There were facilities for postgraduate study and a special relationship in engineering with the N.W. University of Illinois. The library, called after Sir Douglas Newbold, who presented it with 3,000 volumes, left his own books to it, and was more responsible than any other man for the foundation and shape of the University, housed nearly 100,000 volumes. There was hostel accommodation for women students as well as for men.

The Chancellor was appointed by the Head of State on the nomination of the University Council and it was regarded as a good omen that the holder of the office on the occasion of the first degree day was a southerner, Sayed Siricio Iro. Expatriates were still numerous and uninhibited among the faculty members.

Educational expansion at lower levels had been considerable.

Under the first two five-year-plans schools were springing up all over the north and demand continued to outstrip supply. The obvious danger was as usual a decline in quality. The contemporary picture was portrayed, on 11 January 1957, for the Jersey branch of the Royal Empire Society, by the Sudan Ambassador, Sayed Awad Satti, an ex-Director of Education. He began by pointing out that the Sudan had to cut its coat according to its cloth. There could be no question as yet of universal literacy or small classes. Most important of all was perhaps the elementary school because that was all the schooling the average boy got, and it was vital for him to go out into the world with a broad mind, a knack of picking up knowledge as he went along, and a sense of responsibility to his fellow country-men. The objective was variety, and he claimed that thanks to the pooling of ideas at Bakht el Ruda from Sudanese, British, Egyptian and other nations the syllabus was the richest and most varied in the Arabic-speaking world. More than 200 text-books had been prepared there for the guidance of teachers, and since 'in these early stages of education it is always desirable to ... (provide) ... practical illustrations ... there are local visits to historical museums, science laboratories, town council offices and other places of interest'.

After four years of elementary schooling a minority of boys and girls moved on at the age of eleven to an intermediate school.* There were 160 of these, absorbing about 25,000 children, and about 18 following the Egyptian syllabus. Intermediate education followed the same curriculum, at a higher level, but with the important addition of English. Literacy, debating and musical societies, a Farmers' club, a Fishing club, and above all a General Society, or school parliament, were a feature of these schools. This last handled all activities except policy, teaching and discipline. It was responsible to the Headmaster through a member of his staff acting as liaison officer with the student body and presumably strengthened their predeliction for representative institutions.†

The 4-year intermediate course was followed by 4 years secondary, but as there were in 1957 only six full secondary schools for boys and four two-stream schools in the north half the intermediate product could not be accommodated. There was still only one secondary school for girls in the whole country and one two-stream school for boys in the south. One of the six northern secondaries was a Technical School and another a Commercial College.

English was still the language of instruction in most subjects, but boys find it difficult to arrange their thoughts and express them in a foreign language and Arabic was expected to replace English very soon, at all but university and near-university level.‡

Policy in the south was to bring existing government schools up to northern standards of staff and equipment and then take over the mission schools. Expansion plans were concentrated at this stage on Arabic and teacher training. One thing the missionaries had done

---

* Later, during the period of military rule, it was decided to aim at eliminating the intermediate school and substituting for the 4+4+4 system 6 years elementary +4 to 6 years secondary.
† In the excitement following on the October Revolution, however, these societies began to claim complete control over the schools and the position of the headmasters became intolerable.
‡ Progress was hampered by the lack of suitable textbooks in Arabic, according to a statement in the Central Council on 23 June 1964.

well, apparently, was technical education, and the Government was building on this foundation as quickly as shortage of staff permitted.

'Our aim,' the speaker concluded, 'is to bring about an adequate and unified system of education for the country as a whole. It is very clear that the Sudan cannot make sound economic and political development unless its people are educated, but the rate of expansion must not be launched irrespective of the strain on our financial resources and manpower. This is a risky affair in the present age of inflation and scarcity of qualified and trained personnel. Our present plans are considered to be satisfactory in the prevailing circumstances. There is no rigidity in these plans, they are carefully observed and constantly reviewed, and for that we have a system of close co-ordination and consultation between the concerned authorities.'

The ordinary man would add two criticisms. One is in ironic contrast to the clash between tribal conservatism and western liberalism in the education of boys. For girls the boot is on the other foot. Although away at the top of the educational ladder young women are slowly battling through to a measure of emancipation, down in the village schools behaviour is inevitably and very properly conditioned by the strictest notions of Muslim propriety. As a result the child who has been brought up in the free and unselfconscious cameraderie of Kordofan or Upper Nile rural society returns from school enwrapped in veils and modesty, to shun the company of her recent playmates.

The second criticism is tied up with public reaction to the equivalent of the election poster: 'What has the government done for YOU?' The farmer or the grazier, who between them still constitute the bulk of the population, would admit the value of accessible medical facilities, of having a local court to settle disputes inexpensively and in an intelligible fashion and of improved public security since the bad old days; but they might demur about education. They would be all for the education of their own children to occupy supposedly lucrative and definitely prestige-bearing government posts, but the provision of these facilities for *all* children might seem less desirable. After all, as a chief in Sierra Leone once pointed out, somebody has to grow the crops and since no educated African will demean himself by working on the land, universal education would mean starvation! Something of this kind was probably in the mind of Sayed el Awad when he drafted his final paragraph, but tremendous expansion has since taken place without such disastrous results.

To return to what the Government had done for the rural voter, one might be pardoned at first for supposing that his interests had been overlooked in the concentration on industrial and urban development. But quite a lot had in fact been achieved. Westward from railhead at el Obeid stretched a line of waterbores along the various stock roads to southern Darfur. Other bores, strategically placed among the dunes, provided villagers with a shorter walk to water in the summer and facilities for picking gum or harvesting ground-nuts in remote areas without risk of thirsting to death. Dams, contour-bunds and artificial tanks enabled the stock-breeder to make the best use of his grazing. A report on Rural Water supplies and Soil Conservation had been one of the first items discussed by the Advisory Council in 1944 and although many of its suggestions were unpalatable — especially where goat-restriction was concerned — the country had slowly become more erosion-conscious, and in 1956 a special Department of Land Use and Rural Water Development was set up with a regional office in each province. One of the lessons learned over the years was that permanent water bores create an expanding circle of over-grazing whereas a surface reservoir dries up with the grass and forces the grazier to move on elsewhere before it is too late. Experiments in controlling the movement of Baggara cattle along specified corridors from winter to summer grazing were also carried out successfully by the Rizeigat autocrat, Shaikh Ibrahim Musa Madibbo, in southern Darfur. The science of culling and selective breeding was very slowly inculcated. Contagious bovine pleuro pneumonia and rinderpest, the two great scourges of African cattle, were being brought under control.

The cattle man had in fact had a great deal of money spent on his behalf for an export product which only topped a million pounds in value as late as 1956. The camel breeder did rather better than this on his own, exporting his beasts on the hoof and unaided to a value of just over a million and a quarter in that year. He had not so much for which to thank the government, only protection against trypanosomiasis and mange and one or two other diseases and the suppression of theft and raiding, a doubtful blessing in the eyes of the potential participant.

The camel trade with Egypt flourishes on both sides of the Nile. The place of cattle in the economy of the southern Butana of Kassala Province had been filled by a mechanised crop production scheme inaugurated just after the war. There were the usual teething troubles, due mainly to the heavy soil and the refusal of sorghum to conform to the nice regularity of temperate zone grain crops, to say nothing of the attention of the Spanish sparrow, but remedies were found to all these afflictions and by 1957 more than 400,000 acres of prairie cultivation were producing millet and sesame, a valuable basic supply for the central Sudan* to supplement the irrigated grain crop.

Sparrows are not the worst of the Sudanese farmer's enemies. He has also to compete with the locust and with a sucking bug, or pentatomid, called *andat*, which descends in myriads from its winter quarters under the leaves of evergreen trees. Battle had been joined with all three of these pests and the present international locust control organisation may be said to have grown out of preventive measures taken against the desert locust in its solitary state on the Red Sea littoral. The other two pests have also to be attacked between seasons when resting in low bushes or clustering under trees. Various methods have been tried and a fair degree of success obtained.

This is not the place, however, for cataloguing achievement or listing deficiencies. The new republic, it can fairly be claimed, inherited no real problem except that of the south, which will be discussed below.

The best index to a healthy body politic is provided perhaps by the incidence of crime. The prison population of the Sudan remained fairly constant at 11,000 to 12,000 persons from 1949 to 1957, climbing to 13,549 only in the year 1956 after the southern mutiny.

---

* Including heavy annual purchases by the Government itself.

Chapter 9

Military Rule

THE HISTORY of the years 1958–64 covers an attempt by two men to create a new Sudan, economically viable and politically stable, using the army to maintain public security while they worked out their plans.

Both men were well-intentioned; both were of unquestioned integrity. They failed because they had to become more and more repressive. Their scheme for erecting a pyramid of representative councils took too long to mature and its inception was marred by the temporary abandonment of elected representation in its only surviving field of employment, the local council. Growing resistance led to increased curtailment of civil rights, especially the much-prized privilege of public criticism. They were not the men to gild the pill by building up a national hero-image or rousing hysteria against sinister foreign influences. Nor were they naturally ruthless. So when nemesis overtook them in the south and a slight relaxation of pressure led to popular demonstrations in the streets of Khartum they were neither prepared nor able to disperse them with a sufficiency of grape-shot.

I have referred this endeavour to two men only because there is no evidence that the military junta on which they depended was sympathetic to their long term aims. There is indeed every indication that it was opposed to them.

These two men were the President, Ibrahim Abboud, and the Chief Justice, Muhammad Abu Renat.

Abboud was a genial soldier, competent and hitherto popular. He was the kind of man of whom people said, 'They can't have told him what his henchmen are doing. He wouldn't have allowed it.' He was the new regime's best asset, at home and abroad, which is probably why he survived so many vicissitudes. He was to the Sudan what Najib was to Egypt, but he lasted longer.

Abu Renat was notorious for his incorruptibility, as just a judge as the famous seventeenth-century Qadi Dushayn, whose grandson founded Wad Medani. Brought up in Kordofan, where his father had been *omda* of Nahud, his sympathies lay less with his fellow

Shaigia than with the ordinary countryman. His legal training accentuated a natural prejudice against extremism. In 1952 he had found himself in sympathy with the Socialist Republicans and his whole instinct was towards stability at the centre and the avoidance of political vicissitudes. His adherence was important to Abboud and it was granted because he thought he saw the opportunity of constructing a new constitution more indigenous than the old and better representing the feelings as well as the interests of the bulk of the people.

They had at first a fair measure of goodwill. People were tired of political intrigue and disposed to give the soldiers a chance. There was no hereditary prejudice against military interference in politics such as has characterised the English. For the observant there was a recent precedent in Pakistan, though the Army's prestige had not stood quite so high or its efficiency *vis-à-vis* the civil administration seemed so marked as it did in Rawalpindi.

It is doubtful, however, if this disinterested inclination to give the new rulers a run for their money would have prevailed without the agreement of the two Sayeds. Sayed Ali's was equivocal but seems to have been given without much hesitation. Like Abu Renat he had a natural affinity with conservatism, together with a distaste for party politics which involve the public manipulation of strings which could more decently be pulled in private. Sayed Abdel Rahman was a dying man. He was younger than his rival, in his early seventies, but his many vicissitudes and his emotional temperament had taken their toll. Financial difficulties and fear of Egyptian intervention had increased the strain that summer and when reports of the impending *coup* reached him he seems to have found it difficult to make up his mind. He spent the night of 16–17 November on his steamer, moored off Tuti Island. In the morning General Abboud and Major General Abdel Wahhab arrived in a launch with a draft for his signature and a tape recorder. The Sayed refused to speak into the microphone and referred the document to a committee of his representatives in Khartum, who left the decision to Abdel Rahman Ali Taha, sometime Minister of Education. Abdel Rahman finally signed on the Sayed's behalf but relations remained uneasy. Most of the leading politicians had formed part of the Sayed's entourage at one time or another. He was dubious about the length of time likely to elapse before a measure of democracy could be restored, and the inevitability of clashes and repression in the meantime.

On 24 March 1959, he died, and an epoch in Sudanese history came to an end. The crested crane which he had fed from his table for thirty years died the same week, and there was an eclipse of the

moon. 'Old men and beldams in the street did prophesy upon it
dangerously.'

He was succeeded as *Imam* by his son Saddiq, late President of
the *Umma* Party. Saddiq was, as we have seen, irreconcilably
opposed to military rule and under him the Mahdists became the
spearhead of a resistance which included party members, students,
journalists, townsmen in general, communists and militant
labour.

The reaction of the civil servant at this stage was mixed. The
constant succession of Ministers — one department had had six in
two years — had been frustrating and wearisome. 'We used to
watch the files accumulate on the Minister's desk,' said one Under-
Secretary, 'while he gossiped with endless place-seekers for whose
protegés we were then instructed to find jobs.' It was a pleasant
change to be left alone to get on with one's work under a Minister
still sufficiently at a loss to abstain from interfering. As time went on,
however, this advantage disappeared and it became irksome to
serve under a man whose I.Q. was lower than one's own. 'You have
been in there for nearly half an hour,' an Under-Secretary remarked
to an emerging visitor, 'What on earth did you find to talk to him
about all that time?' Many of them also were members of the old
political service, and that service was becoming disgruntled. They
had co-operated loyally with the Marshall policy of transfer of
power but they knew that the machinery of province administration
still depended largely on their experience and professional skill. To
be subordinated to an inexperienced military governor was more
than many of them could stomach. Resignations at the top were
numerous, and meant the loss of valuable and experienced men,
known to the people and understanding them. It is difficult to be
unbiased when considering their loss.

On the morning of 17 November 1958 General Abboud broadcast
to the nation. He told them that the whole body politic was threatened
with degeneration, instability and chaos owing to the bitter strife
between parties interested only in their own advantage and prepared to use any means of securing it, from corruption of the press to
trafficking with foreign powers. The army had waited patiently for
a sign of improvement but when instead the country was brought to
the brink of disaster it had stepped in to restore order in the interests
of the people and to safeguard foreign residents. Its objective was to
restore stability and clean administration, and it was influenced by
malice towards none. He called on his fellow countrymen to keep
the peace and carry on as usual, the civil servant at his desk, the
worker at his bench, the farmer in his field and the merchant at his

counter. Foreign diplomats need have no fears. The new government would continue to maintain cordial relations with the world in general and the Arab world in particular. No effort would be spared to strengthen ties with the closest of all, the United Arab Republic.

The 1956 Constitution was suspended by a Constitutional Order (No. 1). The two ex-premiers, Azhari and Khalil, were pensioned off, and the other ministers each received a letter of thanks and 14 days' pay in lieu of notice. Use was made of the old Defence of the Sudan Ordinance to legalise various enactments. This piece of legislation, known familiarly during the war years as DOSO and regarded much as the British public in an earlier war regarded DORA, had already been resuscitated after the Najib riots in 1954 and again in 1955 during the southern mutiny. A state of emergency was now declared under para. 2 and Area Commanders were vested with temporary administrative powers under para. 5. Publication of newspapers was suspended under Regulation 31. No legal authority existed however for dissolving political parties and trades unions. This was done in the exercise of powers conferred on the President by the new Supreme Council of Twelve, which included nearly all the senior officers with the notable exception of the commanders of the northern and eastern areas, Abdel Rahim Shennan and Muhy el Din Abdullah.

The following day, 18 November, saw further evocation of powers. Sovereignty was vested in the people, constituent authority in the Council, which delegated its legislative, judicial and executive powers, with the command of the Army, to the President. A subordinate Council of Ministers included several civilians, notably the Ministers of Finance and Foreign Affairs, and one southerner, Santino Deng.

On the 19th they all took oath before the Mufti. A statement on foreign policy followed. The new Government accepted its obligations under international law, the U.N. Charter, the constitution of the Arab League and the Bandung agreements. It confirmed existing treaties and undertook to support all nations struggling for their liberty. It recognised the special position of the Sudan with obligations to the African as well as to the Arab world, obligations which it promised to fulfil in accordance with the principles recently laid down at a conference in Accra, aiming at peaceful co-existence, non-interference in domestic affairs, free cultural and commercial exchange and the preservation of peace.

It may fairly be claimed that these promises were kept. In October 1964 no state except Israel, Portugal and the Union of

South Africa regarded the Sudan as hostile.* On more than one
occasion it had been invited to mediate between disputants and had
done so successfully. An agreement between Algeria and Morocco
had just been concluded when the Government fell and rival
delegations from the Yemen were actually discussing peace terms
under Sudan patronage at the hill resort of Erkowit behind Port
Sudan.

The next step was to set up committees to consider methods for
the control of rents, for furthering the employment of Sudanese by
foreign firms, and for the production of revised trades union legislation. On 29 November the American Aid agreement was confirmed.
On 11 December it was decided to remove the statues of Gordon
and Kitchener.†

The new Government's economic policy will be discussed below.
Suffice to say here that a more realistic price policy resulted in the
swift disposal of accumulated arrears of cotton.‡

Early in 1959 a new political crisis developed. National survival
depends ultimately on the national concept, which may be embodied in a saviour of the state, like Jamal Abdel Nasir, or in
established tradition. The image of a Sudanese nation had been
blurred by political strife, by Nile Valley propaganda, by sectarian-
ism and by rebellion in the south. If the Presidency were to become a
bone of contention between the legions the prospect was ominous
and that is precisely what seemed to be happening when, on 2
March, troops from the east and the north moved into the capital,

* Outside the Arab League the closest association was with Jugoslavia. After a
visit by Tito in 1959 a trade agreement was signed and arrangements made for
the training of military and naval personnel and the building of ships in Jugoslavia
for a new joint shipping line. Cultural exchanges and the construction of a tannery
and a cardboard factory were arranged, and Jugoslav experts carried out a survey
of Suakin with a view to the reopening of the harbour to relieve congestion at
Port Sudan.

† This was done with due ceremony. The Kitchener statue may now be seen
at Chatham, the Gordon statue at the school for sons of soldiers founded in his
memory, near Woking.

‡ The figures are as follows:

1958	Unsold on 1 January	235,000	bales (of 420 lb.)
	Crop	259,000	
		494,000	
	Sold	231,000	
1959	Unsold on 1 January	263,000	
	Crop	654,000	
		917,000	

The whole of this accumulation was disposed of by the end of August and shipped
by the end of December together with 30,000 bales held by exporters. Prices had
meanwhile recovered to 1958 level.

surrounded the President's house, arrested Abdel Wahhab and two other members of the Council, and compelled the Council itself to resign.

The President, however, survived, and on 5 March an agreement was announced. A new Council of Ten was set up, including Abdel Wahhab and six other old members plus the two rebel leaders and the Central Area Commander, Maqbul el Amin. This body held together for two months, during which permanent responsibility for public security and provincial administration was conferred on the military governors. At the end of April the rebels' position seemed secure. Shennan was leading a delegation to Ethiopia, where he received the Grand Order of the Star of Ethiopia. Muhy el Din, as Minister of Communications, was in Darfur with the President opening the new railway extension to Nyala. On their return at the beginning of May Abdel Wahhab was retired to pension with 3,000 acres of government land.

But they were still unsatisfied and on 22 May they tried again. Two platoons of the Eastern Arab Corps suddenly appeared on the outskirts of the city, but no support materialised from the north and the Khartum garrison (mainly Engineer troops) stood firm. Muhy el Din therefore realised that the attempt was a failure and sent the Gedaref platoons home again. He and Shennan were tried in open court martial and sentenced to death. After a considerable interval, in September, their sentences were commuted.* Their confederates lost their commissions and one other Council member was deposed, but Abdel Wahhab was not reinstated.

The most important feature of these events was the allegiance of the Army. Were troops recruited in Kassala Province really prepared to open fire on troops from Kordofan? It is difficult to believe. Yet the authorities took the matter very seriously and events in East Africa in 1964 have shown how easy it is to work up mutinous feeling. It is said that Sayed Saddiq el Mahdi was constantly urged to bring pressure to bear on the Government through his religious influence with the troops. He replied that to tamper with the loyalty of the Army is to weaken its allegiance to the State and endanger every succeeding government.

The firm action taken in May and June closed the ranks of the senior officers behind the Council but it still had to deal with the student class, the focus as ever of resentment and criticism. The cadets and young officers at the Infantry Training School in Omdurman were in close contact with their contemporaries at the university and as the first anniversary of the revolution drew near it

---

* They were released from prison after the revolution of October 1964.

became known that some sort of violent demonstration was being planned. So far the revolution had been bloodless and warnings were conveyed to the ringleaders that this time sentences would not be commuted. It was all to no purpose. On 9 November the mutineers broke barracks and advanced across the White Nile Bridge. They evidently hoped for popular support, but the time was not yet ripe. They were easily contained and arrested. The trial, condemnation, and execution of the five ringleaders followed, all in the space of a fortnight. They were hanged by the civil executioner, as it was feared that soldiers would refuse to fire.

Public opinion was severely shocked by the severity and the affair deprived the Government of kudos for what was, *prima facie* at all events, a notable diplomatic achievement. On 8 November, the day before the outbreak, a new Nile Waters Agreement had at last been signed in Cairo. Of the anticipated benefit from the new High Dam, 22 milliards of cubic metres of precious water saved from running to waste in the Mediterranean, the Sudan was to get two thirds, increasing its quota from four milliards to eighteen and a half. In addition Egypt agreed to pay fifteen million pounds compensation for the flooding of the Halfa reach. A joint technical body was to be set up to supervise research into other projects, such as the Jonglei Canal scheme by-passing the *sudd*, and to conduct on behalf of the two governments whatever negotiations might be necessary with other riparian countries.

Considering Egypt's previous refusal to grant any concessions this agreement was something of a triumph, but Sudanese opinion was not disposed to favour it. Sudan experts were known to be opposed to the whole concept of the High Dam, preferring a series of smaller barrages further upstream where there would be less loss from evaporation. It was alleged that Egypt's opposition to this alternative plan was not based upon sound hydraulics but on a not unreasonable political objection to becoming dependent upon works situated on foreign soil. Nor was the amount of compensation regarded as satisfactory. The resettlement of the dispossessed Nubians might well (and did) cost double the fifteen millions allotted.

The Halfawis, who are well represented in all walks of life throughout the northern provinces, joined enthusiastically in the widespread demonstrations after the mutiny. There were strikes by railway workers and processions of students. The University and the Technical Institute had both to close. There were abortive attempts at sympathetic action by secondary schoolboys. When the University reopened on 5 December there were more demonstrations against the executions, and once more it was closed down. This set the pattern for the following years, during which resentment must have played havoc with study. In November 1963 the Minister of Education assumed control, but he was no more successful in keeping order and in October 1964 the students touched off the revolution.

In spite of all this disorder the President had been able to produce on 17 November 1959 an impressive record of achievement during his first year of office. The cotton had been sold and the budget balanced. The trade balance was favourable after two adverse years. Water had been flowing since July into the new Managil canal. The Agricultural Bank and the Central Bank (initiated under the previous government) had been inaugurated* and the former was already financing private growers. Rents and prices had been restricted, land auctions controlled, housing schemes initiated. A new Labour Act was in draft.† Work had begun on a hydro-electric station at Sennar. Two merchant ships and five guarda-costas were building in Jugoslav yards. Many other projects for industrial development were in train. International relations were excellent, especially with the U.A.R. In conclusion he announced the appointment of a committee to revise the local government system as a first step to a new constitution.

Discontent, however, continued and in July 1960 the British press reported that it was coming to a head. Causes given included press censorship, the suppression of the trades unions, and the rigorous punishment of anyone caught criticising the Government. To these might be added an increase in unemployment in the Three Towns (Khartum, Khartum North and Omdurman) consequent on an influx of labour from the south and west, attracted by building programmes which were held up by shortage of imported materials. There was beginning to be talk, too, of extravagance and corruption connected with the issue of import licences, building permits and housing loans. Worst of all, complaint was made of the arrogant behaviour of officers. The northern Sudanese are socially the most democratic people in the world. Men who give themselves airs are regarded with contempt; men who ride roughshod over their fellow citizens are resented fiercely. If a military car collided with yours, people were beginning to discover, it was useless to seek redress, or even to expect a word of apology. So the initial goodwill was dissipated. Letters of protest were addressed to the President by

---

* The Sudan Bank took over the government account from the National Bank of Egypt on 22 February 1960. An Industrial Bank was opened on 17 November 1961.

† It did not become law till 1964 and was not markedly different from earlier legislation.

Ismail el Azhari and Saddiq el Mahdi. Some sort of gesture of appeasement was anticipated. No such gesture was made.

In October trouble flared up in Halfa as a result of the Government's decision to settle the 50,000 dispossessed villagers on the Atbara river, on land to be irrigated by the new dam at Khashm el Girba. The Nubians were desperately attached to the Nile Valley, where they had lived since history began. Great travellers though they were every man carried in his heart the image of his home between the desert and the river. Long ago the Condominium Government had attempted to settle the destitute population of the Botn el Haggar — the Belly of Stone — above Halfa, on virgin land at Qala el Nahl in Gedaref District, but a combination of nostalgia and damp climate brought the experiment to nothing. The emigrants made their way back to the Nile and the settlement was abandoned. Faced now by an inundation which they could barely credit, even though their cousins to the north had been forced to creep higher and higher up the cliffs by successive heightenings at Assuan, they had hoped to be allowed to settle above water level or for extensions to the basin-irrigated oases of Dongola.* Failing these there must surely be some place on the Nile where they could grow their dates, their wheat and their citrus and go on living as they had always lived. Most of them were not professional farmers any longer. Their main income was earned abroad. They were like European businessmen with a cottage in the country to which they hoped to retire. Intensive farming was not in their scheme of things and the upper reaches of the Atbara, the home of Beja and Shukria nomads, were as alien to them as Darfur or the Nuba Mountains. Even the women turned out to demonstrate against the move.

None the less Republic Day 1960 again passed off without incident. General Abboud, who had paid a state visit to Cairo in July, had invited the President of Egypt to attend the ceremonies in Khartum and visit the provinces. Stringent precautions were taken, but the Sudanese were determined not to risk a repetition of the incidents of 1954 and all went well.

In his review of the year's achievement the President announced that the new local government ordinance had been passed into law. After again stressing the Sudan's African ties he had further economic progress to report. The exchange reserve had risen since he took

---

* It is strongly maintained by their leaders that this could have been done at a fraction of the cost. It must be admitted that the Halfawis settled at Khashm el Girba at the end of 1964 seemed to be reasonably contented. Possible difficulties lie ahead in the cost of maintaining their expensive new houses and, judging by experience elsewhere, in the lack of pilot schemes. Conditions of soil fertility, salinity and the like have still to be proved.

over from £20 million to £60 million. The budget outcome showed a £20 million surplus. Work continued on the Managil extension and was soon to start on the new dams at Khashm el Girba and Roseires. Development was going ahead in the south. Legislation had been passed to control the relationship between landlord and tenant in the private pump schemes and to raise the tenants' share to 42 per cent. Factories, schools and bridges were under construction. The railway extensions were going ahead. The industrial bank was soon to open and a special economic planning committee had been set up. The police and the armed forces were being expanded and equipped with modern weapons.

All this, however, was of no avail. A week later, on 25 November, the leaders of the dissolved parties addressed a joint letter to the President demanding the restitution of parliament. Council's reply was to ban press comment on the letter and deprive the two ex-premiers of their pensions of £100 a month. On 7 December the Commissioner for the re-settlement of the Halfa population, Daud Abdel Latif, a Halfawi who had governed three provinces, was dismissed for opposing the Khashm el Girba plan. On the 14th a number of people were convicted in Khartum and Atbara for distributing anti-Government leaflets.

Overt opposition appeared to subside, and early in 1961 a delegation from Halfa was allowed to see the President and informed that there was no compulsion to go to Khashm el Girba. Anybody who wished could draw his compensation in cash and find a home elsewhere as best he might. A six months' lull followed, during which an attempt was made to find a compromise by negotiation. Various solutions were suggested but nothing would satisfy the opposition short of the complete withdrawal of the army from politics and the appointment of a coalition government to draw up a new constitution and hold a general election.

In June 1961 27,000 railway workers struck for a 50 per cent wage increase and stayed out for a week, threatening to repeat the process every month until their demands were met and their union recognised. Again the Government took repressive action and again the politicians struck back. They took as their pretext the alleged torturing of a young communist caught distributing leaflets and despatched a telegram of protest and denunciation. At 2.0 a.m. on 11 July twelve of the signatories, including all the leading politicians, were arrested and flown off to internment at Juba. Sayed Saddiq, the first to sign, was left at large, and indeed it is difficult to conjecture what would have happened if the Imam el Mahdi had been put under arrest. It must have been an anxious time for the President but whatever the personal ambitions of the Mahdi's family they have always been patriots first and foremost. The country did not seem to be ripe yet for revolution and the Sayed made no attempt to divide it.

In August his forbearance was strained to breaking point. At the celebrations of the Birthday of the Prophet the Mahdist Youth, as was their custom, marched in formation through Omdurman to the Mahdi's tomb. There was a general ban on demonstrations and when the column reached the Mosque Square the police were ordered to disperse it. What exactly happened is obscure because the inquiry was never completed; for some reason fire was opened at short range. Twelve young Mahdists were killed and, in the subsequent scuffle, three policemen.

The Government took no action on this incident and Sayed Saddiq had again to reach a decision. Like his father before him he had found the strain of public life in adverse circumstances almost unbearable. Two years of futile negotiations with an opponent impervious to his reasoning had broken down his health. Now he had to decide between acquiescence and a direct appeal to his supporters in the Army. He literally worried himself to death, on 2 October 1961. His brother Sayed El Hadi succeeded as *Imam*. His political mantle fell on the shoulders of his son, Sayed Sadiq.

Meanwhile at Juba the twelve politicians, deprived of contact with the outside world, were taking advantage of their enforced contiguity to thrash out the problem of the future of democracy and to plan future co-operation. Amongst other things they apparently decided to have no more sectarian politics (easier said than done?) and that the American presidential system was a better safeguard against instability and political bargaining than the Westminster model. There was also a general feeling that an Upper House would only be justified if it were reconstituted as a sort of expert committee of elder statesmen and retired officials.

After seven months of incarceration they decided one Friday to go on hunger strike, and asked that the President should be notified accordingly. The following day they were informed that the Supreme Council had decided a few days earlier to release them. On the Sunday they were flown back to Khartoum.

The arrest of the politicians had coincided with the inauguration of the new province councils and it is time to consider Abu Renat's plans for the new democracy.

Judging by an address given in June 1959 by the then Director of Local Government at a conference in Berlin there had been no great change in the system up to that time. The Marshall plan was being implemented slowly. Two thirds of the members of local councils were elected.

The position of the civil governor had however deteriorated. The old unofficial executive committees of the province councils which existed here and there seem to have faded out and ministries had ceased to consult him about their activities in his province. Responsibility for public security was now exercised by the Commandant of police under the Military Governor.

The absence of 'sound democratic institutions' at provincial level had been blamed by the President for the failure of parliamentary institutions. People whose business involved a contact at this level hardly knew whom to approach. There was no representative institution to further their interests and the administration of province affairs had passed into the hands of officials who either acted on their own responsibility or took their orders from Khartum. There was no organisation at province level to co-ordinate official activity and territorial planning was consequently incoherent.

So spoke the President, on 1 July 1961, inaugurating the new councils. The Commission which he had set up in November 1959, under the chairmanship of Abu Renat, had discussed various aspects of the problem in its report.*

The advent of the local council and the resident magistrate had reduced the responsibilities of the District Commissioner in most places to public security, government lands, central government finances and tribal affairs. The time had now come to hand over these powers. Public security was a matter for the police, acting in collaboration with native authorities and court presidents, on whom the necessary powers had been conferred long since. Most of the remaining functions could be exercised by councils on an agency basis or by ministerial inspectors. Tribal disputes could be settled by native courts, whose decision would be passed to the council for enforcement by the resident magistrate. Business Profits Tax could be assessed by councils.

On the face of them these two last provisions sound easier to fulfil in theory than in practice, and in fact this re-allocation created at district level precisely the confusion which the President had deprecated in the province. A man with a complaint used to petition the D.C. Now he applied to the Local Government Inspector, only to be redirected to the town clerk or magistrate or police officer or to some ministerial representative. Until he had learned to write to his M.P., and had an M.P. to write to, there was much to be said for

* Report of the Commission on Co-ordination between Central and Local Governments, November, 1960.

restoring some sort of co-ordinating authority in the district as well as the province.

The Commission expressed its intention of preserving established traditions and profiting from the experience of the past sixty years. It was necessary 'to keep pace with social and economic progress without rushing ahead too far and too fast!' It recommended for each province a statutory Council with legislative, executive, and advisory powers, recruited from the chairman and certain of the members of subordinate councils, together with 'other personalities selected on the basis of their prominence in the area or for their technical, professional and general experience'. Police activities would be supervised by a Security Board or Watch Committee appointed by the Minister of the Interior.

An executive Province Authority should be set up under the Council with the old civil governor as chairman. The Council chairman must in present circumstances be the military governor* but should not in any case be a member of the Province Authority. The civil deputy-governor should be secretary to both bodies, but otherwise legislative and executive powers must be kept separate.

The Commission was not in favour of reuniting the Ministry of the Interior with the Ministry of Local Government because one was concerned with public security and the other with public services. The former had to deal with 'the influence of external organisations which frequently invade countries which have recently become independent' and its officials must be free to devote themselves to this great responsibility. None the less the terms of service of such administrative officers as remained under the Ministry of the Interior should be unified with those who had been appointed Inspectors of Local Government and with the local government cadre of executive officers. It was recognised that in a few undeveloped areas the District Commissioner must remain as chairman of the council as well as regional inspector and retain his judicial powers as well as his authority under the amended Police Ordinance. Such cases, however, would not be numerous and those officers who were not absorbed in the new joint service could be found homes in the judiciary, the diplomatic corps and the Ministries of Information and Commerce. This passage in the Report concludes with a tribute to 'the great role played by the administrators in developing the councils and the great efforts they have exerted to raise the general standard in all districts, the factor which made the system we are proposing an easy task'.

* Abu Renat hoped to replace him in due course by an elder statesman from the ranks of retired governors and heads of departments.

So far so good, but the Commission also recommended the suspension of elected members in local councils. This proposal, which nullified the whole claim to be reconstructing representative machinery, was justified on the grounds that 'citizens are not yet in a position to elect the right representatives. Experience in this country has proved beyond reasonable doubt that the elections to local government councils produced some members who degraded the standard of membership and led in some cases to party groupings inside the council which hampered the interests of the citizens and delayed useful work'.

The phrasing as well as the content of this passage betrays some other hand than that of the Chairman. It must have destroyed any faint hope that the pyramid plan would come to be accepted as democratic by informed opinion. There is something to be said for indirect representation and much to be said against party politics in local government, which is not yet universal even in the U.K. Nomination too has its points in some contexts. The record of 'nominated' peers as a committee of experts in the House of Lords has been excellent. But the trouble about nomination is that however confident the nominator may be of the excellence of his choice everyone else is convinced that they are place men or yes-men. They can only justify their selection by their subsequent behaviour. If a preference on their part for justice over the interest of the government leads to dismissal, as it has done in Ghana, then democracy in any intelligible sense is dead.

Surely therefore it would have been possible to retain at least a third of elected members as an earnest of good intention, an outlet for public opinion and a method of educating the electorate.

The Provincial Administration Act of 1960 embodied most of these recommendations, while allowing for the subsequent loosening or tightening of central control.

The key figure was the Central Government representative appointed by the Supreme Council (now consisting of six members only) and answerable to it for province administration. All government officials in the province were under his authority and in theory any citizen could be appointed to his office. The Province Council over which he presided was to be established by warrant of the Council of Ministers, which would lay down the proportion of elected to nominated members and the quota of delegates from the local councils. The Council of Ministers would also set up the Province Authority. Again the civil governor was not chairman *ex-officio*, nor his deputy secretary. The functions of the authority were defined as being to execute decisions of the province council, to act for it between sessions, and to answer the questions of its members through the appropriate ministerial representative on the Council.

Members of the Province Council were required to take an oath to 'uphold the republican regime with faith and fidelity; to observe the interests of the people and the security of the country; to respect the constitution and the laws, and to carry out their duties with honesty and faithfulness'. The Council was to meet in public, was generally responsible for the promotion of local government, approval of the various local budgets and development plans, and for passing the Province Authority's own budget (the revenue for which was found at first by allocation of a proportional share of the proceeds of the government sugar monopoly). It was empowered to censure the Authority and to formulate and recommend to the appropriate ministry proposals to meet local problems in all branches of administration. It must meet at least four times a year.

In the warrants issued in January 1961 appointing Province Authorities for the Northern Province, Kassala, Khartum and the Blue Nile there was no provision for a representative of the Ministry of the Interior. The civil governor appears as representative of the Ministry of Local Government.

In his inaugural speech on 1 July 1961, already quoted, the President announced that the next step would be 'the erection of a Central Council . . . in a pyramid with the local councils as a base' after reintroducing elections to local councils by 'a reasonable percentage system'. After the inauguration of this Central Council a national committee would draw up a new constitution embodying 'all the principles and fundamental rights as a prelude to a sound parliamentary system by universal election. Thus shall we reach our goal of true democracy free from the errors of the past.'

On 6 January 1962, a new commission met under the same chairman to draft proposals for reintroducing elections to local councils and setting up a central legislative council. It included representatives of the Law, the University, the administrative service, a southerner of Deputy Governor status, Clement Mboro, and a survivor of the old Legislative Assembly in Sayed Fadl Bashir. Within six months its proposals were ready for implementation on the assumption that electoral rolls would be completed by 15 November, local government elections by the end of January, elections to Province Councils immediately afterwards, and the Central Council itself 'on or before June 1963'.

The new electoral rules were rather more liberal than the old, which makes the previous suspension still more surprising. The franchise was extended and the residential qualification reduced.

The number of nominated councillors was not to exceed one third of the membership of the more advanced councils or one half of those in the first three stages of development.

The Central Council Act 1962 provided for a Council of 72 members, 54 from Province Councils and 18 nominated by the President. Council and President together would constitute the Legislature, from which the executive was carefully divorced. The Speaker would be elected by members from their own number or from outside. Council would meet every six months on summons by the President. Ministers were members *ex officio* and were required to answer members' questions. The Council's powers included the ratification of treaties and conventions; the passing of legislation (subject to ministerial veto, which meant in practice the submission of resolutions to the Council of Ministers); the confirmation or rejection of ministerial decrees issued between sessions; taxation; the budget; and the Auditor General's report. It was debarred from interference in debt service charges, the salary of executives, the judiciary, the civil service, and the audit. The Auditor General was the Council's servant but could only be removed by order of the President in pursuance of a recommendation passed by a 75 per cent majority.

The Council met for the first time in November 1963, and although the resistance organisations* had let it be known that patriotic citizens were expected to refuse to serve, there were quite a few distinguished names on the roster. Nor does perusal of the weekly digests of proceedings reveal a reluctance to criticise Government policy. There were some obvious time-servers and sycophants but there were also men prepared to speak out and return to the charge on subjects like the freedom of the press, southern policy — or the lack of it, alleged atrocities in the south, and inefficiency and corruption in administration. The long debate on this last subject, which lasted right through the second session in 1964, reveals a determination to expose scandals and played, through the medium of press reports, no small part in arousing public opinion. It was the Council, too, which pressed for a Commission of Inquiry into the southern problem and so set the ball of revolution rolling. Boycott is more often than not a two-edged weapon and the resistance leaders owe a lot to some of the men who disobeyed their instructions.

But the Government gained little credit either way. The fact that the Speaker and the Leader of the House were nominees and Major-Generals destroyed any chance of that. The Commission on the South did not meet until September 1964. The demand for an

* With the unexpected exception of the communists.

'administrative audit' was fobbed off. Outside the Sudan, however, the creation of the new Council was accepted at its face value and when, in May 1964, President Abboud in an after-dinner speech at Buckingham Palace referred to a shared faith in democracy no violent incongruity was felt at his employment of that much-abused word.

Anxiety was also expressed in the Council from time to time about the economic situation. Basically there was nothing wrong. Crop production was booming wherever the peasant farmer was in a position to take advantage of improved communications and technological advice.* On a long term view the Sudan's endless areas of undeveloped land for the use of an expanding but still comparatively small population insure against real distress. Even the Gezira with its heavy overheads and its fluctuations in yield and price has always succeeded in battling through its various crises because it could show a profit of a kind when rival producers, the U.S.A. for example, were forced to pay a heavy export subsidy. The trouble in 1964 was not just that the cotton crop had been poor, but that the planners had overreached themselves. On the face of it the development was prodigious — new schools everywhere, hospitals, factories, railway extensions, a new bridge from Omdurman to Khartum North under construction and of course the two great dams. But the admiring survivor from an age of bare utility could not help asking where all this money was coming from. Khashm el Girba is a case in point. A fine dam and hydro-electric station, spacious buildings with marble floors and stainless steel doors swinging at a touch on invisible hinges; evacuees from Halfa in the new town and new villages with concrete residences costing more than £2,000 apiece; schools, hospital, administrative and police headquarters, a two-storied office block for the Irrigation Department. It was all breath-taking until a still small voice recalled the legend found chalked on the door of the modest new headquarters of the pre-war Sudan Defence Force — 'C'est magnifique, mais ce n'est pas la Guerre'. 'What about the overheads?' asked critics in Khartum. 'What will the maintenance costs be?' 'Can the peasant farmer afford to inhabit a house of this standard?'

Where was the money coming from? Not, as the cynical observer is apt to suggest, from Russia and America bidding against each other for the good will of the uncommitted. Foreign aid, here as elsewhere, has played a large part in development, but foreign aid

* In southern Darfur, for example, where since the advent of the railway, ground-nuts have begun to replace cotton as a cash crop and other potential money-spinners like coffee are the subject of successful experiment.

K

has usually to be matched pound for pound. At first this was not difficult. The Sudan was still regarded as a good investment in spite of the fiasco over cotton sales. The budget was balanced year after year and there has been no default on debt redemption. Cheap money on 'soft' terms was likely to be available once the immediate 1958 embarrassments were overcome.

These included, in addition to the disposal of the unsold cotton, the reluctance of the commercial banks, which had burned their fingers in 1957–8, to put up money for financing privately-owned schemes. A state Agricultural bank was in process of formation when the soldiers took over and was functioning in time to make the necessary advances for the 1959–60 crop, subject to strict control of costs. The transfer to this bank of the accounts of the Gezira Board and other public corporations provided much of the necessary capital, but it had also to be subsidised as had the Industrial Bank opened in 1961. The money available for general development and the proportionate amount of foreign aid were reduced accordingly.

None the less the Government felt that it was justified, after seven years of productive investment, in launching for the years 1961–71 a highly ambitious Ten-Year Plan with estimated capital outlay of over five hundred millions. A great deal of this would have to be met from budget surpluses and it was obvious that the first five years, when new projects were still unproductive, would be crucial. General administrative expenditure was bound to increase *pari passu* with expansion and revenue must therefore expand still more rapidly. Heavier taxes would not provide the answer. Priority must be given to short-term production projects. In 1961–2 62 per cent of an estimated development expenditure of £38 million was allotted to productive schemes, including the two dams and the Managil Extension, which was to be completed in half the time originally estimated because it would produce revenue as fast as it was completed. More dubious was the hope of saving foreign exchange by the swift completion of factories to supply sugar and cardboard, leather and cotton piece goods, tinned fruit and dried vegetables. All these must at first be uneconomic until they got over their inevitable teething troubles. Of the remaining expenditure 20 per cent was earmarked for social services, 6 per cent to communications, 5 per cent to public utilities and 7 per cent to administration and research.

On the long-term plan the proportion of allocations was adjusted. The productive projects fell on the overall figure from 62 per cent to 30 per cent: social services rose from 20 per cent to 30 per cent; transport and communications from 6 per cent to 20 per cent. The balance went to new industries, public utilities, mineral resources and the like. The aim was to increase national income by 63 per cent and the average individual income by 23 per cent.* The original figure for expenditure over the ten years was £565 million, including £93 million earmarked for replacements. An overall budgetary surplus of £220 million was anticipated, of which £54 million would be needed for debt redemption. Foreign exchange reserves were to be kept replenished at the existing figure of £57 million.

Private enterprise was expected to find, mainly for building, £200 million odd and the remainder would come from the profits earned by public corporations, or by government borrowing. £86 million of foreign aid had already been secured when the plan was drawn up, in the form of loans or grants in aid. It was hoped to raise most of the remaining requirements by soft long-term loans. If the money had to be obtained on the open market it was reckoned that by 1971 the resultant debt service would amount to about 12 per cent of estimated export value.

Such was the plan, inevitably something of a gamble, as are other long-term plans in an era of rising costs. One important criticism at the time was that it did not give high enough priority to remedying a major problem, the bottle-neck at Port Sudan. Considerable improvements and extensions to the harbour and docks have of course been made, and the cotton was now being got away regularly, but imports were apt to be hung up for lack of rolling stock, which has been known to return unloaded to avoid delay in clearing accumulations up country. The Government, prompted no doubt by the President's family connection with Suakin, had shown interest in the possibility of reopening the harbour there, a project which Jugoslav experts estimated to cost £55 million. The Americans surveyed a road to the coast and construction was given high priority as a supplementary project to the Plan. This seems short-sighted. The Sudan Railways Administration is in the unusually satisfactory position of fearing little competition from road transport. Its long new extensions to west and south will have to traverse many unproductive miles for some time to come. Surely it would be wiser not to spend money on the creation of an expensive competitive route to the sea but instead to improve or double the existing railway line, with its double track 'dormant between stations', or to run a

---

* 23 per cent, that is, of the population in 1971 estimated at an annual increment of 2·8 per cent on the adjusted 1956 census figure of 10,263,000. According to the planners the increase in gross domestic product, which had been cancelled out in 1960–1 by the increase in population, was running ahead of it in 1961–2 by 9 per cent.

new branch line direct from Kassala. Road construction and maintenance in Sudan conditions are very much more costly than the railway, and the road allocation could more profitably be spent on building feeder services from production areas to railhead.

On the revenue side difficulty arose from dependence on indirect taxation, which in a country like the Sudan provides a method of regulating the economy in substitution for the control of bank advances utilised in more highly capitalised societies. The fluctuation of price and yield which has been noted as a perennial feature of cotton production can only be prevented from playing havoc with the cost of living if the device of a variable export duty is constantly used. The imposition of import duties whether as producers of revenue or as a check on adverse balance of payments cuts both ways. In addition to affecting the private sector of investment, on which, as we have seen, the plan depended for more than a third of its capital, it has a direct effect on government spending. Not only has the duty itself to be reimbursed to contractors but the resultant increase in service charges and consultants' fees pushes up the overall cost of the enterprise. It might have been wise to grant a customs rebate on all government contracts. Nor were these the only unforeseen increases in costs. At Khashm el Girba itself the presence of rocks on the riverbed, not unforeseen by the original consultants, made the dam much more expensive to build than the estimate. Moreover as time went on more and more supplementary projects were approved. The proceedings of the Central Council reveal constant pressure from local interests for roads and bridges, schools and hospitals. Many of these demands were resisted, but many were approved, and the overall expenditure figure for the ten years began to creep up towards the 600 million mark. The surplus on the ordinary budget, in spite of buoyancy of revenue, failed to maintain the estimated average of £22 million (the actual figure for 1959–60). In 1960–1 it was £15·9 million; in 1961–2 £8·7 m.; in 1962–3, after a good cotton crop, £16·8 m.; for 1963–4 it was estimated at £9 m. Nor did the measure of foreign aid add up to the planners' hopes. In 1961–2 it amounted to £13·4 m. against a target figure of £14·1 m.; in 1962–3 £10 m. against £17·9 m.

As a result of these various factors the convertible foreign exchange reserves fell steadily by more than £30 m. in 34 months. The failure of the 1963–4 cotton crop accentuated these difficulties and recourse had to be made to direct taxation to take advantage of the increased prosperity of certain classes. The scope of Business Profits Tax was widened and Income Tax imposed for the first time on the wealthier citizens. Expenditure was to be rigorously checked but no essential items economised. The 1964–5 budget estimates provided for a surplus of £16,601,891, and expenditure under the development budget was cut from £47·7 m. in 1963–4 to £32·4 m. in 1964–5.* Criticism, however, increased with anxiety. It concentrated on reports of corruption and extravagance. The critic in the café was asking where the money was coming from to complete the ground clearance and irrigation works which alone could convert the new Roseires Dam from a white elephant into a source of revenue. The new factories were alleged to be uneconomic. The canneries, the sugar refineries and the onion drying plant had capacities far exceeding potential production. The cardboard manufactured at Aroma was said to be brittle and costly.

Dissatisfaction was building up everywhere, particularly in the Gezira, where the tenants were becoming not only a centre of disaffection but a potential danger to the whole economy. Early in 1964 they had elected as their president the familiar figure of Shaikh el Amin Muhammad el Amin† who had achieved a new popularity by suffering imprisonment and was chosen mainly because he was against the Government. Their demands for a share in the management of the Scheme are not unreasonable but their continual pressure for a larger share in the profits at the expense of the government share is less justifiable. They have become a highly privileged section of the community, gentlemen farmers dependent more and more on hired labour. The case for retaining a substantial share for the Government over and above the running expenses of the Gezira Board is as good today as it was in 1953. The Sudanese taxpayer financed the Scheme and is entitled to his reward from its product, not only through increased hospital and educational facilities but by reduction in indirect taxation on the commodities which bulk large in his cost of living figures — sugar, coffee, tea, and unbleached cotton goods, and in the cost of transporting them to him and carrying his produce to the trains or the port. The equity of continuing to collect direct taxes from him while the Gezira tenant, who has free access to the Sudan's most valuable commodity, water, still pays none, has been questioned,‡ though in fact the taxes he pays are now part of local government, not central government revenue.§ Ideally it would be better to tax the tenant,

* See the Minister of Finance's Budget Speech to the Central Council, 9 July 1964.
† See p. 114 n.
‡ Notably by Sir John Carmichael, sometime Financial Secretary to the Condominium Government and later Financial Adviser (to whom I am indebted for much information) in an address to the Anglo-Sudanese Association in London on 25 November 1961.
§ Local government in the Gezira has had to rely on other sources of revenue, such as licensing.

who contributes little to the general economy, but that is not practical politics.

As late as December 1963 there were few signs of discontent in the Gezira. One can usually make a fair guess at public opinion from the expression on the faces of the bystanders when a government official drives by. If their enthusiasm borders on the hysterical there is danger ahead for the national shadow-bearer, whoever he may be, and later perhaps for the demi-god who casts the shadow; if they are apathetic the rulers are secure so long as they do not relax the pressure; if they grin and wave and go about their business there is nothing seriously wrong.

Such was the impression created during a drive through the Managil Extension area at that time. Tenants on donkeys, irrigation employees on the regulators, men working on the land, women going to market, all seemed to be in excellent spirits. Yet ten months later they all appear to have been convinced (by communist propaganda?) that the Government had filched a large slice of the tenants' share of the profits.*

Admittedly my cicerone was a civilian, and so were my hosts at Managil, officials of all sorts, Gezira Board staff, and local government employees. These were presumably the men who earned the goodwill, because they obviously possessed it among themselves. There was no ceremony, no hierarchy, no interdepartmental jealousy, no intellectual snobbery. The presence of an old friend, well content to stay at home, employed in 1927 as an accountant in the local provincial service and in 1963 as head of the council accounts section, enjoying the affectionate esteem of the younger men, was a sign that there was not much wrong with the machinery of administration in the north.

The discovery in a council office of a shy unhappy-looking southerner poring over an Arabic grammar was a reminder of the inevitable minority problem. The Six Counties in Ireland, the Turks in Cyprus, the Muslims in India, the Tamils in Ceylon, the Somalis in Kenya, and the southerners in the Sudan. I told him I too had tried to learn Arabic in the same building nearly forty years before, and wished him luck. My companion asked after his wife and family, was there anything he could do for him? He said they were doing nicely thank you.†

---

* In fact the tenants received, in addition to their share (£1,427,000) of the 1963–4 crop of 2·3 *kantars*, a supplementary grant of £763,000 from the reserve fund and an advance of £1,220,000 on the 1964–5 crop.

† Other southerners, it is only fair to record, were holding important administrative positions in the northern provinces without apparent resentment or difficulty on either side.

When we come in the next chapter to consider the problem of the southern Sudan there is a bias to take into account, not necessarily a Christian prejudice against Islam, if one believes that Divine Providence is not restricted in its operation to one body of believers, and has numbered one or two Muslims among one's closest friends, but a prejudice against any form of intolerance. To this must be added the belief that although Islam more than any other religion involves a distinctive manner of life, a Christian can none the less be a loyal and useful citizen of a Muslim state. The complete elimination of Christianity in the south does not seem to have been the objective of the military Government, judging from the proceedings of the Central Government, where any such suggestion was firmly rejected. But it did aim at ensuring that the Christians should become an ineffective minority, like the Copts in Egypt. It is surely essential that they should retain some voice in affairs if the Sudan is to provide a bridge between Muslim and non-Muslim Africa. When, however, we condemn a repressive policy we have to remind ourselves of the results of tolerance elsewhere. The suppression of Afrikaans in South Africa, or of French in Canada, would have paid Britain far better than the toleration on which she used to pride herself. Would not the southerners, unless absorbed into the Islamic world, inevitably turn sooner or later to Uganda? Would they not, if left to themselves, succumb to tribal fratricide like the Congo?

It is possible to detect in the southern resistance a facet of the pan-African reaction against Asia and the Arab which comes second only to the reaction against the West and which has already lifted its head in Zanzibar. Northern anxiety on this head was the last but by no means the least contributory factor to the overthrow of General Abboud's Government. It is now time to turn back a hundred years and trace the history of the southern problems.

Chapter 10

The Problem of the South

THE THREE southern provinces of the Sudan form a segment with its chord stretched along the tenth parallel. There are two southern outposts north of this line in the Shilluk and the peoples of the Nuba Mountains, the fighting remnant of many tribes. Behind them the *sudd* has provided a defence against northern invaders and it is only near the eastern and western frontiers that the land climbs out of the marshes and makes access comparatively easy.

The Ethiopian foothills were too often a battleground between Sudanese and Ethiops for them to provide a regular penetration route, but there was expansion southwards none the less in Fung days from the Blue Nile area, and a string of little states grew up in the country of the Bats (*Watawit*). This area, known nowadays as the Beni Shanqul, developed into an entrepôt for the slave trade, supplying the markets of Shendi in the eighteenth and Messelemia in the nineteenth century,* but most of the victims came from or via Abyssinia. Of Sudan tribes only the Anuak and the Beir suffered much from it.

Penetration was easier at the western extremity. Early rulers of southern Darfur — Taju, Baygo, Shatt and Nyingulguleh — evidently colonised the headwaters of the Gnol, Lol and Pongo rivers before the Dinka arrived from the south-east or the Baggara from the north-west. There they dominated the brown people known to the Dinka as Jur and to the Arabs as Fertit, establishing at an early date agencies for the export of slaves through Darfur to Libya and Egypt.

Between these two prongs stretched the great and warlike nation of the Dinka, lacking only cohesion to dominate the whole area and harbouring in their midst their intractable cousins the Nuer, an even more formidable, because more ferocious, fighting race.

Two other tribes bulk large in southern history. The Azande, believed to be cannibals by the Arabs and accordingly known as

* And the White Nile in the twentieth. See below p. 164.

152

Nyumnyum, are an example of the welding-together of various tribes by a conquering aristocracy into an efficient fighting machine. The basic stock is much the same as that of their docile neighbours but the Avungara overlords could have established a formidable empire if they had refrained from quarrelling among themselves. As it was they never combined enough to be irresistible but never diverged so much as to be an easy prey. Throughout the nineteenth century they were moving northwards on to and over the Congo–Nile watershed on a broad front up the headwaters of the Bangui river.

The Bari owed their prominence to their position on the Nile between the *sudd* and the Fola rapids, an obvious settling area for northern colonists. Gondokoro, Lado, Rejaf, Mongalla and Juba were all sited in the Bari country. Racially they are related on one side to the Nilotics of the swamps and on the other to the so-called Nilo-Hamites of Lake Rudolph and the East African uplands who neighbour them on the east.

Between the Bari and Dinka on the north-east and the Azande to the south-west a number of weaker and less warlike tribes awaited a conqueror.

It was not until 1839 that a flotilla despatched by Muhammad Ali Pasha succeeded in piercing the *sudd* and opening up a potential route from Khartum to Lake Albert. The intruders who followed were of three types — government men, ivory traders and missionaries. Each group distrusted the other two and was not unwilling to incite local prejudice against them. The object of the first was imperial expansion plus private profit, of the second private profit plus a personal *imperium*, of the third brands to be plucked from the burning. One thing they shared, a common contempt for the southerner as an inferior being, coupled with a complete indifference to his religious ideas, his ethics and standards of behaviour, his social and tribal pattern.

At first things went reasonably well. The Bari were friendly and had large stocks of ivory ready for sale to the annual government convoy. But after 1850 European traders from Khartum entered the market and the supply was soon exhausted. Elephant hunts had to be organised and up went prices. Rival firms set up their own supply organisations, leaving a garrison to collect ivory between seasons and live off the country as best — or worst — they might. These bodyguards and the crews of the boats were constantly clashing with the villagers. Warring tribes sold their services in return for military assistance, often to find, like the ancient Britons, that friend was more dangerous than foe. As ivory grew scarcer the expeditions pressed

farther and farther into the hinterland. Friendly chiefs were re-
warded with captured cattle and since prisoners were inevitably
taken as well it was not long before the Nile slave trade began to
rival the older routes and to bulk more largely than ivory in the
profit and loss account. Nor was the missionary at this time more
welcome. The trader disrupted tribal society, but the missionary
severed its roots. Conversion deprived the community of a living
cell, denunciation of ancient religious practices threatened the
continuity of the family unit in life and death, and condemnation
of polygamy threatened to throw large numbers of women on the
rates or on the streets.

So the stage was set for a century of suspicion and misunder-
standing. The same situation existed on the Bahr el Ghazal to the
west. Here Jellaba merchants were already collaborating with the
Baggara and the local sultans in exploiting the traditional overland
route before the arrival in the 1860s of river-borne rivals (the
Bahhàra) at Meshra el Rek. These established stockades — the
notorious Bahr el Ghazal *zareebas* — south of the sultans and pushed
forward until checked by the Azande confederacy. By 1870 the
most famous of them, Zubeir Pasha, had concluded judicious
alliances with some of the Zande princes and with the Baggara
Rizeigat to the north and was building up a slave-state of his own
which eclipsed its predecessors and almost obliterated their memory.
His progress was facilitated by the concentration of Egyptian and
European interest upon the Bahr el Jebel (White Nile). Explorers
returning from the Great Lakes had whetted the appetite of the
Khedive Ismail for expansion and in 1869 Samuel Baker arrived in
Gondokoro with instructions to satisfy it. Baker also had plans for
the economic development of the Bari, but they never trusted him
and the Danagla traders obstructed him in every possible way. So
he became more and more at loggerheads with both and was
finally forced into taking punitive action against the Bari which
made him even more unpopular than his predecessors. Gordon
followed, and got on a great deal better at first but he was too busy
trying to extend Khedivial suzerainty over the Bunyoro and
Buganda kingdoms to follow up this initial advantage. When his
southern adventures proved a fiasco the Bari turned against him,
and when he left in 1876 the expansionist period came to an end.
The Buganda kingdom looked to Zanzibar instead of Khartum, and
Egypt was bankrupt of men and money.

Gordon's period of office as Governor-General (1877–80) was
marked by Gessi Pasha's defeat of Suliman Zubeir and an attempt
by Gessi to settle and develop the Bahr el Ghazal. But the Dinka

were unsubdued and hostile and Suliman's lieutenants at large and uncontrolled. Barely had Gessi's successor, Lupton Bey, arrived at the end of 1881 when the repercussions of the Mahdi's successes began to be felt. The Rizeigat were early converts and Mahdist agents seem to have met with a surprising success among the Dinka. Lupton and his able lieutenant Mahallawi had to compete not only with the Baggara and Dinka and the remnant of the *Bahhara* but with the local sultans as well, notably the Nyingulguleh. Some of these were allies and some enemies, but they all stood to benefit at least temporarily from the overthrow of the Government. Only a prince or two of the Azande remained loyal.

In this situation Lupton was surprisingly successful, inflicting defeat after defeat upon his various enemies. He even succeeded, early in 1884, in capturing and executing his chief opponent, Yanqu of the Nyingulguleh. But the Dinka were unaffected by defeat, and even carried on a successful side war against the Rizeigat. Darfur had capitulated in December and when a Mahdist army under Karamullah Muhammad, a Dongolawi merchant from Deim Zubeir, advanced against him Lupton's men refused to go on fighting any longer. On 28 April 1884 he surrendered.

Karamullah moved on against the Equatorial garrison, which was also ready to surrender, but the Mahdist advance was delayed by Zande hostility and then by a mutiny of the *Jehadiya*. Most of the Danagla merchants went over to join the invaders and the Governor, Emin Pasha, began to take heart. His fifth columnists were gone, and his officers and men had begun to realise that resistance was their best chance of survival. Neither the ex-supporters of Arabi Pasha nor the locally recruited 'Nubis' (as they came to be called in those parts) had anywhere else to go. They were far from popular locally but were still feared if not respected. When therefore Karamullah resumed his advance late in the year he met with unexpected resistance from the garrison of Amadi which repelled all the assaults of his *Ansar* and their Dinka allies, withstood a siege for four months, and when finally forced out by starvation, in February 1885, cut its way through the besiegers and withdrew to Rejaf, fighting rearguard actions as it went. Karamullah got no farther. The *Jehadiya* were in arms again behind him and presently came news of the Mahdi's death, with a summons from the Khalifa to return to Kordofan. There he was sent to deal with a revolt by the Rizeigat, and the Bahr el Ghazal was left for a time to its own devices.

There was a reasonable chance that Emin Pasha in Equatoria would have been left alone too, for the Khalifa had plenty of other campaigns on his hands, had it not been for the entry on the scene of King Leopold of Belgium, operating under cover of the 'International Association of the Congo', the progenitor of the Congo Free State. Leopold and the other powers — notably France, Britain and Germany, each with its associated chartered company, were by now engaged in an intricate and unedifying series of manoeuvres for control of the sources of the Nile, with Italy skirmishing on one flank and Portugal on the other. The Emin Pasha Relief Expedition, headed by the explorer Stanley, which arrived in Uganda at the end of 1887, was a thinly disguised attempt to get Emin Pasha out of Equatoria and ease Leopold in.

The Khalifa seems to have had an excellent intelligence service, and used to pass on information about events in Equatoria to the garrison at Suakin. He decided it would be dangerous and damaging to his reputation to leave these foreigners unmolested and in June 1888 an expedition under the Emir Omar Saleh sailed for Rejaf.

Meanwhile, in spite of a Khedivial decree abandoning Egypt's rights in Equatoria, Emin's troops refused to withdraw with Stanley and put the Governor under arrest when he ordered them to do so. After a crushing defeat by Omar in October, however, most of them changed their minds and withdrew to the south end of Lake Albert, where they were used later by Lugard in his Uganda campaigns and gave him a great deal of trouble by mutiny. The hard core stayed on under an officer called Fadl el Mula, so that the unfortunate Bari had two rival armies quartered on them, to be avoided, opposed, or placated as opportunity might offer or expediency dictate.

Fadl el Mula was hopelessly outnumbered and could only exist by pillage until he allied himself with the Belgians in 1893. The Mahdists were also hamstrung by friction between Danagla and Taeisha, and it was not until the Taeishi Emir Arabi Dafaallah arrived at the end of 1893 to take over from the Dongolawi Abu Girga that they were in a position to take the offensive again. Arabi was probably the ablest general the Khalifa had left and he celebrated his arrival by defeating and killing Fadl el Mula in January 1894.

Meanwhile the Belgians in alliance with the Zande chief Zemio, an ex-ally of Lupton, had pushed up along the Bahr el Ghazal as far as the Arab river, where they contacted the Fur pretender, Sultan Hussain, and were granted concessions to exploit the copper at Hufrat el Nehas. This advance was facilitated by the inactivity of the Mahdists at Shakka, who were recovering from a defeat suffered at the hands of the Dinka. The Belgians were less successful elsewhere, however, and cannot have been altogether disappointed when news arrived in November 1894 that the Bahr el Ghazal was now included in the French sphere of influence. They withdrew southwards and narrowly escaped complete disaster at the end of the year when Arabi, in alliance with another Zande Sultan called Renzi, attacked their post at Dungu on the upper waters of the Uélé River. Arabi's failure cost him heavily and he had to retire to Rejaf and await reinforcements.

These were delayed by two old allies of the south — the *sudd* and the Shilluk. It is remarkable how the Shilluk, whose country lies wide open to invasion and was occupied for most of the Turkia and Mahdia by predatory garrisons, commanded at times by generals as able and ruthless as Zaki Tamal, contrived to survive and preserve their nuisance value after endless defeats. Arabi's own journey south had been delayed by the need to finish off a protracted campaign against them and now his reinforcements had to be diverted on a similar mission. By the time this was completed the *sudd* had re-formed and it was not until the middle of 1896 that one small steamer struggled through to Bor.

Meanwhile the French were on the move. In 1895 Victor Liotard, Governor of Upper Ubangi, established an advanced post on the Sué river in the village of a Zande chief called Tembura and prepared for an advance to the Nile. A force despatched by Arabi at the end of the year to join the Shakka garrison crossed ahead of the French but was annihilated near Tonj in January 1896 by the Nuer, whose first real appearance in history this is. Provided they avoided a clash with Nuer and Dinka the French now had their path open. A steamer was assembled at Meshra el Rek and Colonel Marchand, who arrived in Tembura's village in July 1897, made his way successfully through the swamps to reach Fashoda exactly a year later. Here he expected to contact a party coming down the Sobat from Ethiopia. He was still waiting in September when Kitchener arrived in the gunboat *Dal* to claim the country in the name of the Khedive.*

The armies of the Congo Free State and Arabi Dafaallah, after sundry marching and counter-marching, had met in battle south of Rejaf on 17 February 1897, and the *Ansar* were completely defeated. Arabi withdrew north to Bor, where he held out against the local Dinka and even raided southwards, narrowly failing to recapture Rejaf in June 1898. He was finally forced to retreat in November on the approach of a joint Congolese-British force from the south, and

* For the reasons for the delay of the Sobat party see *Journal of African History*, Vol. III, Part I, pp. 86 seq. (G. N. Sanderson). They were bamboozled by the Emperor Menelik.

set off across country for Shakka, being still unaware of the Khalifa's defeat. He repulsed on the Bahr el Arab a Fur army sent against him by Ali Dinar and was then besieged at Mandowa in his home-land, Dar Taeisha, by the Hamari Abu Dugl, representing the new Government, and Musa Madibbo of the Rizeigat, lately his ally against the Fur. After Abu Dugl's withdrawal he continued to negotiate with the new Government from a refuge in the Kara country (now part of Chad) until his troops mutinied in 1902 and he had to surrender to Ali Dinar.*

After the French had finally agreed, in March 1899, to abandon the southern Sudan and evacuate Fashoda, Leopold of Belgium revived his claim to the whole Bahr el Ghazal and had to be bought off with the life tenure of the area subsequently known as the Lado Enclave, between the Nile and the 30th meridian south of Latitude 5° 30. On the east bank the boundary between the Sudan and Uganda was vaguely left at 5°N.† until Leopold died in 1909 and a series of adjustments led to the definition of the present frontier in 1913. Until 1906 the Bari formed part of the Upper Nile Province, which had a post at Mongalla, just north of the nominal boundary. In 1906 Mongalla District became a province again.

The attitude of the Bari to all these events is reflected in their remarks about the later capital at Juba, recorded in 1933.‡

'Years ago,' they said, 'the white man came to Gondokoro and built his wharf, offices and houses. Later barracks appeared, with English officers and an English District Commissioner. Where is that now?

'The white man also built the station at Lado. Where is that now?

'Later he put up houses and offices and shops at Rejaf to last for all time. This time we thought it really looked permanent. But where is it now?

'Then Mongalla was built with barracks for hundreds of soldiers, lots of homes for officials, beautiful roads all round. They even planted trees and it certainly looked to last for ever, but where is it now? Almost covered with grass.

'Then they started on Juba, and indeed it has got all the appear-ance of permanency, but what are we to say? All the others looked the same to us and where are they now?

'On the other hand our small villages are on the same sites as

---

* For his death see Chapter 4 above.

† They say that Kitchener expressed surprise when confronted with the Uganda delegate in London. 'So it is Uganda we have on the border,' he said, 'I thought it was Nyasaland.'

‡ *S.N. & R.*, Vol. XVI, p. 184.

they always were and what will cause them to change? It is better from our villages to watch Juba grow up and fall down again, and not to take any more notice of it than we did of Gondokoro, Lado, Rejaf and Mongalla.'

The Bari were, however, ready to acquiesce in a government which paid for what it took. The new administration was chiefly engaged during and after the first decade in trying to pacify the Dinka. The procedure is described in the Upper Nile report for 1904, which emphasises the desirability of simply travelling through the country and abstaining from plundering *en route*. This unprecedented behaviour was calculated to arouse curiosity and might later on allay suspicion. Famine relief, it was hoped, might also have good results among the Nuer. But deep-rooted fears caused frequent relapses into violence and recurrent military patrols. The intervals between incidents grew longer and less uneasy as time went on but that was the measure of success. The return of the missionaries — Americans to the Sobat and Austrians to the Shilluk in 1902, the C.M.S. to Malek in 1905 — undoubtedly had a pacifying influence, but in 1912 the Anuak killed five officers and 42 men in battle, in 1919 the Aliab Dinka stabbed to death their Governor, Chauncey Stigand (a Samson whose feats of strength were long remembered), and in 1927 the western Nuer murdered their District Commissioner, Vere Fergusson. Even as late as 1941 J. H. T. Wilson's iron constitution alone enabled him to survive after having had a Dinka spear driven through his back fifty miles north of Lake No.

Most of these disturbances were connected with the activities of witch doctors, two of whom, Gwek and Pok, achieved the distinction of a verse in *Punch*.

This was also a period of continual raiding from Abyssinia, which continued up to the Italian conquest. A boundary had been agreed upon in 1902 providing *inter alia* for a Sudan trading enclave at Itang in the Baro Salient, the precursor of the later post at Gambeila, and also, rather surprisingly, for the construction of a railway line from the Sudan to Uganda through Abyssinian territory. But none of the countries concerned was in a position to administer up to its new frontier and during the hiatus Ethiopian ivory poachers established a sort of Bahr el Ghazal *zareeba* in the hills west of Sanderson's Gulf (Lake Rudolph). This was manned by a force of Swahili and Baluchi adventurers which grew more and more bold during the administrative stalemate of 1914–18 and even penetrated in 1916 to within a day's march of Mongalla. Combined operations by the Sudan and Uganda had to be undertaken against them as soon as the war was over but it was not until 1930 that the area up to the Ilemi Appendix was more or less administered, if not yet pacified.

So it came about that the eastern part of the southern Sudan was only ready for development at the very moment when the world recession in trade made development temporarily impossible.*

The western section, the Bahr el Ghazal, though sharing the problem of the Nilotics, was slightly better off at the beginning. Access overland was, of course, difficult, with Darfur independent again and the allegiance of the Rizeigat undefined, but the channel to Meshra el Rek was reopened by 1902 and posts established at Wau, Rumbek, Deim Zubeir, Tonj and Shambe.

Since Karamullah's withdrawal the Dinka and the Zande had come to grips and by their hostilities had cleared a sort of no-man's land, about 150 miles square, which reverted to uninhabited wilderness, the wretched inhabitants having found refuge with one party or the other, under whom they existed as serfs or slaves.

The Dinka would have nothing to do with the new government. The Zande as usual were more co-operative but, again as usual, at least one of their sultans was hostile. This was the famous Yambio, who had successfully resisted all invaders save Lupton, who captured him in 1882. He even defeated Arabi Dafaallah in 1897, and he was now ready to take on the Sudan and the Congo at the same time. This he did until fatally wounded and captured by a Sudan patrol in February 1905. The Congolese then attempted to occupy the area and a kind of Fashoda Incident developed at Meridi, where the rival forces faced one another uneasily until the Belgians were prevailed upon to withdraw.

The process of resettlement of the devastated areas was facilitated by the arrival of the Central African Catholic Mission in 1904, and an unexpected but valuable means of winning confidence was provided by the twenty-year campaign against Sleeping Sickness which began in 1909. The existence of the disease had been suspected as early as 1903 and fortunately its cause, the bite of the tsetse fly, had just been discovered in Uganda, so that it was possible to carry out a survey of fly areas before infection was in fact discovered — at Raga and Tembura and in the Lado Enclave when it reverted after the death of Leopold. The technique was to settle the people along the roads where they were accessible to treatment and clear the scrub along the river banks, where the fly flourished. But the

---

* The time lag for recovery was inevitably behind the north. When Gezira money was available in the late 'thirties requests for expenditure in the south were countered time and again on Council by the rejoinder that northern money must be spent in the north on e.g. public health measures in the Gezira itself.

areas affected were remote and inaccessible and all the efforts of the British and Syrian medical officers only sufficed to bring the pest under control. As soon as that control was relaxed, in the 1955 troubles, it reappeared.

The resettlement schemes and movement permits and other restrictions were not of course popular, but in the process people ceased to be afraid of the white invaders. 'Some had come out of the forest to become craftsmen, carpenters, builders and blacksmiths. All had learned to obey laws. Superstition waned. Agriculture prospered. The task of extirpating disease had profoundly affected the life of the people.'*

The localisation of southern administration which later developed into a Southern Policy was reflected in various measures taken during this period. A local military force, the Equatorial Corps, was recruited and the last of the northern garrison left in 1917. A by-product of the recovery of the Lado Enclave was the substitution of Sunday for the northern Friday as the weekly day of rest.† An attempt was made to solve the language problem, at a conference held at Rejaf in 1928, by designating a 'group-language' for each area.

Meanwhile the Dinka had been in arms again in 1918, and it was only in the middle 'twenties that southern district commissioners began to struggle up through the swamps to meet their Darfur and Kordofan opposite numbers and start working out a *modus vivendi* for Baggara and Dinka along the Bahr el Arab.‡

The southern district commissioner was usually a soldier or ex-soldier serving on contract. It was desirable in those parts to have a man in the same station for a good few years. Pensionable staff could be and were posted south, but since they were likely some day to be called upon to govern provinces it was thought best to move them round every four years or so to widen their experience. The southern D.C. had to learn a local language as well as local customs. He had to establish himself as part of the background of life, something whose gait and habits and face were familiar, his foibles and prejudices known, his reactions accessible. He often had plenty of foibles to assess, for a contract post in the southern Sudan was unlikely to appeal to an ordinary man. Nor would the ordinary man have survived long if he got there. If he was too imaginative he

* G. K. Maurice. *S.N. & R.*, Vol. XIII, Part II, p. 245.
† The Sudan Government C.O.I. publication *Basic Facts about the Southern Provinces* (Khartum 1964) p. 82, dates the change at 1938.
‡ There is a rather remarkable account, by Captain R. C. Greenwood, in *Sudan Notes and Records*, Vol. XXIV, p. 189, of an encounter with a Rizeigat raiding party north of the Lol river in 1909. To read it is to understand how Southern Policy began.

would suffer from what the French called '*Sudanité*'; if he was unimaginative, from '*le cafard*'. The Bog Barons, as their colleagues called them (the Bahr el Ghazal was known colloquially as the Bog) had to strike a mean between these afflictions, and they certainly had prejudices.

One was a distaste for unnecessary clothing, which brought them into conflict with the missionary and the Muslim, both of whom have inherited the ancient Semite horror of nakedness. Hellenic and Anglo-Saxon tradition regards male nudity as natural and female nudity as something one can soon get used to. The African himself is happy to acquire a garment or two. The Nuba used to paint them on, *faute de mieux*, but the missionary Mother Hubbard or boy scout attire was felt to be derogatory to his natural dignity and to weaken his resistance to extremes of climate. The Arab *jibba* or *jallabiya*, on the other hand, inevitably unwashed, was thought to harbour dirt and lice and so encourage disease. This conflict of prejudice over nakedness is a cause as well as a symptom. It played a part in all the conflicts — 'Southern Policy', government versus missions, northern contempt for the sons of Ham.

Northerners believe that the Government and the missionaries collaborated to convert the south to Christianity and divorce it from the north. 'Collaboration' is hardly the word, as is clear enough from Bishop Gwynne's biography.* The missionaries were allowed to operate in the south free of the restrictions placed on their work in the north. They were encouraged to open dispensaries and schools, for which no government money was available. But they were frequently faced with the old charges of disrupting tribal society. Paradoxically enough the Italian Verona fathers, who took over from the Austrians after 1914 but who from 1935 onwards were suspect and later enemy subjects, tended on the whole to get on better with the barons than their fellow countrymen. They all shared a common suspicion of the northerner, which was later embodied in Southern Policy, but the barons' suspicion had little to do with religion. The northerner for him was either a raider or a trader. Up till the middle 'twenties the Baggara were still lifting slaves south of the river and disposing of them to inaccessible markets far to the north. When not slave raiding they were poaching elephants or hunting giraffe or lifting cattle. When they condescended to do a little trading they usually swindled the unsophisticated Nilote or paid him with counterfeit coins. As for the professional

* *Pastor on the Nile*. H. C. Jackson, S.P.C.K., 1960. See also an article by Richard Hill on "Government and Christian missions in the Anglo-Egyptian Sudan" in *Middle Eastern Studies*, Vol. 1 No. 2, Jan. 1965 (London School of Economics).

trader, the Jellabi, he in baronial eyes was an equally undesirable immigrant, battening on the villages, selling rubbishy goods at a vast profit, and introducing venereal disease. He had always preyed upon the southerner and now he threatened to interfere with progress, as the Indian was doing in East Africa, by monopolising petty trade and cash farming.

The policy of excluding the northerner would not however have been endorsed by Khartum had it not been for another factor. Policy from the beginning had aimed in the south at government through the chiefs but this in practice proved easier said than done. Such chiefs as retained any authority after all the vicissitudes of the nineteenth century owed their survival to toughness, ruthlessness and cunning, none of which qualities was likely to commend them to the new government. Time and again they had to be dismissed for nonco-operation or for practices repugnant to western standards of justice and morality. The average African chief or the rain-doctor or other wizard, whose departmental spiritual authority was imperfectly understood in the days before anthropology, was vested on inauguration with a supernatural sanction. This meant that in the eyes of the people he held office for life. He could not be deposed. Moreover his traditional functions were limited. He was not empowered by his office to collect taxes or perform administrative functions for an alien government. When therefore he was dismissed it simply meant that the tribe had now two chiefs — the real chief in the background performing his sacred office, and 'the Government's dog', as he was called in the Nuba Mountains, the puppet chief who took the blame and whose appointment or dismissal was a matter of indifference to the people. When the tribal elders were asked to elect a chief they usually kept the real man in the background and put forward one of his relations to be their go-between.

As a result administration became more and more 'direct' in spite of the official policy. When in the early 'twenties an attempt was being made to build up a new type of chief by bestowing judicial powers similar to those conferred on nomad shaikhs in the north a very delicate administrative experiment developed. Western standards and a few basic Western notions of judicial procedure (as against trial by ordeal or the use of magic, for instance) had to be inculcated without the court president forfeiting the chance of acquiring prestige and ceasing to be regarded as a stool-pigeon. In this process of progressive conservatism the missionary was a complicating issue for the reasons already given. The process would have been quite impossible if yet another influence had been at work, that of the Islamic north. The introduction of a type of civilisation which the Turkish and Mahdist occupations had made unpopular but which had none the less produced in Equatoria a small half-caste partially Arabicised proletariat was therefore regarded as undesirable.

Even so the official enforcement of Southern Policy did not materialise until after the discovery in 1929 that an extensive trade in slaves was still going on under the nose of the Government from the Beni Shanqul across to the White Nile. This aroused all the old fears and a decision was reached to enforce the Closed Districts legislation, and virtually close the south to northerners, even to northern administrative officials.

The northern reply to this argument was that apart from this local outbreak the slave trade was dead and that the civilised northerner no more thought of reviving it than Europe thought of resuming the trade from West Africa to the Americas. Islam had successfully colonised the Fur and the countries of Ifrikia to the west, eliminating unpleasant customs like ritual murder more successfully than Christianity and providing, in the considered opinion of European writers like Winwood Reade,* a better civilising influence on the African. The real intention of the Government was obviously to cut away the southern provinces altogether and attach them to Uganda, as was later advocated by the Fabian Colonial Bureau in a pamphlet called *The Sudan — the Road Ahead* published in 1947.

Many of the British in the Sudan certainly came to regard this as a sound solution which would be in the best interests of the southerner and no great loss to the north, for whom the south would be an economic liability for many years. Others however argued that the boundary would be almost impossible to define satisfactorily; that the North on its own would find it difficult to avoid absorption by Egypt; that there was a tie in the African blood contributed by southerners through the centuries to every northern tribe; that the south could supplement the northern economy by providing tropical products which the north was unable to grow for itself and which Uganda and the Congo already possessed in abundance; and that if the south, while remaining essentially southern, could yet become an integral part of an independent Sudan it could help to bridge the inevitable gulf between Muslim and non-Muslim, Asian and African, white or brown and black, in the Africa of the future.†

* *The Martyrdom of Man.* Published in 1872.

† The Ngok Dinka, on the Bahr el Arab, had joined Kordofan Province at the reoccupation and had played precisely such a role as intermediaries between the Homr Baggara and the Dinka of the Bahr el Ghazal.

There was no definite decision either way until 1946 but there
was a desire to leave the issue open in case it turned out, in fifty or
a hundred years, as men thought then of the time available, that
one course or the other was obviously right and desirable. The pro-
fessed intention in 1930 was 'to build up a series of self-contained
racial or tribal units with structure and organisation based upon
indigenous customs, tribal usage and beliefs'. Eight years later Sir
Stewart Symes, in a memorandum dated May 1938, wrote:

'More than thirty years of patient cautious penetration by
officials and others, including missionaries, is beginning to yield
fruits in the reintegration of a normal tribal life, in good public
security and a friendly attitude on the part of the natives. These
southern societies are now in process of being reformed along
indigenous patterns in accordance with their natural capacities
and material requirements. This is the simple aim of the so-called
Southern Policy. It recognises that southern genius is distinctly
African and Negroid. It conceives that the desirable nexus
between the peoples of the northern and southern Sudan will be
best established on a firm basis of common interests and mutual
tolerance. As time passes this nexus will undoubtedly be strengthened and extended but whether, initially, by passage of northern
Sudanese southwards or, as seems more likely, by an infiltration
of southerners seeking work in the more prosperous districts of
the northern Sudan, is still uncertain. In either case the primary
urge will be an economic one and intermingling of the two very
different racial stocks need entail a state of political subjection to
neither. Improved relations already prevailing on the fringes of
north and south between Arabicised and Negroid pastoralists
promise well for the ultimate success of a policy which is clearly
well adapted to suit local conditions and by its utilisation of
southern employees has provided a good and most economical
administration of the region.'

Douglas Newbold, broadcasting from Omdurman in January
1944 on the plans for setting up an Advisory Council for the northern
Sudan, referred to

'the fear that behind the Ordinance there is hidden a secret policy
to split the Sudan in two. . . . No such decision has been reached.
Nor is the Sudan Government empowered on its own to make
such a decision. . . . We are not prejudging the future status of
the southern Sudanese. It is simply that the southern Sudanese

have not yet, for historical and natural reasons, reached a degree of enlightenment and cohesion which enables them to send competent representatives to a council of this kind. Nor are there any northern Sudanese who can fairly claim to be able conscientiously to represent the southern peoples. We must look facts in the face. The same difficulty applies in a lesser degree to the Nuba Mountains districts, but owing to their close connection with the north and the fact that they are an integral part of Kordofan Province* we have thought it necessary in spite of some differences of language and outlook and social life, to arrange for their representation on the Kordofan Province Council. ... It has been suggested that District Commissioners or even missionaries might be nominated as southern representatives. A District Commissioner might with difficulty represent the Nuba Mountains but the diversity of tribes and customs and languages and the distances in the southern provinces are such that almost every district would have to have a separate representative, and it is Government's aim that this Council should be a predominantly Sudanese assembly. We have carefully drafted the Ordinance so that later on, when our plans for accelerating the educational and economic development of the south have matured, it can either join up with the northern council or have a separate Council of its own. It is interesting that in several southern areas native local government is developing well.'

This was all very fine, in northern eyes, but it left the door open for secession. Newbold went south that May to look into the situation. The new court chiefs had by this time acquired a respectable status in public opinion under an Ordinance passed in 1931. The social problems created by proselytisation seemed capable of solution on the lines laid down for Free French Africa by Felix Eboué, whose administrative memoranda, issued in 1941, had been translated and circulated at Newbold's direction.† Education was still almost

---

* The Nuba Mountains were absorbed into Kordofan Province in 1928.

† See *Sudan Notes and Records*, XXV, Part II, 1943, and especially the Memorandum on Native Policy. Three of Eboué's more pertinent observations are quoted in the Introduction:
'Native customs are always changing. Let us not freeze them into immobility.'
'Changes of Chief are not just deplorable. They are absurd.'
'The office of chief is not a suitable reward for old soldiers or faithful cornerboys.'
To these might be added a fourth: 'Our object is not to produce a certain number of exemplary Christian households but to diffuse the Christian idea of marriage throughout a society which is living under a different code: to make that society understand little by little the sacred and indissoluble character of

entirely in the hands of the missions, which had been subsidised since 1926, subject to a government inspectorate. In 1937 plans for the complete reorganisation of southern education had been drawn up *pari passu* with the De La Warr reforms in the north. They aimed at a general improvement in the standard of education and the opening of central boys' schools under trained missionary educationalists. Implementation had been held up by the war but there were in existence 3 intermediate schools for boys, 7 central schools, 37 elementary, 3 trades schools and almost 300 village schools. For girls there was one central school, 13 elementary and 7 village. The Government had opened an experimental village school of its own at Tonj and a post-elementary school at Abwong in the Upper Nile Province to train teachers and work out a syllabus. Trained anthropologists (notably E. E. Evans Pritchard*) had been called in to advise on social, educational and administrative problems. None the less Newbold found standards remained low and southern staff not up to northern level. That rates of pay were lower was not unreasonable. Northern rates would have upset the local economy. (Compare the effect of the affluent American G.I. on England during and after the recent war.)

The arrival from Uganda in 1939 as Director of Agriculture of Dr. J. D. Tothill had focused attention on the possibility of developing southern agriculture as an economic asset in spite of the remoteness of the country from the world's markets. An Equatoria Projects Board was set up and the Azande were inevitably chosen as promising material for a pilot scheme, near the village of Yambio. Newbold was anxious that cash crops should not be allowed to prejudice the necessary supply of good and ample food. 'We are a long way from that in many areas,' he remarked, 'especially among the Madi, and east of the river. Yambio must not be allowed to monopolise attention and funds.'

There was talk of the desirability of appointing a Lieutenant-Governor of the South at this time but he thought the plan of doubtful value, likely to cost money which would be better spent

---

* Dr. S. F. Nadel was employed in a similar capacity in the Nuba Mountains.

monogamous marriage freely entered upon: and yet to modify as little as possible existing ideals of family life. We must do nothing which can possibly be interpreted by native opinion as a move towards an entirely new society in which every traditional belief will be called in question.

'It is when this stage has been achieved that I shall be prepared to agree to deny to Christians the right of divorce and to prosecute them for bigamy by virtue of the change in public opinion. Here, as always, the change in opinion must precede the law. ... The law is still Customary Law, re-dressed in Christian guise.'

elsewhere. Economic and social development could be pushed ahead without a new headquarters to control them.

Newbold, however, had only a few more months to live and as it happened, Southern Policy did not long survive him. In June 1946 members of the Sudan Administrative Conference which was discussing the next step in devolution of power at the centre flew to Juba to get a swift impression of the south. A demand for fusion of north and south and for the representation of both in the proposed new legislative assembly followed, and the new Civil Secretary, J. W. Robertson, made up his mind that separation was no longer practicable. Most of the administrators in the south concurred,* but they were far from happy about southern representation in the new assembly and it was finally decided to hold a conference in Juba to discuss the matter. It met in June 1947 and consisted of six British officials, six northern Sudanese and fifteen southerners. The Civil Secretary in his opening address announced that 'the policy of the Sudan Government regarding the southern Sudan is to act upon the facts that the peoples of the south are distinctly African and Negroid but that geography and economics combine, as far as can be seen at the present time, to render them inextricably bound for their future development to the Middle East and the northern Sudan: and therefore to ensure that they shall by education and economic development be equipped to take their place in the future as socially and economically the equals of their partners in the Sudan of the future.'

After considerable discussion the northern representatives persuaded the fifteen southerners not to wait until they were better equipped to meet them on equal terms but to agree to participate in the new assembly. The southern governors and district commissioners were alarmed by this unexpected decision, but relied upon the insertion in the enabling act of some sort of safeguard against the acquiescence of southern representatives in some measure which was against their real interests.

The northern representatives regarded any such safeguard as unnecessary, undesirable, and a breach of trust. They had been greatly disturbed by the publication soon after the Conference of a government brochure drafted months before with an eye upon the Anglo-Egyptian dispute at Lake Success. This publication, written before the decision to abandon Southern Policy was made known, mentioned the possibility of referring the future of the south to an international commission.†

---

* See Document No. 1 appended to this Chapter.
† *The Sudan; A Record of Progress*, 1947. It is quoted in Document No. 2 appended to this Chapter.

The northerners' reaction is reflected in the following extracts from a private letter written by one of them the following October:

'I always said to myself "Never hesitate to co-operate with the Government as long as this was in the best interests of my country". The action which shook my belief and made me much more bitter than ever before was the Government's action over the south. I don't only disagree with the views of the Government but I think they were extremely dishonest. . . .

'When we went to the first meeting of the Sudan Administrative Conference we said we wanted to know whether the word "Sudan" in the terms of reference meant the whole Sudan or the northern Sudan only. . . . It took us some time to get the Civil Secretary to say that the word "Sudan" meant the whole Sudan. Our doubts were again roused when he allowed Mr. Marwood,* during the second day after the recommendation about administering the country as one unit was accepted, to make a long speech in which he questioned the wisdom of the decision taken the day before. . . .

'I did not raise any objection to the purpose of the meeting (at Juba) but when I was told the names of those invited to attend, objected on the grounds that Government was going back to the old detested practice of individual consultation. . . .

'. . . When the C.S. and those with him arrived at Juba the meeting turned out to be another conference in which a form of plebiscite was made. The Agenda included an Advisory Council for the Southern Sudan.

'. . . Then a communiqué was issued in which we were told that H.E. in Council had accepted the recommendation of the Conference but decided to make certain safeguards. . . . We waited eagerly for the type of safeguards that were to be made. While we were waiting "The Sudan: A Record of Progress" was released and we saw there that the Government's policy was declared in no vague terms and in more than one place. The southern Sudanese should not be denied the right to self-determination which was given to the northerners and when an international commission comes to the Sudan that commission will be faced with the south and they will have to decide what is best for the south — to join the north or become part of Negroid East Africa.

'These apparently conflicting actions and statements broke my heart. Had they told us of their real intentions right from the

* Vivian Marwood, Governor of Equatoria. Murdered in Kenya in 1964.

beginning we would have fought the matter with them but we would have respected them.'

In fact the famous safeguards were never included in the Ordinance because the Legal Secretary considered that the Governor-General's power of veto covered the point, but the omission caused just as much heart-burning amongst the southern administrators as the publication of the *Record of Progress* had caused among northern politicians. Nobody foresaw that in less than a decade the south would form part of an independent Sudan without any safeguards at all, and that in the circumstances the sooner southerners had experience in the Legislative Assembly the better.

A narrative of events during these years is prefixed to the report of a Commission of Inquiry into the southern Sudan disturbances of 1955, published by the Ministry of the Interior on 10 October 1956.* Since the impartiality of the proceedings and findings of this Commission has never been questioned relevant extracts are quoted verbatim below, with comment occasionally. The Commission consisted of Mr. Justice Tawfik Cotran, Sayed Khalifa Mahjub (General Manager, Equatoria Projects Board, and an ex-police officer of high rank) and Chief Lolok Lado of Lyria.

After censuring Southern Policy for perpetuating and exacerbating southern prejudice against the north, and drawing attention to the failure of missionary education to produce a reasonable standard of clerical and administrative efficiency in southern staff, the report remarked that on documentary evidence over the past sixteen years the Sudan Government seemed to have been unable to make up its mind between union, separation or partition. By December 1946, however, it was decided to cast the lot of the southern Sudan with the north, and the Juba Conference followed.

'We do not find in the minutes of this conference that any resolutions were passed, but the trend of southern opinion appears to have changed, though agreeing in principle to one unified Sudan, from preferring an Advisory Council [of their own] on the first day (though sending observers to see and learn the workings of the Government in the Legislative Assembly) to fully agreeing to participate by sending 13 representatives to the All-Sudan Assembly in Khartum, on the second day. Some Southern Sudanese whom the Commission heard charged that this conference was nothing short of a fraud inasmuch as the

* Southern Sudan Disturbances, August, 1955. Report of the Commission of Inquiry.

majority of southerners were not agreeable to join the Northern Sudan as a unified country. We are not satisfied that this charge has been substantiated. Very few people could visualise in 1947 what the political developments in the Sudan would be in 1955, and it seems to us that the southerners' dissatisfaction of political affairs and their consequent fear and suspicion, though always present, came to prominence when the results of Sudanisation were known.

'The All-Sudan Legislative Assembly with 13 southern members present opened on 15 December 1948, and until the signing of the Anglo-Egyptian Agreement of 12 February 1953 this period witnessed great economic, educational, and administrative advancement in the southern Sudan; the Zande Scheme, with all its branches, became a going concern; saw-mills were established in Kateri, Gilo and Loka, and communications improved; a unified system of education introduced including the teaching of Arabic; local government was established in practically all districts; permits to trade licences were freely given for Sudanese whether southerners or northerners, and free movements between the two parts of the country were relaxed.

'It must be said at once that in the political sphere at any rate the unified policy adopted by the Central Government was much favoured by all except the few of the British administrators in the southern Sudan.* One of them went as far as accusing the Civil Secretary of "sacrificing his conscience", and no opportunity was left without instilling into the people that northerners will dominate them; will treat them as their fathers did, and that "the sins of the fathers shall be visited upon their children unto the third and fourth generation". Fear and suspicion reigned, as it still does, in the minds of the southerners.

'The most important feature of this period is that through more political contact with Khartum, increase in education, and the expansion of the social services, the southern people have become more politically conscious than they ever were before.†

Period between 1953–5

'When major northern parties went to Egypt shortly before the signing of the Anglo-Egyptian Agreement of 12 February 1953 to negotiate with the Egyptians re the Agreement, none of the southerners were represented in any of the parties. The southerners

* See extracts from private letters appended to this chapter, Documents Nos. 3 & 4.
† For an appreciation of the situation at the end of 1952 see document No. 5 of the appendix.

considered that they had been belittled because their views were not asked for. This has been put forward as a grievance: but we find that this is more of a talking grievance than a real one. In the first place the southerners did not have a party of their own at that time, in the second place we find that the whole thing was an afterthought when it became evident that the Sudanisation of the south was going to be more rapid than at first visualised; and in the third place southern politicians gave their blessing to the steps already taken.*

'Be that as it may, preparations for the elections which took place in November and December 1953 were in full swing and each of the major political parties tried to gain the votes of the southerners. The Southern Party† had the same aim with regard to the major issue of complete independence as the *Umma* Party and little canvassing was done by the latter party in the south. The leaders of the N.U.P. paid a visit during the elections to the southern Sudan. Major Salem‡ also paid a visit. Rash and irresponsible promises were made to the southerners by N.U.P. politicians.

'The first Parliament met on January 1st, 1953. N.U.P. was returned to power with a small majority over all other parties. Twenty-two southern members (roughly a quarter of the House of Representatives) were returned. Twelve were Southern Party, six were N.U.P., and four were independent.

'A Sudanisation Committee was appointed on 20 February 1954, to consider posts in the Civil Service which should be Sudanised, the Public Service Commission advising on the promotion of Sudanese.

'In August 1954 *Umma*-Liberal politicians led by Buth Diu, M.P., paid a visit to the southern Sudan. Several meetings were held where most disparaging remarks to undermine the government were made, including a reference to the omnipotence of the forces that they can muster and the sacrifice made in the bloody incidents of 1 March 1954, in Khartum.§

---

* But see appendix, Document No. 6.

† Formed in 1953. Enjoyed the support of majority of southern intelligentsia and 'it can safely be said (p. 85 of Report) the Southern Party has also got the support of the great bulk of southerners'. Name changed in 1954 to Liberal Party to attract northern members but none were, and names were later used synonymously. Not very active until the Sudanisation Committee's recommendations were published in August and September, 1954.

‡ Major Salāh Sālim, Egyptian Government representative, who, according to p. 113 of this Report, promised the southerners forty posts as Governor, D.C. and A.D.C. when the British left.

§ See above p. 105.

'The N.U.P.s in Equatoria, mostly Jallaba, hurled charges against the *Umma* party and reminded the southerners that the leader of the *Umma* Party (Abdullah Bey Khalil) and his followers were the descendants of their bitter enemies the slave-traders, and that the date of oppression at their hands will be forthcoming if they support it. The *Umma*-Liberal speakers charged the Jallaba with exploitation of southerners; the northern merchants on the other hand interrupted their meetings, and the only out-come of all this seems to us to have been a deterioration in relationship between southern and northern Sudanese.

'The tour seems to have been successful with some southerners and many demanded that their M.P.s who had joined N.U.P. should resign from it. The Government, on 15 August 1954, then issued a warning that "they were fully aware of the conspiracies that are being worked out in the South" and threatened the Southerners that "they shall use the force of iron in dealing with any Southerner who will dare attempt to divide the nation". This angered all southerners irrespective of party; and "Our northern brothers will use force against us" slogan by agitators started. During October the names of those promoted to occupy senior posts were announced* and the result was still further deteriora-tion in southern-northern relationship. Fears of domination became widespread among educated southerners and some southern N.U.P. members resigned and joined the Liberal Party, as the Southern Party then came to be called. A Conference of the Liberal Party was called to meet in Juba in October 1954 where the effect of Sudanisation was debated, a resolution was passed to demand federal status with the north, with a call to all southerners to be ready for sacrifices.

'A tour was then undertaken to the southern Sudan by N.U.P. politicians, including the Prime Minister (Ismail el Azhari). They were booed and ill-received everywhere. Feelings were running high and to counter-effect the success of the Liberal Conference a rise in the salaries of the prison warders, police, and clerks to accord with northern scales, were at once announced. This was regarded by southerners as a bribe and in any case created discontent as it did not include Article III Clerical Category, who form the great majority of clerks in the south, despite the recommendations of the Governors that these should be included.

* Southerners were given 4 posts as A.D.C. and 2 as *mamur* (p. 114 of the Report). Southern N.U.P. members in a memorandum to the Prime Minister dated 25 September had demanded 3 Governors' posts, 3 Deputies, 6 D.C., 8 A.D.C. and 12 full *mamurs* (p. 115).

'A series of blunders followed in the administrative, political and industrial fields. A Governor who seems to have, to a little extent, gained the confidence of the southerners was transferred and the activities of the Southern Liberal Party (to whom practically all southerners belong) increased. In May two southern N.U.P. Ministers left the cabinet (one resigned and the other dismissed) apparently because of disagreement with the Prime Minister on southern affairs. The Liberal Party welcomed them and a call to all southern M.P.s, regardless of party, to form one Southern bloc "to pursue the demands of the southerners" and to meet in Juba in June 1955 was made. Attempts by the Government were made to frustrate the Conference. The Assistant District Commissioner Yambio summoned thirteen chiefs to his office and a telegram (in his name) supporting the Government against the Juba Conference was sent. . . .'*

'The fact that the Assistant District Commissioner himself interfered in politics in such a way is deplorable both in a moral sense and in an administrative sense. When an administrator is appointed his primary duty is the welfare of the community he serves. In the southern Sudan he has got the additional duty of nursing primitive peoples to maturity. It is manifestly wrong for an administrator to allow his party loyalty to carry him beyond his duty to his people and the Public Service.'

'This telegram was used for propaganda purposes by Radio Omdurman and so became known to a Zande member of Parliament called Elyas Kuze. This man was campaigning on behalf of union with Egypt, without much success because he had been elected on the Independence ticket. The telegram provided him with an opportunity to improve his position. At a public meeting held in Yambio on 7 July he demanded the removal of the signatories from office. The motion was passed with enthusiasm, excitement ran high, and the offended chiefs demanded his arrest. He was brought back from Juba, tried with four others by a court of the chiefs he had denounced, and sentenced on 25 July to twenty years imprisonment on a charge of criminal intimidation.

'We are of the opinion,' commented the Commission, 'that the trial was a farce and a usurpation of the machinery of Justice. Its intention was wrong; members were judging their own case; it was *ultra vires* a Chiefs Court; it imposed an illegal and vindictive sentence; and it offended against the oft-repeated gold rule that Justice must not only be done, but MUST BE SEEN TO BE

* The detailed description which follows is from a later part of the Report (p. 88).

DONE. ... Needless to say the conviction was quashed (but the harm had been done).'

After the sentence was announced a crowd of about 700 staged a demonstration. Police and S.D.F. troops were called and tear gas was used. The crowds dispersed, but small groups raided a shop belonging to a northerner and beat up some northerners. At about 6 p.m. order was restored.

The following day (26 July) disorders occurred at Nzara, the industrial centre of the Zande Scheme.

'For various reasons ... this region was chosen for an experiment. The experiment consisted in the main of establishing a cotton industry providing for growing, spinning and weaving within the district and of export from the district of part of the cloth manufactured. The scheme became a going concern in 1949 and it has become a source of livelihood to many thousands of Azande and others who now flocked to find employment in its industrial centre at Nzara, a small village 16 miles west of Yambio. As a result of the scheme together with the corresponding expansion of public services there evolved in the Azande a sense of organisation and discipline and, through contact with other foreign employees, a widening of outlook and a thirst for knowledge. Communist propaganda seems to have penetrated ... by northern and foreign officials ... and since December 1954 their activities increased. The Azande and Moru Districts ... were mostly affected. ... In January and February 1955 Nzara and other parts of Equatoria were visited by prominent northern politicians from the Anti-Imperialist Front and they recruited for the propagation of their views many southerners. ... In spite of this communist activity the evidence suggests that the people of Southern Sudan do not understand or care about the theories of Marx or Lenin. ... The intelligentsia ... also did not seem to care about abstract communist theories, but extracts about "equal pay for equal work" and "three little parliaments in Juba, Wau and Malakal" interested them. ... It is certain that the disturbances of 18–30 August were not communist-inspired either, but industrial unrest due to mass dismissals* plus the political atmosphere then prevailing gave rise to them. ... In our view these dismissals ... were a major blunder in that the decision, though necessitated by reason of economy, did not take into

---

* In June and July the management of the Zande Scheme had dismissed 300 workers owing to redundancy.

consideration the repercussions it might involve in the political situation prevailing.'

The demonstration (for higher wages under threat of strike) on 26 July got out of hand and looting began. Reinforcements consisting of five policemen, each with one tear-gas bomb, and eleven Equatorial Corps soldiers arrived from Yambio and being quite insufficient in number to overawe the crowd had finally to open fire, killing four and fatally wounding two. Two more were drowned in the subsequent stampede for safety. Although the report does not say so specifically, the effect on the morale of the troops of having to fire on their fellow-southerners appears to have been considerable. 'No inquiry was made, and instead a further threatening ultimatum from Khartum was circulated and broadcast.'*

'On 7 August,' the Report continues, 'a conspiracy to mutiny in the Southern Corps (which was the only remaining force the authorities could rely on) involving most of the senior N.C.Os was discovered. The authorities were too weak to make any arrests in the Army immediately but two civilians who appeared to have had a finger in the mutiny were arrested in Juba. A demonstration took place where the mob demanded the release of the accused . . . and it had to be dispersed by the use of tear-gas.

'When the administration lost the confidence of every shade of opinion in the south frantic calls to Khartum to send in northern troops were made. Khartum, neither understanding nor appreciating the situation, was reluctant but finally sent a company by air, whose equipment and support had not yet arrived. Rumours started flying about . . . and the last straw came about when the Army command in Equatoria decided "for its prestige and dignity" to persist in their order that No. 2 Company Southern Corps should move to Khartum when they and everybody else in Equatoria knew that the Company would refuse to obey orders and mutiny, and when the only reliable force left to preserve law and order and protect life and property was a company of 200 Camel Corps Nubas, crippled by lack of equipment, transport and mortar support, in a province as large as Italy!'

Mutiny they did, on 18 August, shot their officers and massacred northern men, women and children in Torit, seventy-eight souls in

* p. 22 of the Report.

all. They then started sending telegrams to the Prime Minister, the Kaid, British Troops Sudan, British Troops Nairobi, and (after his arrival from England) to the Governor-General, Sir Knox Helm.* Finding support from nowhere, they finally agreed to surrender on Helm's personal guarantee of a fair trial, but when on 31 August northern troops reoccupied Torit they found the town deserted. Mutineers and civilians alike had disappeared into the bush, some to prolong a Mau Mau existence for a decade.

The events in Torit had touched off similar troubles elsewhere. All over Equatoria northerners were killed, usually as a direct result of a rumour that southerners in Juba had been massacred. Here and there a loyal N.C.O. or chief managed to save a few individuals. Others made their way into Uganda or the Congo. From Meridi and Yambio the majority escaped to Wau, leaving a number of dead (amounting to 45 in Yambio and Nzara) behind them.

At Wau itself an unusual situation developed. When word was received of the discovery of a conspiracy on 7 August it was realised that the key to the position lay with the Dinka, who as a tribe were not involved in the general malcontent. The senior N.C.O. of the Wau garrison and one third of the troops were Dinka and, with the exception of one man who was incensed at the news from Juba, remained loyal. The Governor cabled to Khartum for a Dinka Minister, Santino Deng, and he arrived by air on 20 August accompanied by another Dinka M.P., Philemon Majok.† As the non-Dinka soldiers and police were beginning to get out of hand the Governor decided that the Minister stood a better chance of saving the lives and property of northern residents if he and his staff handed over to him and withdrew. This they did, on the steamer *Dal*, and after their departure the two M.P.s, assisted by a Dinka officer, the senior N.C.O., the Assistant District Commissioner and the Chief Inspector of Police, restored order. The A.D.C. was a non-Dinka and his assumption of the style of Acting Governor with the appurtenances and 'grandeur of office' irritated the Dinka who 'for some reason regard all other Negroid tribes as an inferior race'. In spite of this friction (an ill omen for 'Southernisation') they succeeded

---

* L. A. Fabunmi, p. 367, argues that this raises suspicion of British complicity in the mutiny and the Prime Minister of the Sudan publicly repeated the charge on 16 March 1965 (see below). Whatever offences the British may have committed, inciting men you have recently commanded to murder officers you have recently served with, knowing that you can in no circumstances save them from the inevitable consequences of their tragic folly, is not one of them. Obviously however the mutineers expected the British to come to their rescue.

† Santino Deng retained his office throughout the military regime. Philemon Majok was later, when a member of the Central Council, to propose, on 4 March 1964, the appointment of a Commission of Inquiry into the problem of the south.

M

between them in keeping the peace until a new northern Governor arrived on 9 September.

In the Upper Nile Province a force of Nuba mounted police provided a stabilising influence. A company of northern troops arrived in Malakal on 21 August and as a precautionary measure it was decided to disarm the southern police and warders next day. This provoked a clash in which four southerners were killed. Attempts to cause trouble in other parts of the province were easily contained because the bulk of the police and tribesmen remained loyal.*

There is no space here to quote further from the Commission's report, which in fact presents a comprehensive picture of the whole southern problem. The strictures on the previous regime can be omitted here because they have already been dealt with. The important points for the future were the comments on north-south relationship — the northern attitude to nakedness; the contempt of north for south and the incorrigible northern habit of referring to southerners as 'abeed' (slaves); the need for exemplary behaviour by northern officials who are judged as representatives, not individuals; southern jealousy of northern standoffishness, officials and merchants sticking together and not 'mixing'; the tactless behaviour of inexperienced officers. Some of these evils were inevitable. All should have been usefully studied in the years to come.

One or two major points emerge. The revolt was political, not religious. The great Nilotic tribes were not involved. The crisis was due to irresponsible political propaganda, both northern and Egyptian, making extravagant promises which could not be fulfilled. Influence outside the Nilotics had passed in five years from the chiefs to the intelligentsia. The whole picture is very similar to that in other parts of Africa, with the northerner unable to realise that he was regarded as just as much a 'coloniser' as the British or Belgian D.C. over the border, with whom he was compared. Here and there the figure of a northern D.C. challenges comparison with the best that Europe could boast. Such was el Fadil Abdullah el Shafi, murdered in Yei in spite of the affection of his people. The influence of the new southern members of parliament is marked. (The reason the original mutiny misfired and became known to the Government on 7 August was because the mutineers' Juba contacts had refused to credit the story of an impending massacre until they could consult Sayed Buth Diu, who was in Khartum.)

---

* Official known fatal casualties of the whole revolt were 336 northerners and 75 southerners, excluding those killed at Nzara in July but including an estimated 55 drowned in the Kinyeti river during a panic exodus from Torit on the night of 18 August.

Sore but still intact, the southern Liberal Party remained an important political factor. Restraint in punishment* accompanied by a readiness to remedy grievances in the spirit of the Commission's report seemed to offer the possibility of permanent settlement and a beginning was made in this direction. Able administrators were hurriedly transferred south. Southern officials were promoted to Deputy Governor status. Buth Diu became a minister. But the southern members still refused to subscribe to the independence resolution.

They had already asked for a local referendum, to be held under UNO auspices or by an international commission, only to be told that under the Anglo-Egyptian Agreement of 23 February nothing of the kind was permissible. The proposed national plebiscite was better than nothing. It would give more time for discussion and for bargaining about the constitution. Something of a federal nature might still be conceded with a measure of regional autonomy. Failing that, the Egyptians had made many promises, which they might fulfil if given the chance. The south could vote, if necessary, for union with Egypt.

A motion in favour of a federal constitution was introduced in the House of Representatives and debated at length. The northern members would go no further than to agree that full consideration should be given to the proposal by the new constituent assembly when it met, and on this rather uncertain promise the southern members finally gave their votes in favour of independence.

Sayed Siricio Iro was one of the Commission of Five which took over the powers of the Governor-General on 1 January 1956 and which, in 1957, assented to the nationalisation of all mission schools in the south and the prohibition of all privately owned schools such as are common in the north.† The process of nationalisation had begun when the schools were reopened after the mutiny. They had remained closed for almost a year and when they reopened, the village schools, which were in process of being taken over by local education committees, were nationalised. Now the elementary, intermediate and teachers' training colleges followed. Only the Bishop Gwynne Theological College at Mundri, and six similar Catholic seminaries (4 intermediate, 1 secondary, and 1 post-secondary) were left in Christian hands.

Meanwhile, in September 1956, a special committee had been set

* Southerners claimed that 300 were executed and 2,000 transported to hard labour in the north. See *Problem of the Southern Sudan* by Joseph Oduhu and William Deng, O.U.P., 1963. About 800 were released in 1961. See below.

† Southern members wanted the mission schools to be left but to be supplemented by more government schools.

up to prepare a draft constitution for submission to the new constituent assembly. Of its 43 members three were southerners.* In their view the committee's first duty was to decide on the federal form of government, but this was instead relegated to a sub-committee of ten members while six other committees discussed matters of principle. The question was argued for more than a year but in December 1957 the majority decided that the disadvantages of regional government outweighed the benefits. The southern case was rejected.

The three southern members took no further part in the proceedings and when the elections of the new parliament-cum-constituent assembly took place in February 1958 a new southern Federal Party fought them on that issue, with the support of the Anti-Imperialist Front in the north and against strong opposition by the *Umma* Party.† According to the *Sudan Times* the party manifesto, drafted by a Mr. E. M. Gwanza,‡ represented the views of a group of young men who were dissatisfied with the old Liberals. In addition to the demand for a federal, or rather a southern regional government, it called for the recognition of Christianity as a state religion on a par with Islam and of English as a state language on a par with Arabic, for the establishment of a separate civil service and educational system, a southern university, and a new development programme. It also called for the transfer of the Sudan from the Arab world to the African. The educational proposals included a specific demand for the return of the three southern secondary establishments, the Juba Training Centre for the civil service, the Meridi Teachers' Training College, and the Rumbek Secondary School. These had been moved north after the mutiny and were housed at this time in the recently evacuated British barracks at Khartum. They moved back again after the elections.

The *Sudan Times* commenting on these proposals, remarked, not unreasonably, that the great Nilotic tribes had little in common with Equatorial politicians, and that in any case the new southern state would not be financially viable without northern aid. If wise use was made of existing democratic institutions for a solid programme of development, tapping the resources of the south, but financed by the north, it would give the south the chance to gain far more than it ever could hope to achieve by bargaining on a basis of independence.

The south had been allocated 46 seats out of 173 in the new

parliament, a figure almost exactly proportionate to its population under the 1956 census. The Federalists won forty of these seats. One or two northerners got in for southern constituencies and the southern party petitioned unsuccessfully against them on grounds of administrative discrimination against their candidates. Relations inside the House had deteriorated. The southern members opposed the new constitution and finally walked out of the Constituent Assembly on 16 June.

Father Saturnino had the last word. 'Sir,' he said, 'the South has no ill-intentions whatsoever towards the North; the South simply claims to run its local affairs in a united Sudan. The South has no intention of separating from the North, for had that been the case nothing on earth would have prevented the demand for separation. The South claims to federate with the North, a right that the South undoubtedly possesses as a consequence of the principle of free self-determination which reason and democracy grant to a free people. The South will at any moment separate from the North if and when the North so decides, directly or indirectly, through political, social and economic subjection of the South.'*

The last sentence is a little obscure but seems to be a threat of secession if the south were not properly treated. As we shall see, the speaker was regarded by the military Government as the main architect of subsequent southern resistance.

According to the authors of *The Problem of the Southern Sudan*, the withdrawal of the southerners was followed by similar 'separatist' requests from the west and the Red Sea area, but before any progress could be made the Army took over. Parliamentary government ceased to exist on 17 November 1958, and with it southern representation in Khartum. The southern parties, like their northern counterparts, became illegal associations, and all the safety valves were screwed down.

It is possible to detect three distinct phases in the history of southern resistance. The 1955 rising was provoked by disappointment at the pace of 'southernisation'; the post-1960 disturbances are remarkable for the involvement of the rural population; the main scene of the struggle during the intervening period seems to have been the mission compound, and the protagonists the senior boys. This was inevitable. Their education and progress had already been interfered with by the closing of the schools. The switch from English to Arabic as medium of instruction hit them hardest of all. The installation of northern schoolmasters in the compound was a religious challenge. The change from Sunday to Friday as the

* *The Problem of the Southern Sudan*, p. 36.

weekly day of rest, to conform to practice in the rest of the country, increased their resentment, although time was allowed off for attending church. Their younger brothers, intent on winning admission to school, found the best qualification to be a smattering of Arabic, to be acquired at one of the new *koran* schools. So they saw a gulf developing between them and the younger generation and their feelings were further exacerbated by somewhat inept northern propaganda in which the Arab boy was featured as holding out a helping hand to his down-trodden southern brother. Nobody enjoys being regarded as a charity boy, still less being asked to play the part in a speech-day drama!

It should be remembered that while a reasonably devout Western Christian is no longer convinced that a convert to Islam is a lost soul, the African enjoys no such comfortable consolation. His brother is not only cut off from him in this world but in the next.

On the face of it, the retention of the mission schools side by side with the new state schools need not have had a disruptive influence especially as the former could have been in no position to compete. The Copt has not shown himself to be a disloyal Egyptian and the Syrian Christian has always been in the vanguard of Arab nationalism. Nor did the old Turkish Government have any qualms about giving the missionaries a free hand in the south.

The military Government however was obviously of a different opinion, and it is time to make an attempt to assess its views and policy.

The 1955 Commission remarked in the course of its summing-up that:

'Some Northern Sudanese, including high officials in the administration, refer to the southern intelligentsia as half-educated. Education is a relative term and largely a matter of opinion, but experience has taught time and time again even nations with a long history of colonial rule that it always pays to gain the confidence of the intelligentsia whether they are fully educated, half educated or quarter educated. The northern administration in Southern Sudan is not colonial, but the great majority of southerners unhappily regard it as such, and as long as this is so it is just as important to gain the confidence of this group as of the people living in the bush. Another point that has clearly emerged from our inquiry is that there is too much mutual suspicion and mistrust between the administration and the missions in the southern Sudan, which is widening ... the cleavage between Northern and Southern Sudanese.'

By 1957 it seems to have been generally accepted in the north that the confidence of the southern intelligentsia had been lost. It could only be recovered by concessions which the north was not prepared to make. The solution must have appeared to lie in taking a leaf from the book of the old Government and putting southern policy into reverse, as it were. The influence of the existing intelligentsia could be weakened by cutting away its feeder system, the mission schools from which it was recruited. Substitute a system of Islamic education uniform with that of the north and within a decade you will have built up a new pro-northern Arabicised student body to replace the now discredited leaders of the nineteen-fifties.

In this endeavour the foreign missionary was an obvious stumbling block. Only a quarter of a million of the three million southerners were thought to be Christians,* but since the departure of the barons, the decline of the chiefs and the rise of the mission-trained intelligentsia the influence of the missionary had greatly increased. Naturally they would object to the teaching of Islam in the schools which they had founded. Try they never so hard to be co-operative (and there is evidence that try they did)† they could not help resenting the change. Nor is the divorce of church from state comprehensible to a Muslim. The statement, in the *Times Literary Supplement* review of Canon Max Warren's *Perspective in Mission*, that the reports which reach the desk of the general secretary of a large missionary society are 'completely untendentious . . . uninfluenced by any desire to further or even to estimate the position of western policies or trade', would strike him as both untrue and absurd. For the Muslim religion is life and life religion, as it used to be in Christian Europe.

The new southern policy, however, whether it existed in this conjectured form or no, was at first no more definite and logical than its predecessor. It depended more on the character of local administrators than on Khartum directives. The change-over from Friday to Sunday was alleged to have only been imposed on the Upper Nile at the insistence of the Governor of Equatoria. Policy over medical treatment varied from place to place. Some hospitals were taken over by the state; some allowed to function unaltered; some, inexplicably, forbidden to provide medical facilities to Africans. It is perhaps as well that Dr. Schweitzer was not operating in Sudan territory!

---

* The official figure, quoted in *The Middle East and North Africa* for 1964–5 (Europa Publications Ltd. London), was 270,251; but the Verona Fathers, in their *Answer* to the Government's charges (for which see below) claim that in 1964 there were half a million converts.
† See below.

The Government's case against the missionaries themselves was set out in a *Black Book* published by the Ministry of the Interior in 1964. It accused the Missions roundly of deliberately obstructing national integration by fostering a civilisation and culture different from what prevails in other parts of the country, 'and by implanting in the southern Sudanese Christianity, the use of English, hatred of the north and separatism'.

'With the advent of national rule,' the charge continued, 'the government maintained a friendly attitude (to the missions). Collective acquirance of firearms was permitted, game licences were granted and further facilities were provided. They were also allowed to barter with natives, sell furniture, plant coffee and fruit trees, and, furthermore, they were left at full liberty to establish places of prayer and trade. Moreover, to foster freedom in religion, Christian government personnel were allowed to absent themselves from official work to attend religious functions.

'But despite all this good treatment the missions continued to operate, through different means, open and disguised, against the public policies of the national government. This was clearly demonstrated by their diehard stand against the government move to assume its responsibilities in matters relating to education, health and other social services.

'The missions' failure, for more than half a century, to educate southerners is a very well known fact. This situation prompted the government to assume full responsibility to handle its most important national service. . . .

'This action on the part of the government aroused rancour among the missionaries. They opposed the Government's decision very strongly and exploited all possible means. Their moral power was behind the students' opposition to the Government's decision to unify school curricula, and was also behind the government employees' opposition when one national weekly holiday was to be observed.

'When the Government took over responsibilities in health services by establishing hospitals, dispensaries and dressing stations, the missions resorted to all means to frustrate this endeavour. They even ignored the laws of the land and supplied medicine and drugs to the natives in order to stop them from going to government medical centres. Contravention of the provisions of the Pharmacy and Poisons Ordinance took place. . . .

'The Government attitude remained, of course, to be one of tolerance. No direct action was contemplated. However, certain precautions were taken to keep the missions' operations within the limits of law. Only those who were either convicted in court or obstructed government policy were asked to leave the country.

'The 1958 parliamentary elections provided a good opportunity for further missionary interference. The missions secretly supported a movement of separation when two of their men entered parliamentary elections. The most ardent of these is Fr. Saturnino who has a conspicuous role to play later. In the ranks of the Southern Liberal Party, therefore, they found their mouthpiece.

'The deterioration in parliamentary life that followed was mainly due to the political activities of the Southern Liberal Party which acted under severe pressure exercised by the missionaries. Moreover, the missionaries' part in the tragic disturbances of 1955 in the south, whether directly or indirectly, is something well remembered.'

The Commission of Inquiry, it will be remembered, was less censorious of the behaviour of the missions in 1955, remarking* that although they regarded the take-over as a challenge to their own work and certain allegations had been made, 'we find on evidence that the real trouble in the south was political, not religious'.

The escape from Torit of the hard core of mutineers rather than submit to trial was disastrous to future peace because it set off a train of punitive operations which never really ceased and which inevitably had a brutalising effect. Repression is the opposite of mercy. It curseth him that gives and him that takes. Whether it be directed against the I.R.A. or the Mau Mau or the *Anya Nya* (southern terrorists) it leads to increased callousness in reprisal. The allegations of atrocities by northern soldiers which appeared with a wealth of detail in the publications of the Sudan African Union (the Liberal Party's heir in exile) are difficult to credit for anybody who has been in contact with them these fifty years, and can only be assessed in the light of experience elsewhere. The military government does not appear to have bothered to refute them.†

It seems that the trouble had spread to Yei District by 1957 and that the Ministry of Defence authorised the burning of 700 huts as a punishment for sheltering wanted men. This is the first intimation

* p. 6 of the Report. See also Document No. 7 appended to this chapter.
† In the Central Council on 11 March 1964 Gobrial Kaw Atir and Alfred Wol made charges of torture with red pepper after the rebel attack on Wau. These accusations, which are repeated with detail and circumstance on pp. 180 seq. of the *Answer* to the *Black Book* to which reference will be made below, were categorically denied by the Minister responsible, Sayed Ziyada Arbab.

of the involvement of the rural population in the resistance movement.* Similar stories occur frequently thereafter, and the security
system appears to have slowly deteriorated. In 1960† something in
the nature of a large-scale migration began out of Equatoria into
Uganda and the Congo. Leading southern intellectuals, including
students at Khartum University, also went into exile. One of these
was William Deng, A.D.C. at Torit and co-author of *The Problem
of the Southern Sudan.*‡ Deng's defection is difficult to understand. He
was known to be on excellent terms with the north, had just passed
his Higher Arabic examination, and as recently as January 1960
had written a letter, quoted in *Basic Facts,*§ supporting complete
integration. It is said that when he took over the district he found
that the Southern Policy files had been removed, and resented this
like his northern colleagues before him, but this seems an inadequate explanation. Possibly, as has happened so often in colonial
history, some act of personal arrogance or nepotism tipped the
scale.‖

Deng and Oduho and the other exiles founded the Sudan African
National Union, and set the Uganda Government a delicate
problem of diplomacy. This body has been active in propaganda
in and out of Africa, canvassing the delegates to the Addis Ababa
Conference in 1963 and generally attempting to rally African
sentiment against the 'Islamic Colonisers'.

Deng's defection alarmed the northern Government and led to
the transfer north of southern officials, whose loyalty could, it was
thought, no longer be relied on. In 1961 the political prisoners in the
north were released and sent home. They seemed to have numbered
about 800,¶ and no attempt had been made to indoctrinate them or
to provide them with a means of livelihood on their return. Most of
them were ex-soldiers, more accustomed to handle a rifle than a hoe,
and after a while they began to drift off into the bush and join the
outlaws. Northern administrators who were serving in the south at

---

* According to a northern District Commissioner serving in the south at this
time the outlaws would conceal themselves in a village and ambush northerners,
who inevitably took punitive action against the villagers. The situation in fact was
similar to that grown familiar in S.E. Asia, where peasants had to be herded into
fortified villages to protect them against intimidation by the rebels.

† This was the year in which the Sunday holiday was abolished.

‡ The co-author, Joseph Oduho, was an ex-Member of Parliament and headmaster of a school. The publication of this book by the Institute of Race Relations
in Oxford caused great indignation in Khartum. The military government refused
an invitation to contribute a reply to the charges.

§ See page 88.

‖ According to a reliable account he was passed over, after being promised a
course of instruction abroad, in favour of a relative of the responsible official.

¶ Compare the southern estimate above of 2,000 taken north.

the time blame the subsequent deterioration of security partly on the return of these men and partly on ill-advised military interference in administration.

In 1961, too, missionary activities were further restricted, catechising and all religious activity outside churches being forbidden. Individual missionaries going on furlough had been liable for some years to find themselves refused a re-entry permit and in 1962 a new Missionaries Act prohibited all proselytising except under carefully restricted licence.* The trouble in the schools came to a head the same year. There were strikes, and pupils ran away or were sentenced to imprisonment. Open revolt flared up in October but was suppressed. Rumours reached the outside world of trouble among the Anuak of the Baro Salient, who were migrating into Ethiopia, where other exiles had already formed a headquarters. In 1963 there seems to have been an uneasy peace until, in September of that year, a new and sinister feature appears in the *Anya Nya*, operating apparently on Mau Mau lines.

In January 1964 the *Daily Telegraph* reported widespread revolt. In the same month a daring and well-planned attempt was made to capture Wau, which might well have succeeded if the signal gun had not been fired half an hour too soon. It was organised, according to local report, from bases in the Central African Republic, whose Government was believed to know little of what was going on in its remoter areas. The allegation that these camps were organised by Israeli agents† is unsubstantiated and seems on the face of it to be more improbable than the rival story that Chinese officers had penetrated into the area from Brazzaville to train the Congo rebels, and were not averse to causing a bit of trouble elsewhere.

The sixty men afterwards brought to trial included one Bernardino, the Roman Catholic son of a Malwal Dinka chief, Joseph Garang, a law graduate of Khartum University, and an unnamed Catholic priest. Bernardino was reported to have a commission issued by William Deng, Garang to be a communist, the priest to be collecting money for SANU. *The Times* of 27 February, which carried the news of the deportation of all the remaining missionaries, also reported the execution of Bernardino and the arrest of the deputy Vicar Apostolic of Wau. The others were still on trial. A ban was also imposed on foreign merchants operating outside district and province headquarters, presumably Greek or Syrian shopkeepers.

---

* Although applications were duly filed it does not appear that any licences were actually issued before the final expulsion of the missionaries in February, 1964.
† Due perhaps to the presence of an Israeli military mission in Uganda.

The *Universe* on 1 May reported that five priests tried at Wau during April had been found not guilty of fomenting rebellion. The *Observer* on 3 May noted that Sudanese refugees in Ethiopia had left hurriedly for Kenya on learning that the Ethiopian Government had completed an extradition treaty.

At about the same time the SANU leaders in Uganda protested to the Secretary-General of the UNO that the people in six southern districts were being exterminated by northern troops, that fourteen refugee settlements on Ethiopian soil had been burned down, and that Ethiopia was preparing to return 4,000 Sudanese refugees. Simultaneously *The Guardian* reported a new influx into Uganda, bringing the total arrivals during 'the last few months' up to 11,000. According to this article Joseph Oduho had been jailed in February for trying to raise an army in Uganda, and William Deng had moved his H.Q. to Leopoldville. The correspondent of the *Glasgow Herald* on 6 May estimated the total number of Sudanese refugees in Uganda at 60,000, of whom 7,000 had crossed the border in the last few days, accompanied by 16,000 cattle and 15,000 sheep and goats. On 7 May Uganda closed the frontier. The figures given in the *Daily Telegraph* (12 May) were 50,000 in Uganda and 25,000 in Ethiopia. Sudanese troops were reported next day to have pursued refugees over the Congo border and attacked the town of Aba.* There were also stories of 'excesses' near Torit. Later in the month an initial UNO grant of £175,000 was earmarked for Sudan refugees in Uganda.†

What part had been played in all this by the missionaries? According to the *Black Book* they busied themselves in preaching against the Government, circulating false allegations in the foreign press, and denouncing the Missionary Societies Act of 1962.

'The campaign was led by Father Saturnino. The Church was evidently the organiser that gave him support. They found in the Government's decision to unify the weekly public holiday good ground to spread propaganda about imminent Muslim suppression. Later, when Fr. Saturnino failed to carry out his plans he escaped the country, in the company of other separatist politicians. Upon their arrival in neighbouring East African countries they founded what came to be called the Sudan Christian Association. Evidently it is a political organisation camouflaging under

* According to a statement by the Uganda Minister of the Interior to a Khartoum newspaper in February 1965, they also pursued parties of rebels into Uganda and shot them there.
† Mostly Christians, according to *The Times* of 28 May, which said the U.N. Commission had asked Uganda to keep the frontier open.

Christianity to enlist maximum moral and material support. In the meantime the missionaries encouraged the southerners to leave the country and join the movement abroad. The deserters were efficiently handled by Church authorities across the border at destination points. This indicates that a well organised plan among missions in the Sudan and neighbouring countries had existed.'

Specific charges follow — against the journal *Nigrizia* for stressing the obligation to resist; against Saturnino and Deng for organising sabotage; against individual priests for aiding southerners to escape, enticing Nuer tribesmen across the border, and generally encouraging and assisting outlaws and rebels.

'Their expulsion, therefore,' the passage concludes, 'became necessary and inevitable.'

Nor was it questioned in any way by southern members of the Central Council, three of whom, Siricio Iro, Philemon Majok and James Bol Kalmal, made speeches welcoming it on 4 March.

Evidence exists, however, for the defence.

In the Church Missionary Society News Letter No. 231, dated October 1960, the General Secretary, Canon Max Warren, quoted a passage from Sir Frederick Eckstein's farewell speech after twenty years as Chairman of the Syndicate:

'Were I asked to define the policy to be pursued by my successor, I would reply — Cultivate to the utmost a loyal and harmonious working, in letter and spirit, with the government in Khartum, and show every consideration to the native population of the Sudan.'

'That was spoken in 1927,' Warren continued. 'It might well serve to define how in 1960 the C.M.S. Missionaries in the Sudan view their relationship to the land of their adoption. The ideal may not always be easy to realise, but in pursuing it with sincerity they best serve the interests of the Christian church of the land.

' "Guard her children; Guide her rulers; Give her peace", is as appropriate as a prayer for the Sudan as it is for the rest of Africa.'

The following is extracted from the opening address of the Anglican Bishop in the Sudan at the Diocesan Synod at Juba on 1 November 1963:

'I would like to take this opportunity of assuring you, Sir, as Government Representative, of our Church's loyalty to the Government, of our sympathetic understanding of their problems, and of our sincere desire to help by our prayers, by our preaching and by our living in bringing about reconciliation wherever there is lack of trust or understanding. We believe the Gospel of Christ which we proclaim is the gospel of reconciliation, and is in the words of our scriptures "for the healing of the nations". We have nothing to hide. Our Bible is an open book. Our Churches are open to all. We believe we have something to give; and we pray that we may be more worthy of our faith and calling.'

The above is quoted from the *Diocesan Review*, Volume 17, No. 48, published in the spring of 1964. The following passage is quoted from No. 49, published in the summer.

'On February 26th, I had arrived at Lainya from Mundri at the close of the Church Conference South.

'At 5.30 p.m. on the 27th, I was handed — by an official of the Ministry of Education — an urgent note from the Inspector of Local Government at Yei, instructing me to proceed at once to Juba to report to the Chairman of the Province Authority. Within an hour I was on the road and when I arrived in Juba, found Mr. and Mrs. Cook, and Mr. and Mrs. Amstutz — of the African Inland Mission — listening to the B.B.C. 8 o'clock news which had just announced that 300 foreign missionaries were being deported from the Southern Provinces. As I had already completed most of my engagements during the previous 5 weeks of my tour of the Southern Sudan, I decided after consultation with the authorities in Juba, that it would be best for me to proceed at once to Khartum, and that this might save further embarrassment to them. So on the Saturday afternoon I regretfully left by Sudan Airways, but with the assurance that when things returned to normal I should be able to return to my Episcopal visitations. . . .

'There were only three married couples of the C.M.S. Gordon Memorial Sudan Mission in the whole of the south at the time of the deportation Order. . . . In each case they were given time to pack their personal belongings, for which we are grateful to the authorities.'

It is difficult to understand why the final expulsion was so hurried — why, for instance, Catholic priests of international repute as anthropologists were not given time to pack up the records of thirty years or more of research.*

* Mention has been made of the Catholic reply to the charges in the Black Book. This detailed refutation is contained in *The Black Book of the Sudan — An Answer*, published in September 1964 in English and Italian by the Istituto Artigianelli at Milan. On the evidence there presented for the defence a verdict of Not Guilty would seem to be inevitable.

On 27 and 28 May 1964, during the President's State visit to London, *The Guardian* published two articles by a Mr. Wright, who had just returned from visiting the South. They placed the blame primarily on the Condominium Government's southern policy and secondarily on the missionaries, who 'readily became the champions of southern separatism, gave the cause a backbone and placed themselves in the way of national unity. Some became active crusaders and from their mission castles flouted the authority of the state'. The *Anya Nya* were recruited chiefly from 1955 mutineers, who had been 'released in an unwise fit of generosity by the military government'.

The extent of the unrest had been greatly exaggerated and foreign journalists were allowed to go where they pleased. Troops were, however, everywhere in Equatoria and Government officials travelled in convoy. There were empty villages and burned villages and 'whole sections of the population' were missing.

The rebels were elusive, and tied down a disproportionate number of troops, estimated at four to five thousand men. They had killed 74 people, including 53 civilians, since September. Little quarter was given by either side and the people were sullen and distrustful of both. Lavish northern expenditure and impressive new schools had elicited little response and some sort of political gesture was badly needed. Negotiation would be difficult because the rebels had no unified leadership and the exiles represented no one but themselves. The older southern politicians were no longer trusted.

The articles concluded with a warning that black Africa could not remain aloof for ever. The 'cautious conservatives in Khartum' had yet to take the measure of the extremists with whom they would have ultimately to treat.

The reference in this article to impressive new schools brings us to the question of the development of the south, on which government publications and resistance propaganda were directly contradictory. According to *Basic Facts*, the following new schools were opened between 1956 and 1964:

One Secondary Technical at Juba
One Secondary Islamic Seminary (*Maahad*) at Juba
One two-stream secondary at Malakal
One new post-intermediate at Meridi
Four intermediate technicals
Six intermediate Islamic seminaries
One girls' intermediate.

The exiles retorted that most of these schools were Islamic propaganda and anyway the Malakal secondary was functioning in Khartum 'for security reasons'.

The Zande Scheme was another controversial factor, flourishing according to *Basic Facts*, moribund according to *Voice of the Southern Sudan*. *Basic Facts* quoted pump schemes and mechanised crop production in the Upper Nile Province, rice at Aweil, increased timber production and re-afforestation, deep bores, dairy farms, tsetse reclamation, virtual eradication of sleeping sickness, improved health service, new hospitals, and development of local government and province councils, all at northern expense.

The exiles denied most of these claims and complained that nearly all the projects approved for the south in pre-independence days had been scrapped or transferred north. Some of these, such as a meat-canning factory in the Bahr el Ghazal and sugar refineries at Mongalla and Malakal, were of dubious viability in any case.

Much was made of a widespread famine at Bor, due to a series of abnormal floods,* with which the Government failed to deal, and which it refused to allow the international relief organisations to handle.

There are discrepancies in both accounts. According to a statement in the Central Council on 23 March 1964 the Umm Delwis M.C.P. scheme, of which *Basic Facts* boasted, had been abandoned owing to inadequate rainfall and a glut of grain in the north. *Voice of the Southern Sudan*, on the other hand, reported the closing down of the textile factory at Nzara more than once.

The answers to these discrepancies will become known in time but meanwhile it is obvious that attempts were made to do something, but nothing really ambitious could be attempted until security improved. The whole northern case was based on the failure of the old regime to give the southerner a fair chance and the willingness of the northern tax-payer to finance it. It would be absurd to assume that nothing was done to implement that promise,

---

* According to a statement by the Minister of Local Government in the Central Council on 19 March 1964 the level was unprecedentedly high for the first time in 1961, when low land in Bor District was submerged; higher still in 1962, when Bor itself and Fanjak were flooded; and in 1963 almost as high as the record, in 1917. He denied that there had been any loss of life and claimed that in addition to remedial and preventive measures £25,000 worth of grain had been distributed in famine relief.

The exclusion of the international agencies was presumably due to doubtful security and reluctance to reveal how bad this was. The Dinka in general were now hostile.

As to the reason for the high floods, given as being due to heavier rains than usual in the Lakes area, a contributory factor may have been the invasion of the water hyacinth, to form a new and formidable *sudd* area farther down stream.

but it is clear that whatever was done completely failed to avert hostility and that hostility in the end prevented anything much from being done. The south grew more and more hostile, and it was even reported that Chief Lalok Lado, the southern member of the 1955 Commission, had been put under arrest.

What went wrong? Even if all the charges against the missionaries had been true they would not account, for instance, for the unrest among the Anuak in the Baro area, let alone the wholesale migration of pagan tribesmen into Uganda and the Congo, where the local rebels were in any case anti-missionary. Events over the border must have had repercussions and the attempted demonstrations by East Africans in London during the President's visit to London in May 1964, show that there was a tie-up with African nationalism of the colour responsible for the ejection of the Arabs from Zanzibar. To this degree the Sudan Government was suffering from the aftermath of the colonial period and there are outside powers which are only too ready to fish in troubled water without nicety of distinction between Muslim Somalis and anti-Muslim Bantus. The eclipse of the political parties in the Sudan was another contributory factor, not because the old parliamentary regime was more successful in dealing with the south, but because it enabled the southerners to blow off steam, and to feel that there was somebody to put their case in Khartum.

In addition to, and perhaps more important than any of these factors, there was the matter of personal relationship. The officer cadre had to provide a Council of Ministers and nine military governors as well as to maintain an efficient military force in being. It cannot in the nature of things have avoided sending south men quite unsuited by temperament to the task of winning the confidence and respect of the common people. History has shown time and again that one man's intemperance can undo the work of a generation of wise governors. What then was to be done? The first requirement seemed to be to stop recrimination about the past and face up to the future. Not the least harmful result of the old Southern Policy was that it provided a convenient excuse for everything that had gone wrong since. However retrograde it may have been, it at least gave the south the only period of peace it has ever enjoyed. If the mission schools were so inefficient why not let some of them carry on unsubsidised as a sop to Cerberus? Surely the manifest superiority of the new government institutions would soon have reduced them to the status of seminaries for the sons of clergy. If anti-northern feeling was simply the result of foreign propaganda, why had it not begun to subside since that propaganda was suppressed?

N

The debate in the Central Council in March 1964 revealed a realist approach in several of the members. Sayed el Fatih Abboud, a relation of the President and one of the most outspoken critics of his administration, took the northern intelligentsia to task for their lack of interest in southern customs and southern affairs. Sayed Bashir Abdullah criticised the quality of the administrators sent south. Sayed Ahmed Yusef Algam noted it as significant that there were no such disorders in the days of colonial oppression. Sayed Hassan Mahjub Mustafa pointed out that this was not simply a matter of combating the influence of colonisers and missionaries, but was part of a world clash of ideologies.

Further constructive suggestions were put forward in a book by Sayed Sadiq el Mahdi, published in April.* The Sayed made a good case for Arabic as the national language and a slightly less convincing case for Islam as the natural religion for Africans. He stressed the importance of economic development in the first place and of the ultimate creation of a national *mystique* in which north and south can share. He also made the point that whereas the collapse of parliamentary institutions had not proved fatal in the north because they lasted long enough to discredit armed revolution as a means of attaining political ends, the south had escaped this discipline, and when deprived of the opportunity of voicing its complaints in parliament had turned to arms as the only alternative. To restore confidence it was necessary first to survey and then to exploit every possible means of raising production levels and standards of living, secondly to choose able and congenial men to serve in the south, and thirdly to employ local men wherever possible. Next came the formidable task of educating northern public opinion out of ideas of racial superiority. He suggested making it a penal offence to call a southerner a slave.

In September at long last a twenty-five-man commission met in Khartum 'to study the causes of disharmony between the northern and southern parts of the Sudan' and submit recommendations for restoring confidence, internal stability and national unity without affecting the constitutional set-up and the principle of unified government. It was directed to take into consideration the views and proposals of the citizens and those of the southern provinces in particular. An undertaking was given that any views expressed would be treated in absolute confidence with a guarantee of immunity to the speaker.

Half the members were southerners, including Sayed Siricio Iro, Deputy Speaker of the Central Council. Other members included

* *Masa'lat Janūb El Sūdān.*

three retired Under-Secretaries, a leading physician who had lived in the south, a Dean of Faculty from the University and a well-known journalist and schoolmaster.

From this point onwards the political history of north and south are merged. The final chapter of this book reflects that merger, an account, it is to be hoped, of the birth pangs of a new Sudan.

Appendix to Chapter 10

1. Extract from a private letter from a senior British official in the south, dated 18 October 1946. (See p.168 n.)
2. Extract from *The Sudan: A record of Progress*. (See p.168 n.)
3. Extract from a private letter from a senior British official in the south, dated 9 November 1947. (See p.171 n.)
4. Similar extract dated 30 November 1948. (See p.171 n.)
5. Extract from a report made for the Governor of Equatoria, dated 27 December 1952. (See p.171 n.)
6. Memorandum of Juba Political Committee dated 13 December 1952. (See p. 172 n.)
7. Letter from H.Q. Troops Juba to Italian Mission at Yei, 5 September 1955. (See p. 185 n.)

DOCUMENT No. 1

The following is a representative opinion, dated 18 October 1946.

'Apart from a certain drift of Zande and Acholi to seek work in the Congo or Uganda, which is discouraged, the economic links of the south are all with the north. One might be able to turn, say the non-Nilotic part of Equatoria, to the south if a railway was built from Seroti to Juba and the Nile steamer service stopped at Bor. But this would cause a terrific upheaval and I don't think it could possibly be in the interests of the Sudan or even more particularly of the south.

'In its origin I don't suppose that "Southern Policy" was any more than the crystallisation of our natural feelings of humanity and fair play. We recognised that the southern peoples had their own personality and that it was only reasonable that they should be given the chance to develop it, as the various groups in the north were. So far so good. But unfortunately in the past ten or twelve years it has developed into an attitude of mind, a negative and sterile attitude of mind, based on an ideology of opposition, opposition to any infiltration of northern ideas and influences. . . . In fact the outcome has been to try to turn the south into a water-tight compartment, a kind of Arcadian Whipsnade, from which the denizens are not allowed to go out in case they get shot, and into which the northerners, though not actually forbidden by law, have been actively and all too often offensively discouraged.

'. . . It is this that has queered our pitch so badly with the better elements in the north and in the long run I can't see how it can do the south any good. . . . I should like to see more contact, always of course on condition that it is on equal terms and that the interests of the southerners are reasonably protected. . . . We need to tell the northern Sudanese more about the south and its problems and seek their co-operation in solving them. If our education in the north has been well founded surely we ought to have been able to instil into some of our northern friends some appreciation of our humanitarian tradition. Can we not persuade them to work with us in our efforts to improve conditions in the south?

'. . . Political is perhaps the wrong word (for feeling in the south) as it suggests conscious expression of group opinion. But as among all primitive peoples — e.g. our own forebears say in the days of Robert Bruce* — racial hatred is a deep-rooted plant which it is very hard to eradicate. To this day the Shilluk are inclined to call their children into the house when *any* foreigner is seen approaching. They are still inclined as Thucydides put it μνησικακεῖν — to remember for evil — their relations with the Arabs of fifty years ago. This is an unfortunate but of course intelligible frame of mind. And we shall get nowhere until it dies out. The northerners must learn to appreciate this and realise that they share our obligation to give the Shilluk a square deal and treat them as full partners in their common country.'

DOCUMENT No. 2
Extract from *A Record of Progress*

'The development of local government in the southern Sudan and the association of that part of the country with the development of central government have not taken place at the same rate as has been achieved for the northern Sudan. The basic reasons for this were that it took much longer to re-establish public security in the south and that it was impossible for many years to find funds to spend on areas which, even now, contribute next to nothing to the normal revenues of the country.

* The correspondents were both Scots.

'The fighting tribes, like the Shilluk, had held the north successfully at bay until the introduction of firearms in the nineteenth
century, during which they were in a constant state of warfare
against the government and the slavers. Those of them who were
accessible were deeply suspicious of the new government while the
rest, like the unconquered Nuer, withdrew into their swamps. The
gentler tribes who lived further south beyond the great *sudd* block
were also accustomed to take to the bush at the sight of a stranger
and in practice it took a quarter of a century before the administration extended itself over the whole area.

'The confidence of these people could only be won by building
up a protective barrier against northern merchants, which later
crystallised into what is called "Southern Policy". This has been
the target for much criticism from the northern educated Sudanese
although in fact exactly the same measures are in force in the
"closed districts" of the north itself, where unsophisticated and
potentially truculent tribesmen are still liable to be exploited by the
cleverer "Gellaba" from the river and also liable at times of inse-
curity (such as 1924) to attempt to get their own back by looting.

'The educated northerner has dismissed the idea of slavery from his
mind (though he still refuses to marry his daughter to a southerner,
however Islamised) but the Arab tribesman has not. In the late
'twenties an extensive trade in slaves from Ethiopia was unmasked
and even today there are occasional kidnappings and the victims
are hurried into the hands of the desert nomads of the far north.

'The Government has therefore been reluctant to throw open the
south until its inhabitants could stand on their own feet and the
process of equipping them to do so has been long delayed. The
principle in force was that the northern tax-payers' money should
be spent in the north and it was not until after the country had
recovered from the world economic depression of the early 'thirties
that the north was sufficiently prosperous to enable it to spare a little
for development projects in the south. Even now the demands of the
south can only be met at the expense of the north, but northern
public opinion appears to be prepared to make the sacrifice,
gambling, it is to be feared, upon the imagined potentialities of the
south as a financial asset instead of a liability. There is at present no
indication that the south can become a financial asset; as a producer
of good human material its possibilities are of course much greater.

'As a result of these economic and human factors the Government has until recent years taken little direct part in southern
education. The Christian missions which had been in the country
before the Mahdia returned after the reoccupation (some of the

individual missionaries survived in Omdurman) and others were given new spheres of influence. Debarred from proselytising in the Moslem north, they were able to provide elementary medical attention and education in remote parts of the south long before government services were set up. They were, and still are, assisted with government subsidies and are subject to increasing government supervision.

'These parallel activities have tended to create a division between the north and south which has been accentuated by the use of English instead of Arabic in the southern schools and the northern Sudanese fear that the ultimate result may be to split the country in half and even to attach the south or part of the south to Uganda. The arguments whether such a course would be to the ultimate advantage of the southern Sudan or to the rest of Africa are many on both sides and the whole question might at some date form a proper subject for consideration by an international commission. Meanwhile, the present Government has made a direct entry into the educational field, has long since established its medical services all over the south, is pushing on with schemes of economic development, is developing local government institutions on the lines which have proved successful in the north and, while doing nothing to prejudice the issue, is proposing to associate sympathetic northern Sudanese with the implementation of a policy which aims at giving the south the same chances of ultimate self-determination as have been promised to the north.'

DOCUMENT No. 3

Private letter from the south
9 November 1947
'If the two are ever to fuse, of which I have some doubts though no fanatical theories, the northerner has to realise that here and now south and north are utterly different countries joined by geographic and economic ties, and that he is more of an alien here than we are. Until he realises that he'll do neither himself nor the south much good.'

DOCUMENT No. 4

Another private letter.
30 November 1948
'It should be realised that the Executive Council and Legislative

Assembly Ordinance came out when a few of the senior D.C.s were on leave; that there is little opportunity in provinces with bad communications to get the provisions of the ordinance round and known to a widely dispersed set of folk living in remote places at a time of year when all are engaged in cultivation and cut off by rains and swamp. In most northern provinces consultation and explanation can be done speedily. . . . It is utterly different down here, and this should be remembered. . . . The workings of democracy can be damned inconvenient and one cannot regulate them. . . . It seems to me that the Bog is far more "alive" politically than either U.N.P. or Equatoria; perhaps this isn't properly realised in Khartum.

'We have at the moment a protagonist of the Black Front, a visitor who is spending his leave in his old stamping ground. He has been holding many meetings with southern staff to get them interested in the Black Front and I think this may quite easily turn into a demand by the southern educated class for "The South for the Southerners and no northern interference". If so I believe it would be a disaster.'

DOCUMENT No. 5

Extracts from a report written for Governor Juba on 27 December 1952.

'I think that the journalists' southern tour has turned out to be a gamble that has come off. Their latest reports have prepared the three-party political delegation for what they have got to expect. I consider it advisable that the political delegation should confine itself to meeting responsible leaders.

'Buth Diu* will presumably ask for federation again. Southernisation of the Civil Service; southern officers in the Equatoria Corps; and a Southern Development Board are all demands which might be put forward. Some of them will presumably be granted by northern politicians in order to effect a *sulh*.† If federation is granted Ibrahim Bedri's‡ plan of offering federation to the east and west too might well arise because it would be difficult to get the north to accept southern federation except as part of a general plan. Ibrahim Bedri wants this to counteract the excessive influence of the Three Towns on the affairs of the country. When I saw him on 21 De-

* Prominent southern politician. See p. 105.
† *Sulh*: Agreement.
‡ President of the Socialist Republican Party.

cember he was prepared to offer the south a development Research Team and a share of any capital available. Southern leaders would be foolish not to accept this offer if made.

This southern development board should be empowered to engage foreign experts for research. It might be necessary to have an Egyptian irrigation expert on it.

'H.E. (the Governor General) told me that the three International experts (British, American and Dutch) who recently toured the Jonglei area to advise the Egyptian Government were most impressed by the work of the Jonglei Team.* I believe that the team's report will provide a blue-print for southern development. Paul Howell† told me that the Egyptian plan would require £25 million for alternative livelihood for the Nuer and Dinka, in contrast to their own, which would cost practically nothing.

'The [main] Jonglei plan (which will require several years and a large amount of capital to put through) provides for a dam at Nimule (immense hydro-electric power); a dam at Bedden Rapids (providing light and power for Juba and a bridge over the Nile ten miles south of the town); a barrage at Jonglei; and a double canal from Jonglei to Sobat mouth with a macadamised road along the bank. The team's plan for Equatorial Nile Projects could thus solve the communications problem of the *sudd* area. With modern machinery it could perhaps be put through in ten years instead of the twenty originally forecast.

'Other possibilities are sugar, coffee, tea, rice, cattle, fish, and minerals. It would be premature and wrong to make a political slogan at this juncture "the south can supply the north with sugar and tea and coffee as its contribution to a balanced economy for the whole country", because we do not yet know what can be done. Research, experiment and pilot schemes are required first of all.

'If only some of these "possibles" turn up trumps there ought to be enough to make a constructive scheme, enough to justify the hope of a partnership between north and south on a complementary basis in a planned economy for the whole country.

'Everybody wants a solution — U.K., Egypt, northern and southern Sudanese. If Egypt could be persuaded to agree that the Equatoria Nile Projects should be designed for the good of the Sudan as well as Egypt and write it into the treaty, that would be her contribution to the reassurance of the south. If the northern politicians could show enough statesmanship to concede the principle of federation they would have made their gesture to reassure

* Team of experts investigating Jonglei Canal Scheme.
† P. P. Howell, Chairman of the Jonglei Team.

southern opinion after forgetting it in Cairo. Details could be hammered out in the new parliament but I believe north and west would both be pleased, and a far more stable government would eventually emerge for the Sudan.

'I have been most impressed by the steadiness and good sense of the senior Sudanese officials here, who realise perfectly well that there is a major problem in race relations to be faced, and that any attempt by the north to dominate the south will eventually lead to trouble as in Kenya. I am full of hope that the traditional good sense of the Sudanese will see us through in spite of self-seeking politicians and irresponsible journalists.'

DOCUMENT No. 6

There was a Political Committee already in existence in Juba at this time, which issued, on 13 December 1952, the following memorandum over the signature of its President, Paulo Logaali.

'The people of the southern Sudan have raised the present political issues because the leaders of the political parties in the northern Sudan after coming to an agreement with the south in 1947, the logical culmination of which was expressed in the Self-Government Statute, made an unilateral agreement with General Neguib without consultation with the south. This made the people of the south doubt the good faith of the northern political leaders and has led the people of the southern Sudan to decide that they must clarify their position by explaining to the northern Sudanese and to the world at large their political aspirations and their views on the present state of affairs.

'The people of the south stand by the Self-Government Statute as agreed by the Legislative Assembly and do not agree to any modifications to that statute unless such modifications are agreed to by a fully representative and democratic body.

'The people of the south are anxious to co-operate with their brothers in the north in the Self-Government of the Sudan. They differ strongly however from the northern view that self-determination should take place in three years. The south considers that it is not yet in a position to enter into an entirely free and democratic union with the north. The south is at the present time behind the north in standard of education and in all spheres of development. The people of the south wish the present Civil Service which has contributed mainly to the standard of evolution reached in the north, to remain to guide the southern people towards the same goal.

SUDAN REPUBLIC

The people of the south look forward to the day when they will be able to join with the north in a free united and independent Sudan. They feel however that this cannot come about until such time when we are in the same footing as the north. There should not be a fixed period for self-determination.

DOCUMENT No. 7

Letter dated 5 September 1955 from H.Q. Troops, Juba, addressed to Father Mazzitelli Salvatore and Father Lonfernini Bruno, of the Mission at Yei, both of whom were later expelled from the Sudan for 'trading in drugs without a licence' (Nos. 4 and 5 in the Government Black List).

'Dear Fathers,

'I have been most pleased to hear the courageous and human services you and your mission staff have so willingly and generously given to northerners during the recent tragic events at Yei.

'It is quite natural that the mission you are undertaking in the field of religion would urge you to help and offer such services to everybody who may stand in need of them, but you and your staff have exceeded all limits. Various reporters have explained to me the amount of risk you have taken in rescuing many, and trying to rescue those innocent victims who lost their precious lives. I must say we are greatly indebted to you all.

'I have sent my Coy. Commander to Yei to resume authority over the District and to reassure all fellow countrymen in the District that northern troops in Yei are there to help them and that they have no grudge or hatred of any of the local people at all. I am sure that the Coy. Commander, by name Lt. Colonel Shannan, would be most delighted to offer you and your staff any assistance you may need. You know that things are not quite good at Yei, particularly as regards food-stuffs. So, please, meet the Commander and ask him for any help, i.e. food-stuffs, etc.

'Finally, words will never suffice to thank you, and I will take the first opportunity to come down to Yei where I will personally express to you our unlimited gratitude for your help.

'Yours sincerely
Colonel Hassan Beshir Nasr
Commander Troops, Juba.'

Chapter 11

October Revolution

'However strong the armed forces are, they cannot override the wishes of the people'

Major General Hassan Bashir Nasr,
replying to a question in the Central
Council on 19 March 1964

AGAINST THE rising tide of discontent, the Government's position was not so strong as it looked. The prison bars had rusted away. When they yielded a little to an angry blow, it required only one concerted heave and all was over.

There was no military caste in the Sudan, though some have accused the Shaigia of ambitions in that direction. Nor was there a national socialist hierarchy to intimidate opposition. Every soldier was in daily contact with friends and relations who disapproved of military rule and regarded his uniform as the badge of oppression. If it came to opening fire on a crowd of his fellow countrymen, his obedience was questionable, except perhaps for the Nubas of the Camel Corps, whose family ties were distant and who had never been known to refuse action. The rest of the army were civilians in uniform.

There were factions too among the officers. Some of those whose seniority had left them just short of lucrative office were anxious to replace the holders. Many of the junior men disapproved of military rule altogether. Of those who did approve, a majority probably favoured a closer link with the similar regime in Egypt and a more active role against the 'neo-colonialists'. Of the Supreme Council itself, only the Minister of the Interior, Major General Muhammad Ahmed Irwa, seems to have been prepared to carry martial law to its logical conclusion.

Members of the Council had been mobbed by students in November 1963 during a social visit to the University, and it was decided, on an Egyptian precedent, to tighten control by appointing the Minister of Education, Major General Muhammad Tala't Ferid, to be Chairman of the governing body. This alienated any remaining support the Government might have enjoyed amongst senior members of the University, without securing any real improvement in academic discipline. The students were well situated to act as a focus for disaffection. They had less to lose than serving officials or householders, and they included supporters of communism at one extreme and members of the proscribed Muslim Brotherhood at the other. There were also a number of southerners, and the situation in the south began to occupy men's minds more and more as the months went by.

Nor could the rest of Africa go on turning a blind eye for ever in the interests of Afro-Asian solidarity. As a speaker in the Uganda Parliament put it in July 'How can we stand on the floor of this House and talk about South Africa and Portugal, when people are being slaughtered like cattle next door to us?' The Organisation for African Unity set up a special commission to investigate, and at the end of September a conference of unaligned states in Cairo arranged for a mediatory visit by the Emperor of Ethiopia on 26 October.

Meanwhile in Khartum University, the Students' Union decided to avail themselves of the new Government Commission's invitation to citizens to give their views by holding a series of debates on the subject. No objection was raised, but when the first meeting decided unanimously that no solution was possible until the Government resigned, the Minister forbade further discussion. The students decided to defy him, and distributed invitations to the general public to be present when the debate was resumed on Thursday, 22 October.

From the government point of view, the timing was unfortunate. Major General Irwa was out of town and so was the Commissioner of Police. The Commandant was in bed with a broken leg. The police themselves were inexperienced in handling civil disturbances. Instead of occupying the ground in advance, they waited until the meeting had assembled and then tried to disperse it with tear-gas, most of which blew back or was thrown back in their faces. Soon they were involved in an unsuccessful game of hide-and-seek with mocking students in and out of the labyrinthine buildings of the old British barracks east of the railway embankment. Reinforcements were called in from a neighbouring post and arrived carrying firearms, which inevitably were discharged, wounding nine students. Thirty-six policemen had been injured.

Early in the morning of Friday, 23 October, one of the wounded students died. The hospital was surrounded by an anxious crowd of friends and relations. The doctors refused to treat the injured policemen, who had to be sent to the military wards, and senior members of the University headed the funeral procession that afternoon. Enormous crowds assembled for the occasion in the square south of the railway station, and after the truck carrying the body had left for the boy's home in the Gezira a violent political demonstration developed. The police were thoroughly demoralised, and stood helplessly by while their broadcasting apparatus was commandeered by demonstrators and one of their vehicles over-turned and set on fire. The crowds then dispersed through the city, shouting, looting, and burning. Some of the damage seems to have been organised — bars, cabarets, and Ethiopian brothels being presumably the objectives of the Brotherhood, petrol stations and unpopular newspaper offices of the communists. But mostly it was due to sheer exuberance and partly, of course, to hooligans.

Next morning a determined effort was made to restore order. Armoured vehicles patrolled the streets and hundreds of arrests were made, but the High Court judges closed the courts and withheld magisterial authority for anti-riot action by the police. On Sunday most of the civil service stopped work and on Monday railway, airport, and radio staff followed suit. Demonstrations took place in the provinces, and students mobbed the Sudan embassies in Moscow, Belgrade, and Beirut.

General Abboud, although aware that his rule was becoming more and more unpopular, seems to have been appalled at the revelation of such widespread detestation. While Major General Irwa, now back in the capital, was arresting two of the recalcitrant judges and threatening that curfew-breakers would be shot down, and taxi-drivers were blocking the roads to prevent his armoured vehicles from penetrating to the centre of the city, the President opened negotiations with a Committee of Public Safety which had come into being overnight.

This Committee was destined to provide the *de facto* Government of the Sudan for three crucial months and it is important to bear in mind that although it assumed power with country-wide popular support, it was not a representative government in the normal sense of the word. It consisted of resistance leaders, men who had the moral courage to declare against the Government before success was assured, who had their own objectives in view and were unlikely to be content with a passive role.

The student body which touched off the whole thing, senior members of the University who backed them and demonstrated with them on the Friday, the doctors who refused treatment to the

injured policemen, the judges and lawyers who organised resistance
on the Saturday, the civil servants who followed their lead — all
these combined to form a National Front of Political Organisations.
The most powerful personality behind them was the new Chief
Justice, Babikr Awadullah, who had the backing of the old People's
Democratic Party and the Khatmia sect. The communists, who had
thrived under persecution as usual, could count on support amongst
the students and intelligentsia as well as the trades unions and were
again in control of the Gezira Tenants' Association,

Through separate representation of these various bodies as well as
of the Party as such, they obtained extra seats on this Committee and
in the subsequent provisional government, though their opponents
alleged that there were only 700 party members on their roll.* The
Muslim Brothers, also accustomed to operating under proscription,
had a strong following in the university as well as a more fanatical
element outside.

The other political parties were caught on the wrong foot and the
Umma, in spite of the activities of the late Sayed Saddiq el Mahdi,
was still under suspicion of having connived at the 1958 take-over.
However, they and N.U.P. and P.D.P. each had a seat on the Committee.

After a desperate effort to avert disaster by sacrificing his more
unpopular henchmen, Abboud was forced to agree on Monday night
to the dissolution of both his executive councils and the formation of
a provisional cabinet pending the proposed recall of the Central
Council on 2 November. Negotiations about the membership and
leadership of this cabinet lasted all through Tuesday and were
resumed on Wednesday morning. The crowds in the streets grew
more and more impatient, and when reports reached the University
on Wednesday that the army negotiators were stalling, a body of
students set off for the President's house. As the head of the procession arrived opposite the gates, a shot rang out. According to one
account, it shattered the window of the guard-room. According to
another it was not a pistol shot at all, but a car backfiring. Whatever
it was, it resulted in an order to open fire with a Bren gun and the
demonstrators withdrew with many injured, leaving fourteen dead
on the ground.

Sullen resentment was now converted into bitter anger, but there
was no further violence, while the negotiations dragged on until
Friday, 30 October, when the names of a cabinet of twelve were

* They were also accused later on of relying on financial assistance from the
Eastern bloc embassies to run their three newspapers and their transport fleet.

announced. The key posts of Foreign Affairs and Finance were held by experienced politicians in Muhammad Ahmed Mahjub (*Umma*) and Mubarak Zarroug (N.U.P.). Clement Mboro was called in from the Deputy Governorship of Darfur to be Minister of the Interior, and Ezboni Mundiri Gwanza of the old Southern Federal Party was appointed Minister of Communications. The communists had three representatives. Ahmed Suliman was Minister of Agriculture, el Amin Muhammad el Amin Minister of Health and Shafi Ahmed el Shaikh, secretary of the Federation of Trades Unions, Minister of Cabinet Affairs. Other prominent left-wing associates were Khalafallah Babikr, Minister of Information, and Abdin Ismail, Minister of Local Government. The new Prime Minister was a civil servant, Sirr el Khatim el Khalifa, of the Ministry of Education, a man enjoying general respect and with many years experience in the south. Abboud was retained as President and Commander-in-Chief, but was subject to the overriding veto of a two-thirds majority in the Cabinet. All were sworn in by the Grand Kadi on Sunday, 1 November.

Their immediate tasks were to conclude a truce with the south, restore the economic situation, and arrange for the early election of a representative assembly to set up a proper constitution. It was assumed that until this was done there would be no major changes in the administration.

No time was lost in restoring the freedom of the press and the independence of the University, raising the ban on political parties, releasing political prisoners, and issuing an appeal to the exiles and rebels in the south to suspend hostilities and open negotiations. The 1956 constitution, with certain modifications, was to be restored. The Central Council Act was repealed and the existing Province Councils suspended. Civil governors, who had already reassumed authority, were invested with full powers as Provincial Commissioners. The Defence of the Sudan Ordinance was repealed and the emergency regulations retained only in disturbed areas. The northern provinces returned to normal without more ado.

It was soon apparent that the new Government had no intention of simply marking time. Its first decisive break with tradition was a declaration of foreign policy. The non-committal attitude which had characterised successive Sudan governments for a decade was consigned to the wastepaper basket, and active support promised to the Congo rebels (whose leaders had recently found asylum in Juba), to the revolutionary government in the Yemen, and to an anti-Ethiopian revolt in Eritrea of which the outside world now learned for the first time. As a gesture of hostility towards the South Arabian

Federation, British military personnel and their families in transit to Aden were denied facilities at Khartum airport.

At first sight, these measures seemed anomalous. The British case for the independence of South Arabia was not dissimilar to their stand for Sudanese autonomy against Egypt and the Arab League after the war. Sudanese politics had been dominated from the first by the fear of precisely such an Egyptian inspired *coup* as had been engineered in the Yemen, where it was maintained in power by 40,000 foreign troops. The Congo rebels had hitherto been regarded as the natural allies of the *Anya Nya* in the south, whom the Leopold-ville Government had correctly abstained from assisting. The declaration of support for the Muslim rebels in Eritrea ended a quarter of a century of unprecedented goodwill and collaboration with Ethiopia. Interference in the domestic affairs of both neigh-bouring states was technically a breach of the Accra agreements.

It must, however, be remembered, as a *Times* correspondent in Egypt pointed out on 24 February 1965, that in the Arab world the head is not always allowed to overrule the heart. The Sudanese had felt very isolated since independence as a result of their neutralist policy. The older generation talked wistfully of the advantages enjoyed by Commonwealth countries like Pakistan and Nigeria, who could talk over their difficulties with disinterested member states from the other end of the earth. To Arab nationalists the Emperor of Ethiopia was just as much an anachronism as the Imam of the Yemen, and a Christian to boot. Tshombe of Leopoldville was a tool of that Western materialism which had so inexplicably, but only temporarily, supplanted the classic Islamic culture on whose survival and restoration depends the salvation of mankind.

As for the British in Aden, they had been the spearhead of that same culture. Goodwill still existed for them, as the Sudanese were to show during the Queen's visit in February, but their Govern-ment was always suspect and they appeared nowadays to be interested only in finding a market for their products. They had paid particular honour to General Abboud during his state visit in May 1964 and apparently approved of his regime. Moreover, the British Press had repeatedly stated that the main reason for welcoming him in spite of the expulsion of the missionaries, was not so much goodwill to the Sudan as the need for staging rights on the Aden route. It was almost inevitable therefore that these rights would be withdrawn as soon as Abboud lost control.* The declara-tion of policy threw the Sudan wholeheartedly into the con-fraternity of opposition to Western influence in all its forms.

* They were, in fact, cancelled on 24 November.

During this first week of power the communists also showed their hand in domestic affairs. A special commission was set up, with Ahmed Suliman as secretary, to purge the civil service and the public corporations of 'collaborators' and persons suspected of corrupt practices or gross inefficiency. That there were plenty of these last had become obvious during the debates on the subject in the Central Council, but it was not going to be difficult to include in the former category anybody who had waited on events during the revolution or was suspected of anti-communist opinions. After all, every official who continued to work under the previous government was a collaborator in one sense of the word. The purge, therefore, though understandable, produced not a little chaos in administration through the forcible retirement of some able and inoffensive men. Scapegoats of various kinds were also easy to find when anything went wrong. Security chiefs might expect to lose their posts after successful rioting, but a managing director is not normally dismissed because a minister's entry was held up by a jammed door.

Dismissals were extended to include expatriate technicians and engineers in the Irrigation Department and public utilities, and in government-controlled industry. With a large expansion programme in hand and most of the new factories still running at a loss, these measures seem short-sighted. The chief criticism of the provisional government must indeed rest upon its indifference to the economic situation, which grew steadily worse during the weeks of political excitement which followed. Every effort was, however, made to contact the various southern organisations, and a commission was set up to prepare for the elections.

During the first week of revolutionary rule, the security situation in the Three Towns remained unstable. The students, fired by their success and high repute as heroes of the revolution, showed signs of wanting to take over full control of their schools and colleges, and claimed to speak with authority on matters of public policy. The police were still demoralised and had tacit instructions not to interfere with demonstrations. The Cabinet was felt to be in no position to resist demands backed by a sufficiently vociferous display of popular support. The general attitude, however, was still one of rejoicing, with much goodwill between northerner and southerner and no especial malice towards anyone. Foreigners began to go about again without fear of unpleasantness and the contrast between revolutionary Khartum and revolutionary Baghdad was again a matter of comment.

President Abboud spent the week in arranging a purge of his own

o

in the armed forces, the ostensible purpose of which was to remove politically-minded officers. On 8 November he decided in his capacity of Commander-in-Chief to put some of them under arrest without consulting the Cabinet. According to him they were conspiring with the U.A.R., but in the opinion of the new Government their only offence was sympathy with the revolution. The Cabinet reaction was immediate. The Minister of the Interior, Clement Mboro, arrested all the members of the late Supreme Council and deported them to Darfur. The former Foreign Minister, Ahmed Kheir, and two senior police officers were imprisoned at Khartum North.

Here was the opportunity the communists had been awaiting to get rid of Abboud. One of them, a lawyer called Farouk Abu Isa, went to Radio Omdurman on the evening of 9 November and announced that a new military *coup* was imminent. All loyal citizens were called upon to rally to the defence of the radio station and barricade the streets.* Within half an hour anxious crowds were thronging into every open space. There was no sign of a move by the army, but sections of the crowd got out of hand and stones were thrown at the embassies of the U.S.A. (by communist sympathisers?) and the U.A.R. (by members of the Muslim Brotherhood?). Demonstrations continued until 15 November when at last Abboud was forced to resign and his powers were vested in a new Council of Five — similar to that dissolved in 1958.

For a space peace was restored, and attention concentrated on the possibility of early elections. The communists held out for postponement† and so did the Gezira Tenants' Association, which asked for delay until the cotton-picking season was over. The question of southern representation was much in men's minds. Proper elections in the south were obviously out of the question until things had settled down, and it was suggested that the southern rump of the 1958 parliament be recalled, and supplemented by nominees of a newly created Southern Front, composed of university students. and southerners working in the north. Towards the end of November, Clement Mboro took off on a fact-finding tour of the southern provinces, during which he appealed again for an armistice.

Meanwhile proposals were put forward, and ultimately approved despite the opposition of the Brotherhood and the old political parties, to add fifteen new constituencies for 'graduates' in place of

*It was alleged that one objective of the manoeuvre was to facilitate the formation of a National Guard.
†They ostensibly changed their minds in mid-December.

the five abolished in 1957, to widen the franchise to include women and to lower the age limit for voters from twenty-one to eighteen. The object was alleged to be to reward the students for their part in the revolution, or to secure seats for the minority parties, according to the point of view.

On Sunday 6 December, Clement Mboro was due back from his tour and the Southern Front arranged a mass demonstration to welcome him. Several thousand southerners, mainly labourers, paraded to the airport. Exactly what followed must remain obscure until the findings of the Board of Inquiry are published.* According to an eye-witness, the bar filled up with southerners demanding liquor which they declared would be paid for by the Minister. By the time word arrived that the plane was delayed at Malakal to enable Clement Mboro to finish his conversations, many of the crowd were fighting drunk and insults were exchanged with the airport staff. The police escort which was awaiting the Minister went away, and so apparently did any responsible representative of the Southern Front.† Somebody started a rumour that the Minister had been delayed by foul play. Telephone messages to the police produced no response and finally, after ugly scenes in the bar and restaurant, the crowd set off in a mood of irrational bellicosity. They spread through the city and across the Blue Nile bridge, growing more and more truculent as they went, overturning parked cars, throwing stones through windscreens, molesting northerners and foreigners, and breaking into houses.

One body, proceeding down the main avenue towards the Republican palace, became involved with a hostile crowd emerging from the Coliseum cinema, and was attacked in the rear by spectators from the Football Stadium. Some rushed into the Egyptian club, but the main body sought refuge in a building opposite belonging to the American Mission. The crowd followed and after missionaries had been manhandled they were removed by the police to a 'place of safety'. After their departure, the building was burned to the ground and a general man-hunt ensued. It will never be known how many southerners perished during the night and on Monday morning. Many bodies were thrown into the Nile and others were picked up outside the gates of the hospital. The Anglican Bishop and his house were only saved from invasion by the determined attitude of their northern servants. The police, whose senior officers were under arrest, made little attempt to interfere before midday on

* The enquiry found no evidence of premeditation.
† A protest by members of the Front at their leaders' failure to appear was published on 23 December.

Monday, when the situation was brought under control. Southerners were then rounded up and given sanctuary inside the high walls of the Football Stadium at Omdurman and in a camp at Kilo Four on the Blue Nile railway.

The events of Black Sunday, as it came to be called, can only be described as disastrous. The allegations that the southerners had been egged on by missionaries anxious to prevent reconciliation is fantastic. After years of frustration, the missions at last had a chance of resuming contact with the churches in the south.* Events in the Congo had shown all too clearly what was likely to happen to the missions if the south became independent. They had everything to lose by exacerbation of relations.

As soon as they could do so with safety, large numbers of southerners, especially Dinka, set off for home, carrying with them stories of massacre which could not help undoing the effects of government propitiation in the south. Northerners began to talk for the first time of leaving the south, or at any rate the south beyond the *sudd*, to stew in its own juice. Foreign residents in the Three Towns were highly apprehensive. Even the Coptic community was reported to have been threatened. Some good, however, came of the evil. Public opinion was again shocked into recognition of the need to restore security. The police emerged from their burrows and began to resume control. Southerners who had clamoured for independence were brought face to face with the possibility of being taken at their word.

Imperceptibly the atmosphere lightened. Christmas was celebrated without incident and so was Independence Day (1 January). Southern students were persuaded to resume attendance at the University, and although the exodus to the south continued in a steady trickle, many southern labourers returned to work (especially, it seems, the Nuer, who as usual took a line of their own).

The situation was reminiscent of England after the death of Cromwell. People were tired of the rule of Major Generals, but unfavourably disposed towards the recall of the Rump Parliament. Parliamentarians and city 'prentices came to blows. There was anxiety about the Scots. Levellers and Fifth Monarchy men bulked larger than their numbers warranted. In the end a tide of public opinion set remorselessly in from the provinces and swept the country along into an inevitable solution.

That was what the parties hoped would happen to the Sudan. They were confident that under an American-type constitution they could provide a stable government and were determined not to

* The Anglican Bishop had just returned from a successful visit to Juba.

repeat the errors of the past. They set about organising themselves for a March election. In the centre stood the two old protagonists, the *Umma* and the N.U.P., with little left to divide them on matters of principle save that the strength of the former lay still in the *Ansar*. The N.U.P. were led by that indefatigable old warrior Ismail el Azhari, the *Umma* by Sayed Sadiq el Mahdi, who was not yet old enough, however, to stand for parliament. Beyond the *Umma*, but sharing many of its principles, was the Islamic Charter Front, including the moderate section of the Muslim Brothers, led by Dr. Hassan el Turabi, also young and highly respected, a teacher at the University and brother-in-law of Sayed Sadiq. Two other Islamic parties completed the right wing. The N.U.P. on the other hand, were in touch with the moderates in the P.D.P., of which the left wing, to the unease of conservative Khatmia, was collaborating with the communists.

It soon became apparent, however, that the politicians were not going to get things their own way. The Federation of Trades Unions and the Tenants' Association, with communist support, were demanding half the seats in the new parliament. The National Front of Professional Organisations, with its nucleus of lawyers, was preparing to set up a permanent organisation to fight the elections, and persevered with the scheme in spite of the opposition and final withdrawal of the Sudan Medical Association, the Islamic Kadis, academic staff, and various student bodies. Meanwhile it was pressing for the abolition of native courts and the liquidation of native administration without waiting for the election of a new parliament. The native courts had handled 130,000 cases in 1963 and the native benches of magistrates nearly 50,000, compared with 21,000 tried by the State courts. To abolish them by a stroke of the pen would create chaos all over the country. The native administration provided the entire machinery for keeping the peace, collecting revenue, and carrying out general local administration under the three successors of the D.C., the Executive Officer, the Local Government Inspector, and the Resident Magistrate. Its disappearance would cause complete anarchy.

The Cabinet resisted most of these demands, but its concessions over constituencies for former pupils and a wider franchise, extending the vote to nearly three-quarters of a million of young people of both sexes, were particularly obnoxious to the Islamic parties. The election manifestos of the Association of Tenants and the Communist Party, published in December, were calculated to cause alarm and despondency in many quarters. The Tenants proposed to take 50 per cent of the profits, while advancing their old and not unreason-

able claim to representation on the Gezira Board. They also wanted
to nationalise private cotton schemes, and to convert them and all
the government schemes into co-operative societies, thereby
eliminating the proprietor's share in the profits. The two Alternative
Livelihood Schemes for persons dispossessed by the Jebel Aulia
reservoir, which had been run since their inception in the 1930s on
native administration lines by 'agricultural shaikhs' were to be
annexed and similarly converted. Native administration was to be
liquidated everywhere, and no elections held till the cotton crop
was in. The communists aimed at placing the state in the hands of
the revolutionary classes — the workers, the peasants (Gezira
farmers?), minority peoples (the south?), and 'the revolutionary
middle class'. There was to be 'a clean sweep of reactionary bureau-
crats in the civil service' and special constituencies for 'workers,
peasants and nationalist intellectuals'.

A press purge was instituted at the beginning of January and
three weeks later the Cabinet approved the suppression of six
journals, alleged to have received subsidies from the military
government. They included the daily *Suhafa*, with a circulation of
25,000, which had twice been suspended under Abboud. This was
followed by a statement from the Minister of Information claiming
to be the only channel of communication to the press for government policy and decisions.

The Public Service Commission was also dissolved, and it was
announced that 'middlemen' would be eliminated from commerce.

The Electoral Commission had submitted proposals for 216
territorial constituencies in addition to the fifteen seats for the
'nationalist intellectuals', but its recommendations were queried on
various grounds and the preparation of electoral rolls delayed in
consequence. In spite of an Amnesty clause in the October agreement steps were taken to find means of prosecuting the imprisoned
generals. A commission of inquiry was set up into the circumstances of
the 1958 *coup*, in expectation of incriminating Abdullah Bey and so
discrediting the *Umma* party. A decision to reinstate all the officers
who had been dismissed during the Abboud regime reflected complete ignorance of the chaos caused in the chain of command by
reinserting 37 senior officers whose juniors had been promoted to
fill the vacancies. A new purge of army and police was instituted
and more dismissals followed.

The *Umma* party was first to react. It claimed that the existing
committee of the Tenants' Association had been elected by *Umma*
votes to oppose Abboud, not to introduce communism. The
President, Sh. el Amin Muhammad el Amin, was accused of im-

proper diversion of water in the Managil extension. Mahdist tenants on the White Nile and in the Gezira demanded new elections. The Professional Organisations were accused of conspiracy to subvert national unity. On 19 January the N.U.P., the *Umma*, and the Islamic parties formed a United National Front to press for early elections and oppose the left wing of the Cabinet. The signatures included Mirghani Hamza, the ex-P.D.P. leader, signing as an Independent. In a letter to the Prime Minister they again denounced the Professional Organisations, maintained that if necessary elections should be held in the north without waiting for southern participation, and demanded the Government's resignation if early elections proved impossible.

The left wing groups retaliated by charging the parties with past oppression in the south, and pointing out that the Islamic parties were disqualified by their religious bias from participation in negotiations. The Cabinet then announced that it was in any case impossible now to hold elections before 21 April. If further postponement was necessary, the Government would seek 'a renewal of its mandate'. At the same time, the Minister of Information, Khalafallah Babikr, made a violent attack on the U.N.F. as counter-revolutionaries.

The U.N.F. in reply demanded his resignation and then the resignation of the Cabinet. *Ansar* supporters, who were coming in from the provinces to take part in the welcome to the Queen of England on 8 February, demonstrated in the streets. On the eve of the Queen's arrival, the situation was serious and members of the Council of Five met the rival leaders and arranged for a truce until after her departure. During the visit Mahdists were conspicuous, lining part of the route to Omdurman and bowing silently as she passed.*

Afterwards the discussions were renewed in a less tense atmosphere but still unsuccessfully. On 14 February the Prime Minister offered to resign. The U.N.F. then suggested that he form a new Government based on representation in the 1958 parliament plus a seat each for the Communist Party and the Islamic Charter Front. This could carry on if necessary for a year without elections. But the communists and the P.D.P. refused to participate unless seats were provided for the tenants and the workers.

---

* The warmth of the welcome extended to the Queen eclipsed all previous visits and surprised the Sudanese themselves. Rumour had it that even members of the Communist Party proposed in future to call themselves the Royal Communists. In local opinion the British Press entirely failed to do justice to the enthusiasm of the crowds.

In spite of an exchange of messages between Sayed Ali el Mirghani, whose influence was still strong with the P.D.P., and Sayed el Hadi, the Imam el Mahdi, the deadlock was unresolved. The Prime Minister tendered his resignation on 18 February and for six days the country was virtually without a government. The P.D.P. suggested that the Chief Justice, Babikr Awadullah, be asked to form a cabinet. The U.N.F. suggested Ismail el Azhari. The ex-Prime Minister proposed a temporary Cabinet of eight Deans of Faculty of the University plus three southerners and five party representatives. None of these proposals was acceptable. The P.D.P., communists, workers and tenants combined to form a Social Democratic Rally in opposition to the U.N.F. and a general strike was called. This was a fiasco. The tenants in the Gezira went on picking cotton; the Railways Union denounced the strike as political; the Motor Transport Union dismissed their Secretary for persevering with strike notices against their wish.

This rather unexpected reaction may have been symptomatic of a general disillusionment reported in the local press. It gave the United Front grounds for hoping that the tide had turned and that the opposition to any government they formed would not be insuperable. On 24 February a new Cabinet was sworn in, consisting of three N.U.P. members, three *Umma*, three Southerners, and one Islamic Charter Front. Three seats were left open for the P.D.P. and one for the communists. Sirr el Khatim was retained as Prime Minister.

Meanwhile new Trade and Communication agreements had been concluded with the U.A.R. and arrangements made to resume sailings from Shellal to the Sudan. (Overland communication with Egypt had ceased since Halfa went under water and there had been talk of running a railway north along the Red Sea coast from Port Sudan.) Egypt also undertook to repay £1 million of six millions owing to the Sudan. The money was badly needed because the economic situation was deteriorating, and international aid was difficult to get until a permanent government had been established. The tenants had been too busy with politics to devote proper attention to their crop and not a bale of cotton had been sold up to the middle of February. Another investigatory committee had reported unfavourably upon the management of a number of government industrial enterprises, but the spate of dismissals had done nothing to remedy conditions. At the University and in the schools, politics were interfering so extensively with study that many of the expatriate teachers had handed in their resignations. On top of everything else, something had gone wrong with the new dam at

Khashm el Girba and the reservoir had to be emptied for examination. The new Cabinet's task was unenviable.

Nor was the southern problem apparently any nearer to solution, after endless attempts to get the various parties round a table. Not only were the northerners at odds, the communists claiming that they alone, being unhampered by religious prejudice, could find the answer, but there was no existing body to represent the south. Neither SANU in Uganda nor the Southern Front in Khartum could claim to speak for the great body of tribesmen, still less a new splinter group founded in Khartum by Philemon Majok and Santino Deng. The Southern Front was ready to co-operate with SANU but the SANU leaders were themselves divided, some demanding complete independence and others regional autonomy. The *Anya Nya* outlaws refused to listen to appeals from all parties to lay down their arms and seemed on the contrary to intensify their activity every time some sort of agreement appeared possible. So long as they were in active operation, it was impossible for Clement Mboro, as Minister of the Interior, to lift the state of emergency in Equatoria and until he did so the SANU delegates were afraid to set foot in Juba. They suggested a meeting on neutral ground, but to this the Khartum government would not agree, though preliminary negotiations took place in Kampala. These revealed another difficulty, as we have seen. The southerners wanted a new constitution before they would take part in elections. The northerners maintained that only an elected assembly could enact a constitution at all.

It is noteworthy that the question of missionaries does not appear to have been discussed, after their return had been expressly barred by the northern delegate, the Minister Abdin Ismail, at the very beginning. Father Saturnino, who had for some reason been defrocked by his Church in mid-December, receded into the background, but attempts by his more recalcitrant colleagues to replace William Deng were unsuccessful. Deng worked hard to get the parties together, addressing a letter to the Prime Minister early in January to explain SANU's *desiderata*, but finding his efforts frustrated by the continued activity of the outlaws. Trouble flared up again in the Bahr el Ghazal, and on 23 January the rebels kidnapped two prominent politicians near Wau, Benjamin Lowka and Abdullah Rihan.

On the 26th an agreement was none the less reached in Uganda between Deng and Daud Abdel Latif, one-time Governor of Equatoria, representing the United National Front. A conference was to open in Juba on 6 February with guaranteed immunity for the southern delegates, and the right to refer back to their headquarters.

Meanwhile SANU were to redouble their efforts to persuade the outlaws to lay down their arms. These proposals were welcomed in Khartum and the Prime Minister undertook to open the conference, with eighteen delegates on each side. The difficulty over implementation was to be overcome by pledging all parties in a legal document to embody the agreement in a new constitution after the elections. The northern delegates would include representatives of all who signed the National Charter in October.

The usual difficulties, however, then arose. The communists objected to a provision for observers from Uganda. The date had to be postponed because of the Queen's visit. The rebels increased their activity round Juba itself and northern delegates pleaded that they in their turn had fears for their security. Why could not the SANU representatives come to Khartum? The Uganda Minister of the Interior undertook to persuade them and the leader of the northern delegation, Dr. Nazir Dafaallah, Vice-Chancellor of the University, flew to Kampala with its secretary, Muhammad Omar Bashir. But SANU was undecided, the northern crisis developed, and the conference had again to be put off indefinitely.

It had, however, become increasingly clear to William Deng and to some of the other SANU leaders that the north was prepared to make considerable concessions. Something had got to be done before the tribes got completely out of hand. Not only were the terrorists defying them, but there was serious fighting going on in the Dinka country and even the prototypes of north-south co-operation, the Ngok and the Messiria Homr, had come to blows. Only a combined effort by north and south together and in agreement could bring these disturbances to an end.

William Deng therefore agreed to open discussions in Khartum at the end of February with a cabinet which now included three of his ex-associates in Clement Mboro, Ezboni Gwanza, and Hilary Paul Logaali,* the new Minister of Works. On 27 February he arrived in Khartum with nine colleagues.

His arrival aroused opposition at first from members of the Southern Front in Khartum and from the extremist group in SANU led by Aggrey Gadain. After a visit to Kampala, however, by Logaali and others, SANU finally agreed to send a delegation headed by George Kwanai. The Southern Front followed suit.

The conference opened in Khartum on 16 March in the presence

* Logaali was son to the signatory of the document on p. 201 (No. 6). Gwanza had unfortunately to resign his post in the middle of the conference. Ministry of Communications staff refused to serve under him after he had come to blows with a telephone operator.

of official observers from Kenya, Uganda, Tanzania, Ghana, Nigeria and the United Arab Republic. Ethiopia was not represented. All parties and groups attended, including that led by Santino Deng. Santino had been a minister under Abboud. He contributed a preface to a propaganda pamphlet issued by the military Government rejecting SANU claims and including a personal attack on William Deng and other leaders. His presence at the conference table was unlikely therefore to contribute to an amicable solution.

If SANU were in fact the creation of the foreign missionaries it was not very tactful of the Prime Minister to include in his opening address a violent denunciation of the missions as agents of imperialism. In fact, however, neither he nor anyone else seriously believed that the movement was anything but political. The speech was a frank appeal to Afro-Asian solidarity against the common enemy — the neo-colonialists. He charged Britain with having aimed at incorporating the southern provinces in a new *imperium* in East Africa and with having instigated the 1955 revolt.* The conference lasted until the end of the month and failed to reach agreement on the political issue, largely owing to the incalcitrance of the extremists. The northern offer was not unreasonable. It proposed to set up a regional government in the south similar to that of Northern Ireland, with its own parliament and executive, public service commission, development committee and university. Representation in the central parliament would be retained, with three ministries and the Vice-Presidency. The Opposition demanded a referendum to enable southern voters to make their own decision between this offer and complete independence, or federation. All northern troops must be withdrawn before the voting. One suggestion was apparently made for a ten-year interregnum under an international commission.

When the conference adjourned at the end of March a twelve-man committee was set up to study these alternatives and report back in three months. Meanwhile a constructive programme of immediate action had been drawn up and agreed upon by all participants. It was signed by representatives of the two SANU factions, the Southern Front, the N.U.P., P.D.P., *Umma*, Islamic Charter Front, Communist Party, and the Professional Organisations. It embodied the following provisions:

(i) Repatriation of refugees and restoration of order.
(ii) Famine relief and control.

* Historians are unlikely to be impressed by either charge, or to envisage the Italian Verona Fathers as agents of British Imperialism.

  (iii) Training and recruitment of southerners for army, police, and civil service.

  (iv) Freedom of religion and unrestricted missionary activity by Sudanese nationals.

  (v) Removal of ban on private schools; return of educational institutions transferred north; re-opening of Yambio Agricultural College, Juba Training Centre, and Malakal Training College; general educational expansion, especially for girls; headmasters to be southerners and not necessarily Arabic-speaking; establishment of a separate southern university.

  (vi) Establishment of a southern branch of the national economic council to review the proposals made in 1954 and revive the Zande Development Scheme.

This programme was to be administered under the supervision of the twelve-man committee. Its implementation depended first and foremost on the suppression of the *Anya Nya*, and it was ominous that George Kwanai still refused to condemn them. The security situation continued to deteriorate and the Prime Minister for the first time was openly criticised for his failure to deal with it. Unrest in Equatoria was believed to be encouraged by SANU extremists from Uganda, who were reported to be fomenting a civil disobedience campaign. Excitement in the Upper Nile Province was running high after the assassination of a southern police officer. Tribal warfare had broken out between the Nuer and the Moru. There were clashes between Nuer and Dinka in Kosti and between northerners and southerners in Dueim. Strikes and labour troubles continued throughout the northern provinces. There was a clash between communist and anti-communist trades unionists in Khartum. In Port Sudan the police opened fire on demonstrating dockers and killed four of them.

The economic situation inevitably continued to deteriorate. Only 33,000 bales of cotton were disposed of in the first three months of the year. Foreign reserves had fallen to £22 million after four successive years of adverse trade balances. Revenue was running £3·5 million short of budgetary expectation.

The new Government's mandate was due to expire on 31 March and not one southern candidate had registered his name for the elections on 21 April. The older parties were none the less urgent that they be held in the north so that a proper representative government could be set up to treat with the south and tackle the economic question. The P.D.P. and the Communist Party, however, held out for postponement.

Meanwhile the tenants and workers organisations, in spite of internal dissensions, continued to press for seats in the cabinet. The Trades Union Federation threatened to call a general strike if a new government was formed without them, but this threat had lost its force after the failure in February. On 1 April the P.D.P. and the Communist Party agreed to take the four seats that had been reserved for them. Presumably they hoped to be able to delay the elections by joining the government, which was now given an extended mandate until 7 June. By that time the other parties still hoped to hold elections.

The proposed prosecutions for complicity in the 1958 *coup* were narrowing down to charges for illegal profiting.

Nearly a thousand candidates had registered their names, including ninety for the fifteen 'intellectual' seats. The *Umma* headed the list with 277, of whom 75 were thought to have a fair chance of success. The N.U.P. came next with 225 (favoured candidates 65). The P.D.P. had 130, the Islamic Charter 81, the communists 22, the Tenants 19, the Social Democratic Rally 5 and the Workers 2. There was a new political development in the entry of eleven Beja candidates on a tribal ticket, and a number of independent Nuba candidates.

A definite effort was now being made to compete with the economic situation. Four million pounds were borrowed from Kuwait and fifteen million dollars from the I.M.F. The Ten-Year-Plan was brought under review and instructions given for the rigorous pruning of all development programmes. 'What is the use,' asked an editorial, 'of building expensive dams when we can't sell the cotton we already have?'

Agreement was reached on 3 April with the T.U.F. to repeal the Trades Unions and Workers Ordinance and the Workers Disputes Ordinance of 1960 and restore the 1948 legislation for the time being. A threatened general strike was again averted and for a moment it looked as though the new all-party cabinet was going to be a success.

But it soon became clear that the Cabinet was not united and the general situation as bad as ever. The Minister of Information publicly denounced the Ministry of Finance. The Minister who combined the incongruous functions of Justice and Animal Resources, announced that in spite of the opposition of ministers who wished to respect the Amnesty agreement he was going ahead with legislation to prevent Abboud's ex-ministers from standing for parliament. He was also proposing to deprive tribal heads of their judicial powers with or without the agreement of the Ministry of Local Government.

The Prime Minister gave no sign of being able to control these dissensions, and when on 6 April the Council of Five decided to go ahead with the elections on the 21st a situation developed in which the P.D.P. ministers were in open rebellion against their own government. The Southern Front, and at first the Communist Party, proposed to boycott the elections, the P.D.P. to 'resist' them.

The southern boycott was due primarily of course to the impossibility of holding elections there, but they were also unhappy because the new assembly was primarily to be a constitution-making body. Its legislative powers were subsidiary. Once it met the southern members might be outvoted, as they were in 1958, and an unwelcome constitution imposed. That was why they held out for an agreement in advance, pledging the northern parties to implementation. Meanwhile they wanted an assurance that persons of northern origin standing for southern constituencies would not be accepted as unopposed entries.

The communist desire for delay was also intelligible. As elsewhere, their strength did not lie in the ballot box. Of their 22 candidates only one was thought likely to get in, though four had a sporting chance of winning an intellectual seat.* They could not hope to retain a seat in the Cabinet. None the less the party finally decided to contest the election.

The P.D.P., who had had only 26 seats in the old parliament, now held three ministries, on a par with the *Umma* and the N.U.P. They too had every reason to favour postponement, but neither desire for power, nor sympathy with the south, nor the personality of their leader can account for the violence of their opposition. The Khatmia sect is an essentially respectable and highly conservative body. Why were they now more revolutionary than the communists? It can only be supposed that they too were afraid of a new constitution and an American-type president who might well be a Mahdist. Was this possibility sufficient to justify any sort of opposition? And were responsible citizens beginning to believe that violence would pay better than constitutional action?

Violence was certainly becoming more common. There had been a new outbreak of strikes, one of which involved essential hospital staff. 'Surely this is the only country in the world,' an editorial complained, 'where this sort of thing would be tolerated?'

Legal-minded gentlemen devoted themselves to undermining authority by attempting to prove that this, that or the other act of government was unlawful, a task facilitated by the dubious constitutional basis of the revolutionary cabinets. The Bar Association

* They won eleven, to the general surprise.

held that the Council of Five had no power to hold the elections without express authority of the Council of Ministers. The Attorney General expressed the opinion that since the new parliament was properly speaking a Constitutional Assembly elections in only a part of the country were invalid. The Minister of Justice persuaded his colleagues to ban the candidature of the ex-ministers. The Electoral Commission declared that it could find no legal authority for deleting their names.

In spite of these domestic anomalies no hesitation was apparent in the field of foreign policy. The Prime Minister at a lunch party for lady Rotarians threatened to break off relations with Western Germany. The President of the Council of Five, at a Bandung Anniversary celebration in Djakarta, refused to extend them to Malaysia. The first threat was implemented on 16 May, the second rescinded a week after it was made.

William Deng, who emerges from these events as a man of states-man-like integrity, was busy reorganising SANU to operate as a political party inside the Sudan, absorbing the Southern Front if possible. Their objectives were defined as being

  (i) to ensure that no law be made binding on the south unless approved by a two thirds majority of southerners, in parliament or by referendum.

  (ii) To work for self-determination or genuine federation.

  (iii) To ensure the social and economic development of the south 'within the framework of black African culture'.

  (iv) To uphold the U.N. Charter and the Organisation of African Unity.

  (v) To secure all-party agreement to the new constitution before elections were held in the south.

It began to look, however, as if Deng, like other moderates, had been outpaced by events. Aggrey Gadain was working against him in SANU, and since the cease-fire the rebels had virtually taken over the administration of the southern provinces outside the three province capitals. They were reported to have set up their own courts, to be collecting taxes, and to be deposing or executing any tribal chief who denied their authority. Every attempt by the province authorities to restore the situation gave rise to threats of resignation by the three southern ministers, and finally by the southern representative on the Council of Five, Luigi Adok. The Cabinet dared not support punitive action and inevitably the law-lessness began to spread.

The appearance of separatist movements amongst the Beja of Kassala Province and the Nuba of Kordofan had been forecast by the authors of *The Problem of the Southern Sudan**. It was probably due to observation of the privileges enjoyed by the south in the way of ministerial posts and communal representation. The Nuba were talking of a restoration of the old Nuba Mountains Province. They were in touch with SANU and evidently looked forward to incorporation in the southern rather than the western region of any federal government that might emerge. Their loyalty was of military importance, for the Sudan could as little afford to lose its Nuba troops as the Government of India its Gurkhas. No one could have foreseen this possibility thirty years before, when the Nuba seemed well on the way to being absorbed by Arab society. The inevitable allegation that the movement was mission-sponsored is inconsistent with newspaper reports that one of the first acts of the Nuba patriots was to burn down a church.

The fact that Darfur, which had had a strong secessionist element† was to return only one local candidate, against 16 *Umma* and 7 N.U.P., is a testimony not only to the strength of Mahdism in the west but also to the success of Sudanese administrators since independence.

Such was the general background against which the P.D.P. issued their challenge at election time, a challenge which might well have caused widespread disturbances. The Minister of the Interior, Clement Mboro, banned all demonstrations and succeeded in preventing them except at Abu Ushur on the Blue Nile and at Khashm el Girba. The Abu Ushur riots were not important, but at Khashm el Girba a party of Arabs rode in from the Butana and attacked the polling station with sword and spear. After losing four men killed the police opened fire. There were 14 fatal casualties in all.

The P.D.P. were unrepentant. Their leader Ali Abdel Rahman said the Prime Minister was to blame for allowing elections to be held against the will of the people. He was arrested and charged with incitement to violence, and his newspaper suppressed. The police magistrate in Khartum quashed both charge and ban.‡ Sayed Ali refused to intervene. It was now 25 April and the elections in the Three Towns, held a week later than those elsewhere, were due on the 28th. Demonstrations were promised in defiance of the order

* p. 181.
† A local patriot marred the Fasher celebrations of self-determination on February 12th 1953 by announcing that "now we have got rid of the British we must turn our attention to ejecting the Jellaba."
‡ Ali Abdel Rahman was again charged after the elections.

and P.D.P. supporters were sufficiently numerous to present a very ugly threat.

Wiser counsels prevailed. Just as in February the Queen's visit had provided a breathing space when tension was high, so now the sudden death of the Finance Minister, Mubarak Zarrouq, carried men's minds back to the early days of Congress and the *Ashiqqa* Party. The funeral of a statesman long associated with Khatmia politics was not to be made an occasion for bloodshed, and the demonstrations were called off on the eve of the poll.

A summary of the election results is given below.*

The *Umma* and the N.U.P., in that order, emerged as the only national parties with a real following in the country. It was upon them that the responsibility now rested. An alliance between them would obviate the necessity of angling for the support of the various Irish parties, without ruling out the possibility of giving them representation of some kind in the Government.† A constitutional method had also to be found for retaining the southern ministers until elections could be held in the south.‡

Failing such an agreement, it was obviously going to be difficult for the *Umma* Party to provide the sort of government the country needed without perpetual bargaining and compromise with an opposition which would be possessed of power without responsibility.

On matters of policy co-operation was to be expected in normal circumstances but a coalition government was none the less desirable in order to provide the confidence necessary for determined action and, incidentally, a wider choice of ministers.

Both parties were in favour, though the N.U.P. was understood to prefer something more widely based and representing every party

* Results (a) in territorial constituencies, (b) in special seats were as follows:—

Umma	76 +	0	= 76
N.U.P.	53 +	2	= 55
Beja	10 +	0	= 10
Communists	0 +	11	= 11
Nuba independents	9 +	0	= 9
Other independents	6 +	0	= 6
I.C.F.	3 +	2	= 5
P.D.P.	3 +	0	= 3

Communists returned included the Sudan's first woman M.P., Sitt Fatma Ahmed Ibrahim. The appointment of Azhari to the Council of Five involved a by-election with a possible communist gain from N.U.P.

† The Beja members went into opposition when they failed to get a place in the Cabinet.

‡ The Southern Front wished to retain all three ministries and withdrew when its request was refused. So did Santino Deng's splinter group and the rump of the old Liberal Party, led by Stanislas Paysama. Ministers finally selected were Andrew Wiu (SANU), and two independents, Benjamin Lowka and Alfred Wol.

in the House. The danger of this was, of course, a lowest-common-factor government, stultified by demulcents.

The main bone of contention was reported to be the Premiership, which the *Umma* as the largest party felt unable to concede to Ismail el Azhari, despite his seniority. If for this, or for any other reason, the situation was allowed to revert to that of 1958 then both parties would forfeit the confidence of the electors.

At the eleventh hour a compromise was reached. Azhari was to be permanent President of the new Council of Five and Mahjub at last achieved the Premiership to which his abilities entitled him.

The coalition inherited two crises, one with Ethiopia provoked by the discovery of a consignment of arms from Syria destined for the Eritrean rebels,* and the other by an alleged conspiracy to overthrow the Government of Chad from a base in the Sudan. The new Prime Minister took an early opportunity of affirming the Government's adherence in future to the Accra pledges of non-interference.

The remaining political prisoners and Major Generals were released and the ban on certain newspapers raised. In a broadcast on June 24th Mahjub outlined the agreed general policy — to deal firmly and justly with the problem of the south, eliminating terrorist organisations while implementing the resolutions of the Khartum Conference; to maintain freedom under the law, to tackle the economic situation, control banking, encourage foreign investment and legislate for tenants,† trade unions, and terms of service.

The programme seemed sensible and encouraging. Men were relieved to find themselves under a strong and wary government again.

In the long run there is only one criterion for judging the worth of a government and that is the happiness of the governed. In new countries the ruling class has to adopt discontent as a pattern of life, embracing the frustrations of education and ambition as conditional for the achievement of national viability. That achievement loses most of its value if the discontent is shared by the bulk of the population.

Ideologies are unimportant from this point of view. Are the Cubans happy under Castro? Do the Yemenites prefer Egyptian rule to that of their Imam? If so, then the revolution was justified whatever our views of its nature.

So in the Sudan. Whatever may be said about the Condominium

* It was supposed at first that the objective was to stage a *coup* in Khartum. Two ministers and Brigadier Shennan were arrested, but released when the truth emerged.

† The tenants were promised the 50 per cent share of the profits which they had demanded for so long.

the Sudanese were not unhappy under it. They were happy for quite a while under Abboud. They are happy now, but if they are to remain so they must be allowed to develop in their own way and their own good time, without revolutionary changes and with a government sufficiently self-confident to check violence and keep the peace.

That is what the electors decided. They were tired of the licence which follows upon revolution. They thought the *Umma* and the N.U.P. had had the benefit of experience and would not make the same mistakes twice. Both had their roots in local tradition. They would not introduce sudden reforms in deference to imported theory, or be misled by foreign economists into premature and extravagant development schemes. In the field of foreign policy neither was likely to be found shouting Hullaloo in the rear without having first discovered the destination of those performing in the van.

Both parties were bound, on pain of ultimate extinction, not to disappoint these anticipations in the north and both parties had the overriding task and duty of finding a solution for the south. If federation proved to be necessary, then federation must be attempted, however wasteful it might be of personnel and money. It was vital for the future of Africa that north and south should hold together, each with its own genius and both essentially Sudanese.

This book has had perforce to come to an end *in mediis rebus*. Any summing-up made in June 1965 must necessarily be out of date by the time it appears in print. I take leave therefore to go even farther back and to end by quoting from an address given seventeen years earlier, to the Union of what is now Khartum University, on 'The Sudan Fifty Years Hence'. (As usual, in the light of events, twenty-five would have been nearer the mark.)

'Africa is divided not only into a number of potentially hostile states, which it should be the duty of the world organisation to bring together into some form of federation; but into two main groups of states which are just as likely to come to blows as the individual members among themselves unless they are able to learn from the fate of Europe that victory and conquest no longer pay.

'You may think, and I agree with you, that the prospects of peace in these circumstances are small, but that is where the importance of the Sudan emerges. There are two progressive countries which bestride the rain-belt, where any future war might be fought. One is Nigeria; the other is the Sudan. No one can underestimate the importance of Nigeria, with its great

wealth and its big population. It presents a curious contrast to the
Sudan because it has developed during the last fifty years on
reverse lines. The seat of government is in the south; the centres
of education are in the south; the focus of national sentiment is in
the south. It may be of interest to read you an extract from a
speech made by a northern Nigerian leader in the Legislative
Council last year.* It was shown to me because of its obvious
resemblance to similar sentiments which have sometimes been
voiced by southern Sudanese. I think you will agree that if we
substitute north for south and the Sudan for Nigeria the parallel
and the contrast are clear enough.

"There are many people in this country, Sir," he said, "who
have taken upon themselves the responsibility of speaking for the
whole country. The Nigerian people would like it to be known
that these southerners do not and never will represent them. A
delegation of these people toured parts of the northern provinces.
We did not understand their real intentions and mistook it for
one of friendship. We never dreamed, Sir, that they would have
thought of becoming our mouthpiece. If the southern people
feel that they are representatives of their own people in their
agitations and demands they must know that our case is different.
We do not know them or recognise them and we share no responsibility in their actions. We shall demand our rights when the time
is ripe. We want independence and we shall demand it then, and
even be prepared to fight for it if necessary."

'Now this southern orientation of Nigeria makes it, in my opinion a less likely country for the purpose which I have in mind than
the Sudan. That purpose is to play the role of intermediary between the north and centre of Africa. Geographically it is better
suited, since the Nile flows first through negro Africa and then
traverses the Sudan for the greater part of its length before
linking up with Mediterranean civilisation in Egypt. Moreover its
situation on the ancient pilgrim route to Mecca ensures continual
contact with other Sudanic states to the west. . . .

'. . . If the Sudan is to fill this role she will need two qualities:
one, toleration, both racial and religious; two, non-aggressive
nationalism. The first quality will enable her to set her own house
in order, the second, to co-operate with her neighbours. . . . A
Sudan linked to the Arab League on the one hand and to a central
African confederacy on the other, and allied, Saadabad fashion, to
a chain of rain-belt states stretching across Africa must one day
play a vital part in the preservation of world peace.'

* In March 1947.

Bibliography

Introductory

For detailed Sudan Bibliography see:

R. L. Hill, *A Bibliography of the Anglo-Egyptian Sudan from the earliest times to 1937*, O.U.P., 1939.

A. R. el Nasri, *A Bibliography of the Sudan, 1938–1958*, O.U.P., 1962.

For information about personalities see:

R. L. Hill, *A Biographical Dictionary of the Anglo-Egyptian Sudan*, Clarendon Press, 1951.

General

The leading authority on the early history of the Sudan is Dr. A. J. Arkell, who served his time in the Political Service before becoming Government Archaeologist and moving on to higher academic distinction at London University. Some of his views are controversial and some have been revised since the publication of his *History of the Sudan from the earliest times to 1821* by London University in 1955; but it remains the main authority on the subject.

A History of the Arabs in the Sudan by another distinguished Political Servant, H. A. (later Sir Harold) Macmichael, published by the C.U.P. in 1922, is a pioneer work which assembled a vast amount of information about the early history of the country, its pre-Arab and non-Arab peoples, as well as describing the Arab invasion and listing the contemporary tribes and sub-tribes. The second volume contains translations of MS and genealogies assembled to the great convenience and comfort of later investigators.

The Fung Kingdom of Sennar by O. G. S. Crawford, printed for the author in 1951 by John Bellows of Gloucester, is another mine of original information with splendid illustrations. Crawford's views on Fung origins have not yet been accepted by all scholars but are more convincing than any other theory yet put forward.

Andrew Paul's *History of the Beja Tribes of the Sudan* (C.U.P. 1954) supplements the above from the Beja angle. A useful and readable contribution to knowledge.

A Modern History of the Sudan, from the Fung Sultanate to the Present

Day by P. M. Holt (Weidenfeld and Nicolson, 1961) is the most up-to-date modern history, but the author's determination not to be associated with the colonisers sometimes leads him into inaccuracy.

Nineteenth Century
It would not be possible to include here the vast library of books about Gordon and the Mahdi, or Stanley and Emin, or the works of the explorers from Burckhardt and Petherick to Speke and Nachtigal. The Khalifa's regime has been described by three of his captives — Slatin (*Fire and Sword in the Sudan*), Ohrwalder (*Ten Years' Captivity in the Mahdi's Camp*), and Neufeld (*A Prisoner of the Khalifa*) as well as by Wingate in his *Mahdism and the Egyptian Sudan*.

The classic history of Egypt in the Sudan is G. Douin's monumental *Histoire du Régne du Khedive Ismail* which was published by the Royal Geographical Society of Egypt in a series of volumes before the recent war.

The best account of the re-conquest is Churchill's *River War*. *England in Egypt* has been portrayed not only by Milner in the volume quoted in the text but by Cromer himself in *Modern Egypt* and, a little later, by Lord Edward Cecil in the brilliant persiflage of *The Leisure of an Egyptian Official*.

The following three modern books adequately cover the period:
Egypt in the Sudan 1820–1881, Richard Hill, O.U.P., 1958.
The Mahdist State in the Sudan 1881–1898, P. M. Holt, Clarendon Press, 1958.
British Policy in the Sudan 1882–1902, Mekki Shibeika, O.U.P., 1952.

The Condominium
For the early days see Ronald Wingate's biography of his father *Wingate of the Sudan* (Murray, 1955); for the troubles of 1918–24, *Survey of International Affairs 1925 Vol. I. The Islamic World since the Peace Settlement*, O.U.P., 1927; for the 1924 mutiny in Khartum, *Imperial Policing*, by General Sir Charles Gwynn, published in 1934.

General accounts of the Condominium have been published by Macmichael (*Anglo-Egyptian Sudan*, Faber, 1934, and *The Sudan*, Benn, 1954) and J. S. R. Duncan (*The Sudan*, 1952 and *The Sudan's Path to Self Government*, 1957, both published by Blackwood of Edinburgh). Other favourable accounts are *The Winning of the Sudan* by Pierre Crabites, an American judge in the Cairo Mixed Courts (Routledge, 1934); *A Foreigner Looks at the British Sudan*, by Odette Keun (Faber, 1930); and *A Great Trusteeship* by M. A. Nejumi, a Sudanese resident in Nigeria, (Caravel Press, 1957).

For the opposition see Holt (loc. cit.) and *The Sudan in Anglo-Egyptian Relations* by L. A. Fabunmi, of Nigeria, published by Longmans in 1960. This book, which puts the case for Nile Valley Unity, but makes a determined effort to give the British devil his due, contains a great deal of detailed information and provides an invaluable reference book. Another doughty supporter of the Nile Valley is Abdel Fattah Ibrahim el Sayed Baddour, whose *Sudanese-Egyptian Relations* was published by Martinus Nijhoff at The Hague in 1960. This book includes useful quotations from Arab and Egyptian sources and some surprising statements, such as that 'if the money which has been spent on the Gezira Scheme had been used for exploring the very rich natural resources in the Sudan, such as the wood industry, the Sudan could benefit more'. Doubtless the author would agree with the American visitor who remarked on discovering that his neighbour on a flight from Khartum was the Chief Conservator of Forests, 'if you will forgive my saying so, Sir, you appear to have been neglecting your duties'.

For the Sudanese point of view see *The Sudan Question* by Mekki Abbas, published by Faber in 1952.

The Making of the Modern Sudan, edited by the present writer and published by Faber in 1952, gives a portrait of events from 1924–44 through the eyes of Douglas Newbold, Civil Secretary from 1939–45.

The South
The following are the most convenient modern references:
History of the Southern Sudan 1835–1889, R. Gray, O.U.P., 1961.
The Southern Sudan 1883–1898, Robert Collins, Yale U.P., 1962.
The Problem of the Southern Sudan, J. Oduho & W. Deng, O.U.P., 1963.
Basic Facts about the Southern Provinces of the Sudan, C.O.I. Khartum, 1964.
For the northern case before Independence see Mekki Abbas, op. cit. Appendix C.

Specialist Books
Gezira by Arthur Gaitskell (Faber 1959). An account of the Gezira Scheme which is also an economic history of the Sudan and an indispensable *vade mecum* for all persons seeking to promote agricultural development in tropical territory.
Agriculture in the Sudan, edited by J. D. Tothill, O.U.P., 1948.
Sudan Geography, Robin Hodgkin, Longmans, 1951.
The Republic of the Sudan (Geography Illustrated), K. M. Barbour, London U.P., 1961.

Sudan Medical Service, H. C. Squires, Heinemann, 1958.

Experiment in Education, V. L. Griffiths, Longmans, 1953.

Pastor on the Nile (Biography of Bishop Gwynne), H. C. Jackson, S.P.C.K., 1960.

Islam in the Sudan, J. S. Trimingham, O.U.P., 1949.

Sudan Arabic Vocabulary, S. Hillelson, Sudan Government, 1925.

Sudan Arabic Texts, S. Hillelson, C.U.P., 1935.

Savage Sudan. Its Wild Tribes, Big Game and Bird Life, Abel Chapman, Gurney & Jackson, 1921.

Birds of the Sudan, F. D. Cave and J. D. Macdonald, Oliver & Boyd, 1955.

Game Animals of the Sudan, H. C. Brocklehurst, Gurney & Jackson, 1931.

Pagan Tribes of the Nilotic Sudan, C. G. Seligman, Routledge, 1932.

Flora of the Sudan, Broun & Massey, S.G., 1929.

The Nuer, E. E. Evans Pritchard, O.U.P., 1940.

The Nuba, S. F. Nadel, O.U.P., 1947.

Divinity and Experience (The Religion of the Dinka), Godfrey Lienhart, O.U.P., 1961.

The Fighting Sudanese (military history), H. C. Jackson, Macmillan, 1954.

Information on practically every subject connected with the Sudan will be found somewhere in the forty volumes of *Sudan Notes and Records*.

Lighter Reading

The Sudan's widest public in 1964 is reached through the various editions of Alan Moorhead's two books, *The White Nile* and *The Blue Nile*; its widest public over the years has been the readers and viewers of a famous novel, *The Four Feathers* by A. E. W. Mason, four times filmed. Based on Slatin and Ohrwalder, the book presents a fair portrait. Two other famous stories deal with the dervish period, Kipling's *Light that Failed* and Conan Doyle's *Tragedy of the Korosko*. More modern stories, both worth reading, are Edward Atiyah's *Black Vanguard* about politics in the north (Peter Davies, 1952) and John Sawkin's *Jangara* about the south just before the 1955 mutiny (Longmans 1963). Both these tales are, however, more imaginative than documentary.

The best of the travel books this quarter century have been: *The Gentle Savage* by Richard Wyndham (Cassel, 1936) about the Bahr el Ghazal; *Death by Moonlight* by Robert Henriques (Collins, 1935) about Darfur; and *Sudan Sand* by Stella Court Treatt (Harrap, 1930) about filming the Baggara.

Finally, of reminiscences by ex-officials:

Sudan Days and Ways, H. C. Jackson, Macmillan, 1954 (D.C.)
Behind the Modern Sudan, H. C. Jackson, Macmillan, 1955 (D.C.).
The Camel's Back, Reginald Davies, Murray, 1957 (D.C.).
The Kindling Fire, Alex Cruickshank, Heinemann, 1962 (Doctor).
Sudan Doctor, L. Bousfield, Johnson, 1954 (Doctor).

For events in the Sudan from January 1965 onwards I am indebted mainly to the columns of the *Sudan Morning News* and to its excellent editorials.

Index

N.B. Where the customary spelling differs little from a more correct transliteration, this has been substituted; the latter has been shown in square brackets.

Abbreviations: M. = Muhammad
M.A. = Muhammad Ahmad

Printed in Great Britain by C. Tinling & Company Limited
Liverpool · London · Prescot

DATE DUE

FEB 8 1967			